BEARING UP

BEARING UP
THE LONG VIEW

FRANCIS FULFORD

TIMEWELL PRESS

First published in Great Britain in 2004 by
Timewell Press Limited
63 Kensington Gardens Square, London W2 4DG

ISBN 1 85725 203 9

Typeset by Antony Gray
Printed and bound in Great Britain by
Biddles Ltd, King's Lynn

Contents

To my mother, whose commonsense and courage ensured the survival of Great Fulford after my father died and from whom I have learnt much of the wisdom imparted in this book.

Introduction

Six years ago the first edition of *Bearing Up* was presented to the public by my long-suffering publisher to – as they say – minor critical acclaim. Now he seems to think that the public might appreciate a fully revised and expanded edition. Whether or not he is correct in his assumption remains to be seen. Nevertheless, he is right to say that the last six years have seen great changes in the country, and in the way rural estates are run and managed. They have also witnessed the odd casualty among the older landed estates, while the casual onlooker will have observed that the popularity, among the *nouveaux riches,* of owning an English country estate has grown inexorably.

The last six or seven years also neatly coincide with those of the Blair government. How will future historians judge it? I think with the same degree of puzzlement that they look back on the regime of Ted Heath in the early 1970s. Heath tried to manage the economy by making rules, which he called his Prices and Incomes policy. Blair tries to govern by targets and league tables. In rural Britain we have, like everyone else, suffered from this form of management control, which is gradually trying to force each and every person in the country to conform to some New Labour model of what a Briton should think and what he can do. In short, the Blair government will be looked back on as the era of the bureaucrat, of an attempt to govern us by rules. In rural Britain this became abundantly clear during the foot-and-mouth crisis, when the rules were enforced by ridiculous officials to the detriment of the aim of eradicating the disease. One example will suffice to show what I mean. A team of slaughterers turned up on a farm to cull cattle, only to be told to go away by a MAFF official as the Portaloos – which had to be available under some obscure Health and Safety rule – had not turned up. Britain is now ruled by people like this official. It is the new socialism. We in the country have to learn to live with and adapt to its pettifogging rules and regulations if we are to survive. So this is one of my reasons for revising *Bearing Up*.

The other is, of course, that my own knowledge on the subject has grown considerably. Some will consider it cheating to write a book and then heavily to revise it and reprint it six years later. I hope those who bought the first edition of *Bearing Up* will not feel too cross; instead I would like them to think of this edition as a new model of a motor car. Six years ago they purchased a Ford Sierra; now they are being offered a new, all-singing, all-dancing Ford Mondeo, with air conditioning, leather seats and, of course, a walnut veneered dashboard.

When I started to write the first edition, some eight years ago now, my primary motivation was the frustration that I felt at reading, and viewing, a veritable avalanche of publications, not to mention TV documentaries, produced on the subjects of landed estates, stately homes (how I hate that term), the environment, agriculture, forestry and, of course, 'heritage'. Reading or viewing these over the years had given me an inkling of what it must be like to be a gorilla in a zoo, stuck behind bars and observed all day by experts, or, alternatively, pursued by the self-same experts in one's jungle fastness. They are, sometimes, well researched and lucidly written, but their conclusions are all too often so much garbage. The reason is, of course, that they are not written by a gorilla. Well, this book is.

The result of all this mass of publicity is that there has probably been more rubbish talked and written about the countryside of Britain in general, and about country houses and estates in particular, than about any other single topic; this book will try to set the record straight.

In short, that is the reason for this book. I am bored by people talking and writing on something called 'the environment' when what they really mean is the countryside. I am equally bored by experts pontificating on the subject of the so-called 'national heritage' when what they mean are people's private homes, and I am particularly bored by a Parliament packed with lawyers, bankers, social workers and the like caving in to every urban-based pressure group with a bee in its bonnet about rural affairs.

What else bores me? Being patronized by the self-same groups of people who seem to think that because one lives in the country one is thick (or, as they would probably say, intellectually challenged); and who have also invented a whole new language in which they speak to you (sorry, I mean with which they 'engage' with you) the only purpose of which seems to obscure completely in a fog of verbiage what they are actually saying, so that they inform no one, but – and this is most important – offend no one. Well, they offend me. I am also offended by having to read page after page of close-typed rubbish written by the self-same people without the faintest ability to write English and whose knowledge of the subject they purport to be experts on is infinitesimal, but who are paid to churn out reports; and having to listen to the leaders of many organizations which represent rural-interest groups as they grovel to some of the above people in the hope of getting some crumbs from the taxpayers' table. These are just some of the things that irritate me and have inspired me to put pen to paper. There are many others, as you will see.

I make no apologies for discoursing on the history of how great landed estates evolved and why so many have disappeared over the last hundred years, since, until the 1920s, the landed estate to all intents and purposes *was* the English countryside, just as the Scottish estate still is – by and large – the dominant factor in the Highlands of Scotland.

Over the coming pages I will argue that landed estates throughout Great Britain have been a force for good in the countryside and that the problems of the countryside today are chiefly attributable to a misguided vendetta waged against them over a span of a hundred years.

I have attempted to set out the reasons for the demise of so many estates since the turn of the century, and have tried to draw lessons from the mistakes our ancestors made, with the aim of helping to ensure future generations do not fall into the same traps. In short, this book contains, among other things, a survival guide for estate owners.

This book is not designed for scholars (though some may benefit from reading it) or politicians (though many would undoubtedly benefit from reading it), but for the general public. I am fully aware that the subject of every chapter could in itself make a lengthy book, but my purpose is to provide a quick and, I hope, amusing overview of how the countryside has developed, and is still developing, and of the role played by the country estate in that development.

CHAPTER 1

History

The history of England is emphatically the history of progress.
LORD MACAULAY (1800–59)
Essays Contributed to the Edinburgh Review, 1843,
Vol. 2, 'Sir James Mackintosh'

Let us start at the beginning – which for the purposes of land-ownership and country houses is 1066. To understand the present, a keen knowledge of the past is crucial; nowhere is this more evident than in understanding the reasons for the existence of England's great buildings, parks and landscapes.

We all know, because such matters were taught in school, that William the Conqueror introduced the feudal system to England after he won the Battle of Hastings. The basis of feudalism was the possession of land: in essence a simple and logical concept.

With victory secured, all land in England became the personal possession of the king. Although this might have worked in theory, in practice he not only had to reward his principal followers, who had accompanied him on his venture, but he also had to be able to rule his new-found kingdom. And for that purpose he needed men. William I, as has been the case with most monarchs throughout history, was short on cash but long on land. So the simple solution was to pay men in land in return for certain basic duties.

Accordingly, the king's best and most trusted companions received great swathes of England, which they held directly from the king, and thus these men became known as *Tenants in Chief.* They too were confronted with the problem that had beset the king, so they, in turn, divided up their estates among their own followers. The smallest area of land given was a manor, which varied in size and wealth, but was some eight hundred acres on average. Later, each manor came to be assessed in terms of a knight's fee. Rich manors might be worth a whole knight's fee, poor ones only a fraction of one.

Richard Carew, the sixteenth-century Cornish antiquary, wrote of Cornwall: 'Commonly thirty acres make a farthing land, nine farthings a Cornish acre and four Cornish acres a knight's fee – but this rule is overruled to a greater or lesser quantity according to fruitfulness or barrenness of the soil.'

In essence 'a knight's fee' meant that a manor worth one knight's fee could support the medieval equivalent of a modern main battle tank: one armoured knight and his necessary retinue. It has been estimated that the result of this division of England was that the king could, if every knight answered the feudal summons, put into the field a force of five thousand armoured and mounted knights.* Each layer of the feudal system swore an oath of fealty, or homage, to the man who had bestowed the land, and agreed to provide him with a certain number of armed men on specified occasions. In effect, William I rewarded his followers and ensured – at least in theory – that all England was held by men loyal to him; thus his writ ran throughout his realm and gave him an inexpensive army to call upon. A neat, simple solution to a complex problem – providing, of course, that everyone obeyed the rules and abided by their oaths.

Although feudalism may have worked in theory – or in line with the latest teachings of modern business schools – in practice, it had severe faults. Yet under a strong king it worked. A Saxon chronicler wrote, on William's death, that 'any honest man could travel across his kingdom without injury with his bosom full of gold'. It is not the purpose of this

---

* This figure of five thousand becomes the rough estimate of the total number of country houses and estates scattered over the face of the English countryside at the end of nineteenth century, some eight hundred years later.

book to look at the practical effects of feudalism or at how it worked, but it should be explained how the system evolved and why the ownership of land was so important.

The concept of a warrior class or race is probably as old as time itself. It is fair to say that some people like to cultivate things and live in peace with each other, while others want to biff their neighbours on the nose. Even today, when we are all meant to be peace-loving traders whose only concern is to make enough money to buy a better car, there is a sizeable minority among us who would prefer to cross the Channel and rape and pillage France rather than take a day trip on the ferry and pay our Gallic neighbours for goods which our ancestors habitually took by force of arms.

Warriors, however, were not necessarily stupid, and most of them could work out the simple economics that told them that, however much fun raiding your neighbours was, you would be considerably richer if you could enjoy some form of peace and stability on your own patch. Your peasants, who ploughed the fields and worked the land, would be able to pay you bigger rents if they were left to get on with the job in hand and, with the money raised, the warrior could equip a bigger raiding party for his autumn holiday spree.

If warriors were not stupid, neither were the humble men of the land: they could see the logic of effectively paying for their defence by having a strong lord who could ensure that they were left alone to lead their lives in relative peace. In other words, the system was symbiotic in its true sense. Logic also dictated that, as the lord of the manor had so much to lose, he would fight hard in any battles against invading forces in order to protect his revenue base, his tenantry.

Of course, things often went dramatically wrong, as when the Saxon thanes went off to fight at Hastings and lost. Then new landlords appeared hotfoot from the battlefield to take over the defeated land-lords' manors. But because the Normans' aims were those of conquerors and not those of raiders they left the Saxon peasantry – with some exceptions – unmolested, and allowed them to continue to farm the land. Moreover, the Normans appear to have been avid agricultural reformers: the Domesday Book of 1086 is littered with entries such as, 'When Odo received it it was worth ten shillings; now it is worth thirty shillings.'

So the ownership of land became the mark of the warrior élite. Without land you did not have the money to finance a decent fighting retinue, and without a fighting retinue you were a man of little account. As the Middle Ages advanced and armour improved and became more expensive, so more land was needed to provide the income to pay for the equipment necessary to put a mounted knight in the field.

The concept of the landowner being part of the warrior élite runs throughout our history, and even today a casual flick through the pages of *Debrett's* will show that a far larger percentage of landowners than of any other category of people serve some time in the armed forces, and are proud of it. Old habits and traditions die hard, and the concept of serving one's country in return for owning land is still alive and well. The armed forces aside, landowners continue to spend an inordinate amount of unpaid time on local committees of worthy causes, as magistrates, as elected councillors (though very much less so now than forty years ago) and, of course, on the committees of those various bodies whose *raision d'être* is to protect and promote the interests of landowners such as the Country Land and Business Association, the Forestry and Timber Association and the Historic Houses Association. In fact, it is a matter of considerable irritation to me when I attend some 'consultation' meeting arranged by some non-government organization (NGO) to discuss some government proposal pertaining to rural England to realize that I am the only one at the meeting who is not being paid! Everyone else – the RSPB man, the National Trust agent, the county council tree officer and Uncle Tom Cobbleigh and all – are, without exception being paid (for the most part by the taxpayer); and to them a good meeting is a long meeting. To me a good meeting is a short one. I used to wonder what would happen to country life if landowners suddenly demanded to be paid for the vast amount of work they do for free. Now I know. The meetings would be longer, the reports produced even less intelligible and, of course, the suburbanization of rural Britain would move ahead even faster.

Today there are few 'big houses' that predate the Tudor period and for this there is a variety of reasons. Partly it is because most of those that did exist prior to 1500 were castles, and Cromwell blew the majority of them up during the Civil War. But there was another more fundamental cause: most medieval landowners' estates tended to be scattered over the whole country and not concentrated in a single mass. There were two reasons for this. First, William I, when he dished out vast estates to his principal followers, seems to have made a deliberate decision to allocate a few manors in one county and then a few more in another and so on. The assumption is that William I, a shrewd man, wished to avoid any of his newly created Tenants in Chief getting ideas above their station and thinking they could set up proto-autonomous earldoms, as their Anglo Saxon predecessors had done and as their cousins in France did with apparent impunity. The second reason was the system of inheritance that evolved after the Norman Conquest. It is often stated that one of the greatest gifts of the Norman Conquest to the evolution of the British country estate was primogeniture: the rule of inheritance under which the eldest son takes all. But actually evidence seems to suggest that this was not at first a fixed rule, and only became so some hundred-odd years after the Norman Conquest. What was a fixed rule, however, was that in the event of there being no son but only daughters, then the estate would be divided equally among those daughters.

Since the easiest way for any ambitious knight to expand his estates was to marry an heiress, even if she was a co-heiress (i.e. had sisters) it is easy to see that, by this means, a family might, over the centuries, accumulate pockets of land and odd manors scattered over several counties. And this, of course, led said knight and his family to being constantly on the move, as it was important to visit the far-flung outposts of your estate as often as possible; there is nothing that deteriorates more quickly than the finances of an estate never visited by an owner. Our ancestors knew this well, even if some people today have forgotten it.

But what of all those younger sons who found themselves disinherited when primogeniture became the rule around the middle of the twelfth century? Some went into the Church, of course, but others looked further afield and established new landed dynasties in Ireland and Scotland. It is a tribute to the brilliance of the Norman race as conquerors and colonisers that within a generation the Scots would regard Robert the Bruce as a great Scottish hero, when in fact he was just a baron on the make, descended from a Norman immigrant a hundred and fifty-odd years earlier.

But back to the 'big house' or rather the lack of it. The medieval equivalent of our eighteenth-century squire lived in a small manor house, in which the most important room was a large hall shared with his retainers, dogs, wife and children. The hall, in other words, was the equivalent of the large family kitchen where today's squire lurks, warming himself beside the Aga, feeding his dogs scraps from his table and finding his peace constantly interrupted by a stream of visitors and children, no doubt much as his medieval forebear did.

The frequency of civil war and rebellion must also have militated against any lavish building enterprise. It would, to say the least, have been decidedly tedious to have spent rather more than one could afford on erecting a grand house, only to have it burned down by the revolting peasants or by one's next door neighbour who, just happening to be on the opposite side, fancied a bit of rape and pillage with his chums after a particularly good dinner. Politics was considerably more fun in those days – though it has to be said the penalties for getting things wrong were rather more severe.

So the chances are your 'big house' will date not much earlier than to the 1540s, built on the back of some astute financial dealings in the days of bluff King Hal, probably by a *nouveau riche* courtier with his greasy hands firmly in the till. It was the dissolution of the monasteries in 1536, possibly the first historical privatization ever executed, that provided such a boost to the country house. Suddenly, about a quarter of the acreage of England was up for grabs, and grabbed it was. Some of it was given in large chunks by the king to deserving courtiers and civil servants, but the vast majority was sold off on the open market at knockdown prices. Sounds more and more like a modern privatization, doesn't it? Anyway, it provided a unique opportunity for many landowners to buy big blocks of land marching with one of their estates. They seized this chance with alacrity, often paying for it by selling outlying land to other buyers. Thus the dissolution of the monasteries caused a major restructuring of the pattern of land ownership throughout England.

Those who accumulated land at this time quickly found that they had made astute purchases. The population of Tudor England was growing, and agriculture, by the latter part of the sixteenth century, was booming. It is perhaps an obvious point, but one sometimes overlooked, that on the whole, the periods of great country-house building and improvements mirror those of agricultural prosperity.

So with rents rising and estates restructured the stage was set for the advent of that peculiar invention of the English: the country house. Only one other factor was needed to prime a building boom: peace and political stability. This, the Tudors – after a fashion – provided.

Once the idea had caught on, it took off with a vengeance, and England must have reverberated to the sound of the hammer and saw. The most spectacular houses were those constructed by the parvenu men of business recruited by the Tudor monarchs to manage their affairs in the place of the old aristocracy, whose numbers had been sadly depleted by the blood bath of the Wars of the Roses. Families such as the Thynnes of Longleat, the Cecils of Burghley and Hatfield, and the Cavendishes at Hardwick and Bolsover Castle, erected great mansions (which the architectural historian, John Summerson, called prodigy houses) to advertise to all that they had now arrived. One suspects that the local gentry, viewing these edifices, sniggered among themselves at their vulgarity and scoffed at their modern conveniences, much as we do today when we hear that some multi-millionaire has spent tens of thousands of pounds on installing sunken baths in his house or paid £750,000 to have a kitchen installed (quite true!). It is one of the great jokes of history that every generation regards the buildings of the previous one as supremely tasteless. Indeed the only reason why so many old houses survive at all is because the original builders frequently nearly bankrupted themselves constructing an over-grand house, thus removing the wherewithal from their heirs to knock it down and start again. This rule did not, of course, apply to the mega-rich families, like the Grosvenors, Dukes of Westminster, of whom the Duke of Bedford drily wrote in 1960, after seeing the plans for a new country house to replace the Victorian Eaton Hall: 'It seems to me that one of the virtues of the Grosvenor family is that they frequently demolish their stately home. I trust future generations will continue the tradition.'

The desire of those grown rich in trade or public office to buy an estate and build a country house is one of the themes running throughout English country history; another is the English aristocrats' love of the country. As early as the fifteenth century, an Italian observer, Poggio Bracciolini, reported:

> The English think it ignominious for noblemen to stay in the cities. They live in the country, cut off by woods and fields. They devote themselves to country pursuits, selling wood and cattle, and they think it no shame to make money from agriculture. I have seen a man who has given up trade, bought an expensive estate, and left town to go there with his family, turn his sons into noblemen, and himself be accepted by the noble class.

Defoe, writing at the beginning of the eighteenth century, noted how 'the present increase of wealth in the City of London spreads itself into the country, and plants families and fortunes, who in another age will equal the families of the ancient gentry, who perhaps were bought out.' This is an observation which, come to think about it, could have been made in the mid-1990s.

There was a pause in country-house building during the reign of Charles I and the Commonwealth for obvious reasons and inevitably a boom when Charles II came to the throne in 1660. But this time very different houses were constructed, for many of those busy building had spent years in exile on the continent and had seen what the Dutch and French were up to and wanted to replicate the style in England's green and pleasant land.

Connoisseurs consider the period 1660–1730 to have produced many of the most beautiful country houses. It saw a unique flowering in architecture, producing such giants as Hawksmoor, Vanbrugh, Wren, Archer and Talman in England and Bruce in Scotland, among many others. Houses were built which today are still eminently liveable in; they had not yet reached the pomposity and pretension that later architects, followers of Palladio, achieved for their clients.

Much has been made of the love of the countryside and of his estates which caused the English nobleman and squire to devote so much time and money to his home in the country. There is some justification for this, but it is also fair to say that the size of the English country house grew, in the eighteenth century, in direct proportion to the power of Parliament, at the expense of the Crown, which meant that ensuring that your man was elected to one of the local seats became more important. The franchise being strictly limited in those far-off days, it was possible for a nobleman to help his cause by entertaining lavishly, impressing the electorate with his grandiose mansion and park. This resulted in a 'virtuous circle'. Once the aim of having a number of MPs in your pocket was achieved then ministerial office would probably follow, with all the many opportunities attendant upon it for filling your coffers; you could then spend your ill-gotten gains on further embellishments to your pile. Sir Robert Walpole's grand house at Houghton is the quintessential example of how the system could be made to work in this way.

Such was the growth in the building of large houses that it is hardly surprising that the authorities sought ways of taxing such naked displays of wealth and success. This had been tried before, back in Tudor times, when a hearth tax had been introduced; not surprisingly, this had proved unpopular and had the added disadvantage that the tax assessor had to gain entry to the property to count its hearths. So in 1697 the hearth tax was replaced by a new stratagem, the window tax. Like many ideas, this looked good on paper – it was easy to assess and virtually impossible to avoid – until, that is, mean bastards such as my ancestors simply blocked up sixty per cent of their windows! The tax was finally abolished in 1851, but it was not until 1992 that I finished opening up all those windows. Such are the long-term effects of stupid taxation policies.

When we admire the glories of country houses, it certainly does not do to examine too closely the means that enabled them to be built. Our ancestors were as grasping and immoral in their business dealings as the worst type of modern financial fraudster; Robert Maxwell would have been very much at home in eighteenth-century England. Two hundred and fifty years later we would, in all likelihood, be wandering round his house, after paying our fiver, admiring his good taste and pictures and perhaps subscribing some of our hard-earned cash to a fund launched by English Heritage to save for the nation a picture painted by an Italian which, via some shady dealer, has miraculously metamorphosed into a important part of the British national heritage.

The various reform acts of the mid-nineteenth century destroyed much of the political power of the gentry and nobility, but by then the aristocracy was so deeply in thrall to the romance of the country house that the building craze hardly faltered; indeed, it was to receive new impetus from the Industrial Revolution, which provided the engine house for estates in two ways. First, the rapidly expanding urban population had to be fed, and in spite of the repeal of the Corn Laws in 1846 the price of wheat and food remained high, on the whole, right up to the start of the great agricultural depression in 1873. At the same time, many landowners found, to their delight, that they had coal under their land or a port from which it could be exported and, as a consequence, riches in the form of royalties flooded into their bank accounts.

Meanwhile, a new class of people was beginning to cast envious eyes at what it saw as the *beau idéal* lifestyle represented by an English country gentleman's existence. Industrialists, mill owners, shopkeepers and the like were making serious money and, like their predecessors throughout history, the one thing they desired more than anything else was to become gentry. To achieve this they were willing to spend any amount on buying an estate and erecting a grandiose house. Consequently, as the nineteenth century progressed houses became bigger and grander – not this time because a large house might bring its owner political influence, but because, with the advent of the railways, the era of the house party had arrived, coinciding neatly with the surge in popularity of driven-game shooting.

If, towards the end of the nineteenth century, the traditional land-owner with his agricultural estate was feeling a chill wind blowing from across the North Atlantic as British markets were flooded with cheap food, causing his rents to fall, industrialists were wallowing in cash and finding that, provided they could lay on a good shoot and lavish entertainment, they could buy themselves into the first circles of society. Once again, I suspect that the old aristocracy sniggered at the parvenus in their neo-Jacobean mansions – but no one turns down a good day's shooting. You may by now begin to see the purpose of casting a quick eye over history: it has an uncanny habit of repeating itself. After all, most of those doing the sniggering were themselves descended from the Tudor or Georgian *nouveaux riches*!

It was, of course, not only in England that the new rich spent money. Queen Victoria had made the highlands of Scotland fashion-able and there were many impoverished Scottish landowners with hundreds of thousands of acres of barren hillside which they could be persuaded to relinquish. Scotland had one other great advantage: a unique architectural style, Scottish baronial, tailor-made for your rich industrialist who had read the works of Sir Walter Scott and who was of a romantic frame of mind. The love affair with Scottish sporting estates started by Queen Victoria continues today, and many rich Europeans, as well as Englishmen, are willing to buy thousands of acres of barren scrub and happily spend hundreds of thousands of pounds, if not millions, on their new-found romantic dream-world – owning a Scottish sporting estate having been accurately described as the equivalent of tearing up ten-pound notes all day under a cold shower.

The houses these nineteenth-century plutocrats built had to be substantial, for the late-Victorian and Edwardian era was the high point of domestic service: in 1900 it was the single biggest source of employment in the UK, involving over two and a half million people. Houses had not only to be big enough to accommodate the small army of servants who lived there, but also to allow for the fact that people who came to stay tended to bring their own maids and valets.

Meanwhile, as the *nouveaux riches* made hay the traditional land-owning squirearchy and nobility were beginning to feel the pressure of falling incomes and rising taxation. The year 1873 marked the start of a disastrous hundred-year decline in the fortunes of the landed classes. The agricultural depression alone they could no doubt have handled, but gradually they were to be assailed by punitive increases in taxation. Death duties were introduced in 1894 and as the twentieth century progressed, income tax was to rise to confiscatory levels. At the same time, the real wages of workers rose inexorably, and during the First World War legislation aimed at controlling rents on houses and agricultural land was introduced. Squeezed between controlled incomes, rising wages and rising taxation, the owners of landed estates and large houses could see the writing on the wall. Fortunately, few of them could read, while many of those who could were either optimists or simply refused to accept what everyone else forecast about the inevitable destruction of the great estates. What a debt everyone now owes to those ostrich-like landowners who buried their heads in the sand and refused to admit defeat, thus preserving so much of the landscape and architecture of rural England for the enjoyment of so many.

Which brings us to the present day; but before we start looking at modern country estates and houses we ought first to consider what a country estate is in contemporary terms. After all, it might be a small red-brick house in the Home Counties with twenty-five acres of land which, when put in the hands of an estate agent and advertised for sale, metamorphoses into 'a desirable small self-contained estate situated in the unspoilt countryside of rural Surrey'. This is no more an estate than 'a property situated in a select development on an exclusive estate'. (Incidentally, the one thing anyone who is anyone wants to run a mile from is something called 'an exclusive estate'; the only thing likely to be 'select' about the development is the amount you are going to be overcharged for living there.) No, an estate in our context means a large country house with a park and a thousand acres or so of farmland and woods, plus a few cottages.

One cannot be too doctrinaire about this definition. Many would argue that an estate can be much smaller than this, but I would draw the line at anything much less than a thousand acres, since its income is likely to be so paltry that its owner has to work elsewhere; in these circumstances, how can he be a country gentleman? Strangely, this definition fits the parameters of a manor established by William the Conqueror over nine hundred years ago. Not that a thousand acres of land is going to produce enough income for most people to grow fat on, but it might just enable its owner to live the life of a rather poor country gentleman.

We thus arrive, reluctantly, at the subject of money, but then being a country gentleman and keeping up an estate is all about money, so I am afraid the subject will crop up with monotonous regularity. Someone – probably that arch-charlatan Sigmund Freud – once said that a man thinks of sex at least once every five minutes; this may or may not be true, but I do know that a country gentleman thinks of money every five minutes. If he did not, the family pile would soon find its way into the 'for sale' pages of *Country Life*.

A thousand acres may be the minimum size for an estate, but there is no upper limit, nor is there such a thing as a typical estate. It is estimated that there are only some twelve hundred estates left in the United Kingdom and although these range in size from enormous Scottish fiefdoms of a hundred thousand acres composed of little more than heather, to highly valuable English agricultural estates of twenty thousand acres and upwards, the majority of estates range between one and five thousand acres.

Just as estates vary in size, so they vary in every aspect of their make-up, but perhaps they fall into two distinct categories: those that are lavishly maintained and are, ostensibly, well managed thriving entrepreneurial establishments, and those that appear to be anything but. The first category is characterized by an immaculate house, smooth tarmac drives and gleaming farm machinery in the home farm, the latter by rough drives, peeling paint and worn carpets within the house and probably the complete absence of an in-hand farm. Strangely, it is often the *immaculate* estates that end up in the pages of *Country Life*, while the knackered numbers muddle through and survive.

Having defined what an estate is, the next thing to do is to break it down into its constituent parts. These are often called, in estate parlance, 'departments'. A landowner may be heard to say, rather grandly, that he is meeting tomorrow with the head of his 'woodland department', which will impress nearly everyone except those other landowners present. They will smile wryly and mentally subtract twenty-five thousand pounds from their friend's net income. For it is a lamentable fact that few departments seem to make any money; the reasons for this will be examined later.

But back to salient features of our estate. There is, of course, the big house, then come the shooting or game department, the woods, the home farm, tenanted farms, cottages and perhaps a garden. Involved with each of these departments there will be people who fall into two categories full- or part-time employees and outside professionals – consultants, land agents, accountants and the like. We will be looking at all these people and their roles in later chapters, so don't worry.

CHAPTER 2

The Big House

Hail to thy pile! more honour'd in thy fall
Than modern mansions in their pillar'd state;
Proudly majestic frowns thy vaulted hall,
Scowling defiance on the blasts of fate.

LORD BYRON (1788–1824)
'Elegy on Newstead Abbey',
from *Hours of Idleness*, 1807

So much for the past. Yet what of the present? Let us begin by looking at what for most people is the central and most visible feature of an estate, the 'big house'. It goes without saying that most stately-home owners are today saddled with houses several times too big for their everyday needs. Gone is the requirement to entertain the monarch on one of their progresses through her realm. No longer, sadly, can we hope to bribe and impress a small electorate into returning our choice as member for the county. As for the armies of servants, they have almost totally disappeared.

Hardly surprising, then, that over the last eighty years or so a great many owners have bitten the bullet and had their houses demolished or arranged for them to be accidentally burned down – a sensible solution, not only relieving the owner of a monstrous liability but also entitling him to a bonus in the form of an insurance pay-out. Many owners, right up to the early 1980s, would, I suspect, have subscribed to the thoughts of the fictional Sir Murgatroyd Sprockett-Sprockett in P. G. Wodehouse's *Young Men in Spats* (1922): 'Here we are and here we have got to stay, mouldering on in this blasted barrack of a place which eats up every penny of my income . . . ', and given joyful thanks for an opportune fire.

The roll-call of casualties was graphically illustrated by the exhibition in 1975 at the Victoria & Albert Museum entitled 'The Destruction of the Country House'. It estimated that some eleven hundred houses in England, Scotland and Wales had been demolished, burned or substantially altered since 1900, of which 423 were demolished or burned between 1922 and 1955.

A grievous loss – especially if you agree with the view of the architectural historian John Harris: 'The unity of a great house with its furnished interior, collection of great pictures and sculpture, its library and family and estate archives, tied within a garden and set in a landscaped park, is perhaps the supreme example of a collective work of art.'

But the purpose of the exhibition was not just to catalogue past losses but to focus attention on the threat to those houses remaining in private hands. It is easy to forget just how grim things looked only thirty years ago. There was a newly elected Labour government whose Chancellor of the Exchequer, Denis Healey, had announced his intention of squeezing the rich 'till the pips squeaked', and to that end was intending to introduce a wealth tax, on top of the reforms to death duties which was intended to make them virtually unavoidable.

At the time it looked as if communism, masquerading as socialism, had triumphed, and that the long delayed death of the English landed estate was finally at hand. Few, if any, saw that this was the last gasp of a discredited economic and social dogma or recognized in the new leader of the Conservative opposition, Margaret Thatcher, the heroic figure who, almost single-handed, would have the guts, five years later, to take on the task of rolling back some fifty years of socialism. For if there is one person who has done more than any other, over the last hundred years, to stop the disintegration of the remaining great estates, it is Margaret Thatcher, the daughter of a shopkeeper.

But the list of destruction catalogued at the V&A is only half the story. The other half concerns the many houses which, in a sense, have suffered an even more ignominious fate: being converted for various forms of institutional use – as schools, training colleges, hotels or company headquarters – or carved up into flats. At a guess I would think this has been the fate of at least a further thousand houses. It is true that occasionally a house reverts from institutional use back into private hands. My favourite example is the current Lord Portsmouth's ancestral home, Farleigh House. It had been let as a prep school, to which he was sent as a boy. He so hated the school, and most of the masters, that he vowed if he was ever in a position to do so, he would send them packing. Years later the lease came to an end and, much to the surprise of the school, it was not renewed.

So from a figure (admittedly debatable) of approximately five thousand country houses and estates in private hands at the turn of the century we are now down to around twelve hundred, a reduction of some seventy-five per cent. I say the figure of five thousand is debatable because no clear definition exists of what constitutes a country house and estate; consequently no comprehensive catalogue exists either. Various people have tackled this subject using a variety of sources, however, such as the 'Index to the Principal Seats in the United Kingdom' contained in Walford's *County Families of the United Kingdom*, which lists 3,321 such places in England and a further 1,974 in Scotland, Wales and Ireland; and Bateman's *The Great Landowners of Great Britain and Ireland*, which listed, in 1873, 1,323 estates in England with more than three thousand acres and a further 617 estates with between two and three thousand acres. Hence a total of five thousand existing in the United Kingdom around 1900 looks about right and is, as I said in the first chapter, a figure that roughly corresponds with the estimated total number of knights' fees in England some nine hundred years ago.

I suppose the time has come to address the problem of why, over the last hundred-odd years, so many owners threw in the towel. There are many reasons for this, mainly financial, but the one which no one really addresses is the most important: defeatism. From 1873 onwards, land-owners had been under almost continuous attack from increases in taxation, falling agricultural incomes and enormous inflation in wages, at a time when most of their incomes were static or falling. They then had to suffer the impact of two world wars.

The Second World War may have been, in some ways, the finest hour of the country house, but it was also to hasten the death of many, a consequence of their role in the war. Houses built and maintained for the pleasure of their occupants or to impress the neighbouring gentry were converted into army headquarters, training camps, officers' messes and the like. Over two thousand houses were requisitioned for use by the armed forces and when, in 1945, their owners returned from the fighting to take back their ancestral properties they found, more often than not, that they had been barbarously treated. The compensation offered by the government to put right the damage was, in most cases, derisory. John Harris, in *No Voice from the Hall*, tells the story of Roll Park, in Essex. It was requisitioned by the army in 1939. When Andrew Lloyd (the owner) returned from the war, he discovered that no fewer than eighteen different regiments had occupied the house; they had hacked up the delectable Tudor back staircase for firewood, and had begun on the Grinling Gibbons front staircase. In the saloon, Allan Ramsay's famous portrait of Emma Harvey had been used as a dart-board and she had been endowed with a moustache. The conservative estimate given to Lloyd for repairs was £50,000, a huge sum then; the government offered £8,000. He wrote to me: 'I threw in my hand in 1943 and allowed the house to be demolished. It was all too much.'

Low levels of compensation were only part of the problem; in post-war Britain draconian building regulations severely limited the supply of materials, so even those owners who had both the will and the cash to restore their properties were often unable to do anything about it.

One hammer blow after another had hit them and none of them could imagine in their most optimistic moments that their heir would ever want to live in the house anyway or, even if he did, would have the income necessary to maintain it. But they were sometimes mistaken. The case of Sir Francis Dashwood is by no means unique. He was on exercise with his regiment in Germany when he received a telegram from his father: 'Hurray! The National Trust have agreed to take on the house.' Sir Francis was furious but there was nothing he could do – the deed had been done.

It is easy to forget how appalling the future looked then to country-house owners. A flavour of the despair felt by many can be gained from reading the late James Lees-Milne's riveting diaries of his travels round England and Wales, on behalf of the National Trust, during and after the war. This extract on Lyme Park is typical:

> Lord Newton is hopeless. The world is too much for him, and no wonder, he does not know what he can do, ought to do, or wants to do. He just throws up his hands in despair. The only thing he is sure about is that his descendants will never want to live at Lyme, after an unbroken residence of six hundred years . . . Lady Newton is as languid and hopeless as her husband. Both said they would never be able to reconcile themselves to the new order after the war. They admitted that their day was done, and life as they had known it was gone for ever. How right they are, poor people.

This air of defeatism remained a major factor for many years after the war. As recently as 1973, James Lees-Milne predicted that: 'The English House is an archaic osprey. The few left fulfilling the purpose for which they were built are inexorably doomed.' Ironically, since those words were written, both the osprey and the country house have taken on a new lease of life.

Consider these words spoken in Parliament on the subject of taxing houses and landowners:

> They employ hundreds of people and labourers of every description, and they give amusement and enjoyment to thousands. In the summer months the means of conveying the people who go to see these places becomes an absolute industry in itself. But if properties like these, which are blessed or encumbered with a Chatsworth, are to be mulcted in the manner which you propose, the inevitable consequence will be that one after the other they will be shut up, their contents will be sold and dispersed, the whole army of people

to whom they give occupation throughout the year will be dismissed and their employment gone, and money will no longer be attracted to the neighbourhood.

Prophetic words indeed – spoken in 1894 by Henry Chaplin MP, during the debate on Sir William Harcourt's finance bill, which brought in death duties.

Incidentally, in a nice touch of irony, the heiress of the 2nd Viscount Harcourt, direct descendant of Sir William, was hit by massive death duties on the death of her father. David Littlejohn, in his book *The Fate of the English Country House* (1997), chronicles the misery which these taxes caused the Honourable Mrs Gascoigne. She told him: 'There was no possible way we could pay the death duties when my father died in 1979, so we reluctantly agreed to permit public access. It is very upsetting and frustrating – every item exempt from taxes must be kept available for the public to see! They tell you how many days you have to open, where you have to advertise. They simply ignore the fact that a house this size is *lived* in – there's nowhere for the family to withdraw.'

My sympathy for her plight is considerably reduced when I recall the misery and impoverishment her ancestor's policy has wrought on so many other families. A quote from Horace seems apt: 'Undeservedly you will atone for the sins of your fathers.' Perhaps Mrs Gascoigne should have it carved in stone above her front door.

But back to the doom-mongers. This quotation is from *Rural Estate Management* by Charles Walmsley (1948): 'The large country house with its surrounding estate is doomed by death duties and taxation.' This extract is from the Historic Buildings Council's report (1954): 'It is unlikely that many of the large historic houses, even those at present in a good state of repair, will remain much longer in private ownership, maintained entirely at the owner's expense.' Lawrence Stone, in his book *An Open Elite* (1986), wrote: 'The alternatives of survival are manifold, but the efforts seemed doomed.' In short, the obituary of the country house has been written repeatedly for almost a hundred years, yet strangely the patient has refused to die. Why?

There is only one reason why there are still some twelve hundred country houses with estates in private hands left in the United Kingdom today: pure bloody-minded determination on the part of the owners; that old-fashioned word 'guts' springs to mind, something most inhabitants of this country are now sadly lacking as they go squealing to lawyers or MPs with the slightest grievance, real or imagined. For the best part of a hundred years these families have held on grimly to their inheritance as the various governments of the day have done their level best to force them to sell or demolish their houses. Now they find, to their surprise and amazement, that their properties are part of the 'national heritage'.

It is a peculiar thing, this 'national heritage'. 'The nation' decrees that a building is part of its 'heritage', but in spite of this, as we shall see, makes no contribution to the costs of maintaining it – in fact, it taxes those who *do* maintain it! Odd. Even odder, though, is the concept that something should belong to the nation when the nation has not spent one penny on building it or buying the items it contains. Personally I do not believe my house is anything to do with the 'national heritage', as the only time the nation took any particular interest in it was when Cromwell's cannons tried to knock holes in it during the Civil War. But then the devaluation of words and the changing of their meaning are characteristic of the times we live in.

But let us look more closely at the country house today and at how the modern owner can ensure its survival for his own posterity.

Whatever the date or size of your house, certain things will be common to all. It will of course be *big*. There are small country houses, of course, little gems of the Queen Anne era, for instance, with a few acres of land, but we are not concerned with them. How big is *big*? People often ask how many rooms a house has, forgetting that the number is frankly irrelevant. A decent-sized great hall or state drawing room may, quite possibly, be large enough to swallow an entire detached five-bedroom executive home! In other words, the number of rooms is no indication of a house's size.

A better measure is to take the square footage of the floor plan, but even this is fallible as many of the grander rooms will soar the entire height of a house. A line must be drawn somewhere, however, so let us draw it at twelve thousand square feet, which would be the area covered by a reasonably spacious family-sized house. So we have our big house. It will come with the customary mixture of large state rooms, family quarters and attic accommodation, as well as kitchens, larders, pantries and the like, designed for when the house was run by a small army of servants. If your house is Victorian or Edwardian, the area devoted to the space behind the green baize door is likely to be vast and a continuing headache (unless you were fortunate and your father demolished it).

So what do you do with this rambling barracks? The simple answer: live in it and enjoy it. Big houses are marvellous in many ways. You can, for instance, take a walk inside when it is raining; your children can ride their bicycles around the corridors and rooms and play endless games. A lot of fun can be had by all the family exploring and looking through old chests in derelict rooms in the hope of finding something valuable to sell at Christie's. In short, big houses should not be taken too seriously.

Sadly, that is what people do now: they worry about the maintenance, about the running costs, they worry about the damage the children are doing using the Elizabethan bed hangings as climbing ropes. Life, in fact, ceases to be any fun at all.

A lot of this worry is caused by the 'cult of the country house', which over the last twenty-odd years has grown enormously – ever since, in fact, that V&A exhibition which predicted the eventual demise of the whole shooting match. There is a lot to worry about, too, if you are that way inclined and actually bother to take seriously what the so-called experts say. A few years ago, I bought a book entitled *The National Trust Book on Housekeeping*. In my innocence, I thought it might contain helpful hints on how to look after my things. Not a bit of it; every time it got on to something interesting the paragraph ended with the depressing advice: 'consult an expert'. It was rather like reading a Jackie Collins book with all the sex scenes cut out.

Experts, incidentally, are the bane of a country-house owner's life. Strangely, they all have one distinguishing feature: none of them has ever lived in a big house. They ponce around one's home, shaking their silken locks dolefully at the peeling wallpaper and the decrepit paintwork, look learnedly at the bulging masonry and crumbling rendering and pronounce that the bill to put it all right will run into millions. Relax. They are ignorant gits who know nothing; your house will stand for many years with a minimum of maintenance, provided you keep the water out.

The real trouble with most of these 'experts' is that they haven't a clue what they are talking about. They rave over the ghastly chair-covers Great Aunt Agatha installed and ask you what you doing to 'preserve' them! Then they are horrified to learn that the only reason why these monstrosities have not been consigned to the bonfire years ago is that you have not got enough money to replace them. They admire the fact that you seem to live in a time-warp, forgetting that it is financial necessity, not choice, that stops you ripping down walls, painting ceilings, hanging new curtains and re-covering the chairs. They forget also that what they admire today is the result of several hundred years of past generations behaving in exactly that way. Of course the danger of this attitude to 'heritage' properties is that in the future all innovation and eccentricity will be banished from country houses. This is a potential tragedy, as the English country house is nothing if not eccentric. Already if your house is Grade 1 or Grade 2* theoretically you cannot touch either the exterior or interior without the approval of the great and good of the 'heritage' world. The idea that 'taste' is the preserve of a committee of so-called experts is laughable.

This brings us neatly to the subjects of listed buildings, English Heritage and its Scottish and Welsh equivalents. Virtually every pile is 'listed' and most are either Grade 1 or Grade 2*. Now, quite often, ignorant people take pride in the fact that their house is listed – at which one raises one's eyes to the ceiling and sighs. English Heritage actually has the nerve to state that listing increases the value of a building. This is rubbish, and, even if it were true, it is totally irrelevant from the point of view of owners who have no intention of selling. No, the sole reason the value of listed buildings is high is that they happen to be, by definition, rather beautiful buildings. Listing, though, is one of those pernicious forms of covert nationalization without compensation which, like a cloud of poisonous gas on a damp morning on the Somme in 1916, has been slowly creeping over the countryside, destroying everything in its path.

The aim may be laudable – to stop unscrupulous people destroying the architectural heritage of this country – and when one looks at what the local authorities, planners and developers have managed to achieve since the war one has to agree that some such legislation was necessary. But here is the irony: guess who is in charge of giving consent to planning applications on listed buildings? Why, the local authorities, of course! the very same bodies which have succeeded in ruining most of our historic towns.

The origins of the listing process can be traced back to 1943, when the then Ministry of Town and Country Planning drew up a national inventory of historic buildings. In 1947, with a Labour government firmly in the saddle, an act was brought in to control the alteration and demolition of listed buildings and, if necessary, to allow for their compulsory purchase.

It is, however, one thing to pass an Act of Parliament and quite another to make it effective. Even 'intellectually challenged' individuals, such as the then chancellor, Hugh Dalton, began to realize that with taxation at stratospheric levels (he had recently raised death duties to seventy-five per cent) owners of many listed buildings simply did not have the cash to maintain them. Some writers hold that Hugh Dalton was the great saviour of the English country house because, in his 1948 budget, he invented the Land Fund. This was to consist of some £50 million, raised by the sale of war surplus. The intention was that this money would be used to buy important houses, land and works of art for 'the nation'. Since the only reason the owners were having to sell them in the first place was that 'the nation' was taxing them at such a high level, what he was actually proposing was a sort of Alice in Wonderland situation in which the nation bought land and buildings from owners who had to sell them to pay the taxes the government needed to pay for the land and buildings.

He introduced this wizard scheme in his famous budget broadcast to the nation, saying: 'I want to help the Ramblers' Association, the Youth Hostel Association and the National Trust in the fine work they are doing.'

The sudden concern of Hugh Dalton and his successor as chancellor, Sir Stafford Cripps, for the future of historic houses was strange, but even stranger is the rapturous applause which their acts attract today. Some even credit them with 'saving' the stately home. I find this perplexing. It is rather as if someone who had been doing his best to drown you suddenly lets go of your head just as you are about to snuff it and allows you to come up for air.

Be that as it may, Cripps it was who set up the Gower Committee to report on the future of the historic house. Its conclusions were published in 1950, and they are well worth quoting:

> In past times great houses . . . were maintained by their owners . . . now we are faced with a disaster comparable only to that suffered at the dissolution of the monasteries . . . Taxation is primarily responsible for this impending catastrophe. The present rates mean that no individual, however much his gross income, or whatever its source, can have much more than £5,000 to spend. Only seventy taxpayers in the country are left with more than £6,000 a year; and that sum represents a gross income of about £100,000. Many great houses need not less than £5,000 a year, some as much as £10,000 a year, to maintain them, not to any luxury standard, but to the minimum necessary to preserve them and their contents from deterioration . . . Particulars were given us of one case in which a gross income of £140,000 is reduced to £3,500 after income tax, tithe, surtax and expenses of maintaining the agricultural estate from which it comes. Out of this the owner has to maintain two historic houses, as well as himself and his family. He can only do this by drawing on capital at the rate of £8,000 a year.

Every estate owner should read this report, if only to help him understand the appalling situation his father or grandfather was faced with at that time. No wonder so many sold their land and demolished their houses; the wonder is that so many did not.

The Gower Report made many radical recommendations, many of which were acted upon, and virtually all legislation regarding stately homes and listed buildings can be traced back to this document. In spite of the legislation, however, the unchanging tax regime meant that houses continued to disappear. Between 1950 and 1975 a further two hundred and fifty were to be demolished.

One of the primary reasons for the continuing destruction was that, as with much legislation designed to safeguard something for the public good, the public was (and is) not prepared to pay for it. As recently as 1995, Stephen Dorrell, then Secretary of State for Heritage, said: 'The principal responsibility for caring for listed buildings rests with the owners. But others have an interest.' Quite so. But when I have an interest I normally expect to pay for it, not to make a thumping great profit.

Let me explain. There are some 440,000 listed buildings in England and Wales, of which 6,067 are Grade 1 and around 17,250 Grade 2*, the remainder being Grade 3.

Now, let us, for amusement's sake, do some basic arithmetic, concentrating on the Grade 1 and Grade 2* buildings, for which the planning requirements are most stringent. Assume for the sake of argument that on average each one of these 23,300-odd buildings requires a minimum of £10,000 spent per annum on essential maintenance and building work. The total amount spent annually therefore comes to £230,300,000 – chunky money by any standard. We have already seen that the public considers it important that these buildings are kept up and indeed owners are forced by law to ensure this is done. But what financial help does the taxpayer give? None. Instead the exchequer takes 17.5 per cent of the total spent on essential repairs in tax. So the taxman's 'profit' on listed buildings is running at approximately £40,330,000 per annum. Of course, if I grease enough palms and get planning permission in a unspoilt village to build an excrescence of a bungalow, complete with a Marley tile roof and PVC windows, plus a modern 'Georgian' front door, then no VAT will be charged. Somehow it doesn't seem quite right.

There is a simple solution: make repairs to listed buildings exempt from VAT. Successive governments, however, have resisted this. Their main excuse is that any changes to VAT have to be approved by the relevant European commissioner, but I suspect that they also think that, if repairs were VAT-exempt, an awful lot of unimportant building work, such as painting and decorating, installing a new Jacuzzi in a bathroom, etc., would be put down as 'essential repairs'. It is an argument that I have some sympathy with. The answer is that only approved repairs should attract no VAT, but then that would result in an explosion of bureaucracy, something everyone is understandably keen to avoid.

Is there a solution? I think there is, and it is one that would have all the advantages of being cheap and easy to administer. One would also not need the dreaded European Union's permission. It is called 'depreciation'. This is a trick well known to accountants and businessmen. If you buy a machine with a working life of ten years, you are allowed to depreciate the cost of the machine over its anticipated lifetime and set the annual amount of its depreciation against your profits for tax purposes.

My idea, which I offer free to the Heritage Secretary, is that listed buildings should be allowed to depreciate the anticipated cost of their repairs according to a simple formula. Those of us who live in these buildings know that the lifespan of most repairs is between fifty and a hundred years. A slate roof, for instance, should last the full hundred and, roof lead, slightly longer, but electric wiring needs doing every thirty-odd years, otherwise the chances are the entire house will go up in smoke – and so on.

The square footage of every listed building would be measured by a reputable surveyor and a tax allowance granted to that building on a square-foot basis. So, a twenty-thousand-square-foot building might need, at today's prices, something approaching £2 million spent on essential repairs over a hundred-year period, or a hundred pounds per square foot (unless, that is, it is owned by the National Trust – but we will be looking at that in more detail later). Each year, the owners would be able to set against tax twenty thousand pounds' worth of repairs or –

and this is important – roll the tax relief forward for the big job they know will need doing in ten years' time.

Unfortunately, the very simplicity of this idea, its good sense and the fact that it is relatively free of bureaucracy, render it automatically a non-starter.

Actually, the profit to the treasury on listed buildings is even greater than I have estimated, because on the other side of the equation is what it would cost the taxpayer to keep most of these edifices in existence if their private owners gave up the unequal struggle. Presumably, since the government insists they are part of the National Heritage, the taxpayer would have no choice but to pay. Admittedly, taxpayers would be unlikely to be willing to take on all Grade 1 and Grade 2* properties, but surely no one is going to suggest that they could look quietly on as houses of the quality of Chatsworth, Blenheim and the like were sold and converted for institutional use. We will get a better idea of the cost savings involved when we examine the workings of the National Trust in a later chapter, but we can safely assume that they would be vast – hundreds of millions of pounds a year.

The threat of stately homes falling into ruin if the current owners were forced to give up and sell has receded in recent years. Estate agents have books full of *nouveaux riches* businessmen and bankers wanting to buy estates and large houses, and not just Englishmen either: Europeans, Arabs, Americans, all seem to want to sink their ill-gotten gains into the bottomless pit of a large house and its surrounding estate. Luckily for estate agents and their clients, there is still a steady stream of such properties coming on the market. Hugh Montgomery-Massingberd, in *The Disintegration of a Heritage*, reckons that around twenty great houses, with their accompanying estates, were being sold each year. I do not dispute these figures, but I do wonder if the only reason behind them is high maintenance costs. In my experience, sales occur mainly for five reasons: the heir/owner is a drug addict or a spendthrift or, perhaps, horror of horrors, a combination of the two; the owner has lost a packet in a disastrous business venture; the owner has married a very expensive wife; the estate has been left in such dire straits that it is no longer remotely viable, e.g., the daughters and younger sons have been given legacies that are too generous; and, finally, the owner has been quietly selling his capital assets for years to finance his lifestyle and now, his income reduced, has only the house and the rump of the estate left to sell.

Actually, there is a sixth category of seller: those who have recently bought a stately home and its land. Estate agents relish selling stately homes, because not only are they prestigious but the chances are they will be back on the market within ten or, at the very most, twenty-five years. Indeed, one large house in Devon called Whiteway has been sold no fewer than five times in thirty-five years! The reason for the inability of most new buyers to put down their roots is simple. By the time they are rich enough to afford their dream their own children are grown up, and when ten or twenty years later they suggest to their eldest son that he might like to take over the estate he is totally uninterested, so back it comes on the market – having in the meantime gobbled up a significant amount of money.

In 1988, Nicholas Ridley said, in a speech to the Historic Houses Association, 'There have to be some opportunities for today's *nouveaux riches* so I am not impressed by the case for the *anciens pauvres*.' To which Lord Shelburne, then president of that august body, replied: 'Potentially there are many hundreds of owners who cannot hold on financially much longer . . . When they admit defeat, beaten by the challenge, will there be queues of *nouveaux riches* to take over where they left off? Of course not. Most successful entrepreneurs have more sense!' Nicholas Ridley was proved right and Lord Shelburne wrong – as he would soon find out today if he put his house, Bowood, on the market.

The reasons behind the sudden appetite of the *nouveaux riches* for country life are many and varied, and most of them probably have not changed since the aforementioned Italian, Bracciolini, wrote in the fifteenth century: 'I have seen a man who has given up trade, bought an expensive estate, and left town to go there with his family, turn his sons into noblemen.'

Part of the reason, however, is probably something to do with the mechanical revolution that has occurred over the last thirty years in house management. Efficient dishwashers, cooking implements, cleaning devices and the like have revolutionized life below stairs in the big houses and have enabled owners to exist in the height of luxury with what before the war would have been considered a skeleton staff. And it is not only inside the house that the mechanical revolution has wrought its work. In the gardens, ride-on lawnmowers and patent weedkillers have enabled large staffs to be reduced. In short, big houses no longer need big staffs to keep them up.

A further factor is that old favourite saying of estate agents: 'Property is about three things: location, location, location.' To which I always respond: 'Yes, and location is about three things: communication, communication, communication.' In other words, the vast improvements in communications over the last fifty years have, from a house buyer's point of view, 'shrunk' Britain. Although we continue, as ever, to complain about the roads and the railways, they are an improvement on those of fifty years ago and the cars we drive are vastly superior in both comfort and safety. But communications are not only about the means of physical travel but also about the electronic transfer of information. First the fax machine and now the Internet have revolutionized rural life, allowing a high-flying banker to work at home and to enjoy country life for rather longer than he would have been able to in the 1960s.

One further factor was needed to make the price of estates with large houses rise dramatically and stay high: the vastly increased monetary rewards bankers and businessmen suddenly discovered were theirs for the asking. Some time in the late 1970s the old City finally died. With it went the traditions of 'my word is my bond' and the concepts of looking after your staff and other old-fashioned practices, denounced as 'paternalistic' rubbish by the new City, which laughed at the old custom of feeding the horses first, then the men, and only then looking after yourself. In the new City you not only fed yourself first, you gorged and, as you made your men redundant and paid them the bare minimum, you ensured that, if removed from office for gross incompetence, you went away with enough boodle to keep you in the manner to which you considered yourself entitled for the rest of your life.

The result of all these factors has been a dramatic inflation of prices for such establishments. Back in 1967, a chartered surveyor, John Taylor, was flicking through *Farmers' Weekly* when he saw an idyllic house in a one-thousand-acre estate; it was called Cricket St Thomas. The asking price was £245,000 and he bought it. Over the next thirty years he developed the estate into a leisure complex and wildlife park, and in 1997 put it on the market looking for offers in excess of £8 million. The house and grounds were eventually brought for a little less than this by a hotel group, but it had still proved a cracking investment, even taking into account the fact that John Taylor had transformed an idyllic gentleman's estate into a glorified entertainment complex along the way.

Part of the reason for the escalation in the price of such properties is their rarity. If you are a super-rich man you can wait quite a long time for your dream estate to come on the market, and when it does arrive you must seize your opportunity. This simple truth has percolated down to the sellers, who have ratcheted up their asking prices, as Knight Frank did with Easton Neston in Northamptonshire. This is baroque master-piece by the brilliant architect Nicholas Hawksmoor, together with 3,300 acres of land, Towcester racecourse and a further twenty-five-odd houses, was put on the market by Lord Hesketh for the princely sum of £50 million. His excuse for doing so, after some 450 years of family ownership, was that it was the only way he could see of preserving what was left of his family's fortune as it was costing him 'at least £500,000 a year to maintain the house and estate but in a bad year this might rise to as much as £1.5 million'. It may well have been costing Lord Hesketh this, as his generosity was – and is – legendary, but frankly you cannot expect to live like a lord on an estate only big enough to accommodate someone with the spending habits of a squire.

But to get back to the cost of maintaining these rambling piles. I seem to be hearing muttering about grants, those marvellous things dished out by English Heritage. Whenever an owner of a historic house spends any money on it, the first thing his friends say is, 'You must have got a big grant.' When said owner has recovered from being quietly sick, he is forced to explain that the chances of getting a *good* grant from English Heritage are similar to those of winning the lottery. In 1992, English Heritage proudly disbursed £118,328 in grants to houses belonging to members of the Historic Houses Association. This worked out at an average of £85 for every member of the HHA which, bearing in mind the association includes such mammoth establishments as Blenheim, Longleat, Chatsworth and Castle Howard, is an interesting statistic. Another interesting statistic: between 1953 and 1973 the predecessor of English Heritage, the Historic Buildings Council, made grants to private owners totalling only £2.5 million, or a paltry average of £125,000 a year! Even if we allow for inflation and multiply these figures by a factor of ten to get somewhere near the modern value of these amounts, it will be seen that rarely have the private owners ever received more than the modern equivalent of £1 million in any one year since the grant system was set up.

Even these derisory sums are now under threat. Under the new regime, grants are going to be managed on a 'regional' basis. In other words, the same amount of money will now be distributed by nine Regional Heritage bodies rather than one National one. Helping the regions to decide how to spend the money will be helpful 'guidelines' produced by English Heritage. A whole new range of criteria has been introduced. Properties applying for grants will have to demonstrate not only that they are 'buildings at risk' but also that they provide – or intend to provide – 'social benefit', 'skills development', and that they contribute to 'regeneration', plus a host of other buzzwords. In short, the days when seriously important privately owned buildings, could and did, apply for and receive grant aid for vital structural repair are over. The *Affaire Tyntesfield*, as the French would call it, has demonstrated that only bodies such as the National Trust are geared up to make the right noises to get the lolly today, and in any event their appetite for spending other people's money is so vast that, after they have taken their snout out of the trough, there is frankly nothing left worth having.

Getting a grant was never easy; many an owner who opened up communications with English Heritage or its predecessor in the hope of getting one lived to rue the day. A typical case history will demonstrate. The owner of a Grade 1 house decides the time has come to put the roof right, an essential repair and one that would certainly qualify for grant aid. His first port of call is likely to be the local builder, who has years of experience of working on the property and comes up with a quote of around £200,000. Our hypothetical owner rubs his hands with glee; he has £100,000 in the bank and, with every expectation of getting a fifty per cent grant from English Heritage, he gets in touch with them. So far, so good, and so simple.

Now for the problems. Has he got an architect's opinion? No, he doesn't think he needs one. Wrong; you must get one if you want a grant, so kiss goodbye to a minimum of £5,000. Does his financial situation warrant a grant? You don't know? Perhaps you were not aware that grants are means tested. There are two bases for assessing financial worthiness for a grant. First is the property's market value. Under this formula you will get your grant provided the cost of the repair schedule exceeds the market value of the house. When this rule was first introduced, large country houses, frankly, were worth very little, so it was of purely academic interest. An example: when my father died in 1969, our house – quite a substantial number – plus three lodges and a cottage, were valued at £12,000 for probate. Since those days property values have shot up and, except in the more inaccessible parts of Britain, it would be hard to find a large house technically valued at under £1.5 million. In other words, you have to be into a pretty substantial essential-repair programme to qualify.

The second basis is a historic estate assessment. This is more complex, as you would expect, so stand by for some serious accountant's bills if you choose this route. To begin with, it is open only to houses that have been owned for at least three generations by the same family. To find out if you qualify for a grant, English Heritage will look in detail at your last three years' accounts and assess whether you have sufficient surplus of income over expenditure to fund your repair programme out of your own resources. So now get your accountant to do the work – bang goes another £10,000 (or far more if you are stupid enough to employ one based in London – of which more later). Next:

is your builder competent, in English Heritage's eyes, to do the work? Perhaps not, so get other quotes from approved builders and discover that, instead of the job costing £200,000, it is now likely to cost £250,000. You are now, I trust, beginning to understand why grants are such a waste of space.

Here is my advice to anyone who still thinks that applying for grants from English Heritage is a good idea: don't even think about it! Unless, that is, your restoration programme is so vast and your house so important that you are talking serious money, i.e. £500,000-plus.

The real joke, of course, is that, since a grant has to be 'approved', you might, after doing all that work and spending all that extra money, not get the grant anyway! Then you really are in trouble. In a worst-case scenario you won't get the grant, but the experts from English Heritage will discover some rare aspect of your property which no one previously knew about and force you to forgo the modernizing of the old kitchen and preserve the 1880 kitchen range you were about to replace with a modern Aga.

You may now be wondering why, if they are so obscured by obstacles, grants are still in existence? A good question. Not only are they virtually valueless as far the vast majority of house owners are concerned, but their very existence causes confusion in the minds of the general public, the latter being under the totally mistaken impression that many stately homes are kept upright only by enormous injections of taxpayers' money. As we have seen, this is decidedly *not* the case. Personally, I believe the Historic Houses Association ought to campaign for the abolition of grants to private owners in exchange for a depreciation charge. This would focus the public's attention on the paucity of grant money available for private owners.

A last word on grants from Sir John Smith, chairman of the Landmark Trust: 'Accepting a grant from English Heritage is like marrying for money. In the end you earn it. I am not saying you should never do it, but you should do it only for what the French call an "important sum".'

Now is a good time to look at listing. It is a pernicious process. If you are in possession of a Grade 1 or Grade 2* property, the restrictions on you are onerous – if you bother to abide by them, that is – because listing extends to all buildings within the curtilage, not just the part of your property that attracted the attention of the inspector in the first place. To quote:

> The ground which is used for the comfortable enjoyment of a house or other building may be regarded in law as within the curtilage of that house or building and thereby as an integral part of the same, although it has not been marked off or enclosed in any way. It is enough that it serves the purpose of the house or building in some necessary or reasonable way.

So, technically, you require listed-building consent to alter or demolish any structure predating 1948 within land that fits the above definition.

This inevitably leads to ludicrous situations. Let us assume that a building is listed Grade 1 because the central block of it is an exceptional Queen Anne house. Sadly for the owners, their ancestors were rolling in loot in the latter part of the nineteenth century and decided to add on a couple of ghastly wings to house the masses of servants they now needed to look after their good selves and their weekend guests. These wings are no longer required and anyone with a brain can see that their demolition would be enormously beneficial both to the family and to the original Queen Anne house. Because they are attached to a Grade 1 building, however, they are themselves Grade 1. And to get permission to alter a Grade 1 building is a lengthy and costly process, especially today, when every obscure architect and style of architecture attracts a vocal and well-financed interest group.

But let us move on. In addition to construction work there are also running expenses, all those ghastly brown envelopes that arrive in the post just as you are settling down to your breakfast. Bills for insurance, electricity, maintenance agreements on servicing the Aga, the boiler, the burglar alarm and so on. They all add up to a considerable annual sum, but some of them you can at least reduce to manageable proportions. Electric lights, for instance, need to be turned on only when you are in a room, while the central heating need never be switched on at all except when the temperature slips some way below freezing. The best investment anyone can make in a big house is in installing a manual on/off switch in the boiler room and removing the timer clock.

Central heating is in fact more a curse than a godsend. The worst thing about it is that all one's friends have it installed these days. They seem to turn it on automatically – regardless of the weather – in October and turn it off only in April; it must cost them a fortune. When they come to stay with me, instead of remarking on the healthy, bracing atmosphere in the house, they start to shiver ostentatiously and make weak jokes. When I suggest there is a simple solution to the problem, which would cost me nothing and would do the British wool industry a lot of good – namely the donning of a jersey – they look at me as though I were a dangerous lunatic. The other side of the coin reveals itself when you go to stay with them. You walk into a wall of heat from which there is no escape. In your bedroom, you find the window does not open, or if it does you are too drunk to work out how. You then try to turn off the radiator, only to find that it needs some special key which you are too cowardly to go down and knock on your host's bedroom door to ask for. The result: you collapse into your bed and wake up with a splitting hangover.

There is one very good joke about central heating: it causes dry rot. This is a nasty fungus, which thrives in warm, damp conditions. It is not native to this country but arrived here in the nineteenth century from the Himalayas, courtesy of plant collectors. One thing dry rot hates more than anything is cold and draughts, so I have no problems; but I know of a man who spent a fortune renovating a reasonable-sized Cotswold manor house, and to ensure his comfort put in double glazing, roof insulation and central heating. To his horror, within a short time the entire building was riddled with the fungus; it cost him a tidy sum to put right.

Apart from central heating there are, of course, many other unnecessary costs. Window cleaning springs to mind. I once read of some peer complaining that it cost him ten thousand pounds a year to keep his windows clean. This struck me as odd, because surely the outsides of the windows get washed by the rain while the insides can be left to fester until one can't see out of them any more, after thirty or even fifty years of saving said ten thousand every year!

In short, a country-house owner needs to look at his costs carefully. What he must *not* do is what all too many try to do: live in the house as though it were a nice cosy five-bedroom house in the Home Counties. You need to be seriously rich to do this, which sadly most country-house owners are not.

After the last war, several owners came up with an alternative to just living in their houses: opening them to the public. This was not a new idea; many houses had opened their doors before – indeed, in the eighteenth and nineteenth centuries it was common practice for those with large houses to allow visitors.

In 1871 *The Times* made the following comment:

> The British public have much to be thankful for . . . Wherever they go they have, within an easy drive, some great place, with park, gardens, very fine oak trees, natural curiosities, and some fine pictures. A moderate gratuity to the servants will often purchase for them as much pleasure as the noble or gentle owner has in a year for enormous expenditure. He only goes down, perhaps to bleed money at every pore, to scold, to give orders, to entertain, and convert his house into a hotel, with the privilege of paying all the bills. The public, a chartered libertine, steps in and enjoys a glimpse of Paradise – as much as is good for any of us – at the moderate cost of a shilling a head for a party of five, perhaps . . . A Fifth Monarchy man of the sternest Communist type used to admit that there was one good in our gentry – they made the country picturesque. The truth is England would be naked without them.

Once again we see that nothing changes. *The Times* could print virtually the same leader today and find few to quarrel with it. It is true that towards the end of the nineteenth century many owners had to rethink their open-door policy, as improvements in communications allowed thousands to visit where before only a few hundred had come.

Some owners though, even before the First World War, had already embarked on the commercialization of their houses. In 1905, Warwick Castle had forty thousand visitors a year paying a shilling a head, providing a healthy income to the then Earl of Warwick. But Warwick was, and remained, a rarity in its pursuit of profit. For most owners who, after the last war, embarked on opening their houses, the pursuit of profit from showing visitors round was a radical and, in some instances, an exciting new concept. Impetus to this idea was added when grants for repairs became available, as grants were usually conditional on the house being opened to the public.

The leaders in this field were, perhaps inevitably, the descendants of the once hugely rich and corrupt old Whig families whose ancestors had built massive piles with their ill-gotten gains in the sixteenth, seventeenth and eighteenth centuries. Men such as the Duke of Bedford and the Marquess of Bath entered eagerly into the spirit of the business and, while some of their fellow peers sniffed at the vulgarity of their antics, on the whole they made a success of it and achieved the aim of saving their houses from sale or demolition.

Just because the scheme paid off for owners of some of the premier-division houses did not mean, however, that every house could successfully follow the same path. Unfortunately, many owners did not realize this obvious fact and, as house followed house in the rush to open, many found, after spending tens if not hundreds of thousands on providing 'facilities' for the public, that said public obstinately refused to be tempted to visit in sufficient numbers to pay the running costs of opening the house to them in the first place – let alone give any return on the capital invested. In short, opening your house did not prove to be the gold mine that had been envisaged.

Of course, not every house opened because the owner wanted it to. In many instances he had no choice in the matter, either because he had accepted a grant for a major repair, and opening to the public was a condition attached to that grant, or he had been forced, on the death of his father, to apply to the Treasury for 'conditional exemption' from death duties, under the terms of which the house, contents and grounds had to be on view, for a specified number of days a year, to the general public.

Owners who resigned themselves to opening for these reasons sometimes invested considerable capital sums in trying to establish a money-making business – only to find, after a number of years of losing substantial sums, that they would have been better off if they had coughed up the cash to the Treasury and never gone into the business in the first place.

The reasons behind the failure of many houses were simple. The cost of setting the whole thing up in the first place was high. The public, it seemed, demanded tarmac roads, 'toilet facilities', restaurants, etc. – all extremely expensive; on top of all this, the staffing and extra running costs were often ruinous, far exceeding the amount coming in. Even worse, unless you could demonstrate to the Inland Revenue that you were actively trying to make a profit (in which case you needed to make a profit at least once every five years), the running costs of the house could not be set off against tax. This is why, gradually, many houses have been slowly restricting their opening times, or have shut down to the general public totally and gone in for yet another venture: corporate entertaining. This – for some – has proved a good wheeze. The caveat, though, is that, once again, to make serious money you need to be near large centres of population.

Other businesses tried, with varying degrees of success, have been wildlife parks, children's adventure playgrounds, and so on. Many of these went well at first, but recently problems have arisen. The public is becoming increasingly sophisticated and demands better and larger attractions every year. Consequently, owners find that in order to continue to attract punters they are having to make major investments on an annual basis in new rides, animals, etc. In other words, to keep the business going the profits from it have to be ploughed back.

Whatever business a house owner decides to go into, the location of the property is the key to success or failure. If you live in a house forty minutes or so away from London or in the Midlands then opportunities abound, but if you live out in the sticks then frankly you might as well forget the whole thing and put your money into the stock market.

Over the last fifty years, stately-home owners have invested many millions of pounds in commercializing their properties. At the best about a dozen have made regular taxable profits; most of the remainder would probably, with the benefit of hindsight, have been a lot better off putting all their available spare cash into stocks and shares. As for those poor saps who actually sold property and land in order to raise the capital necessary to open their houses, all I can say is that they made a very bad deal indeed. Not only has the loss of precious capital sometimes caused the sale of the house itself, as happened to Lord Brownlow at Belton, but also the pressures of commercialization and the need to try and make money have destroyed the very ambience and setting the owner was trying to save for his family.

I often recall the words of an American officer in Vietnam who, when asked by a reporter, during the Tet offensive of 1968, why he had just blasted some village off the face of the earth, replied: 'We had to destroy the village in order to save it.' This was an unfortunate remark, which was relayed round the world and did the American military PR machine no good at all. Yet many country-house owners seem to follow his advice. They open their houses to the public, have various events in their parks on a regular basis, hold great corporate functions in their state rooms and end up by moving out and living in the stables or in a nearby farmhouse. All this is done in the name of 'saving' the house, but in fact all they have achieved is to turn what was a home into a cross between a sterile museum and an up-market hotel. The words of the American officer turn out to be apt after all.

Frankly, I am of the unenterprising school of country-house owners. I am aware of the irony of the situation that, as we have seen, in spite of all this enterprise many of these operations do not make much money and some actually lose it. It is doubtful if even those who claim to make a substantial trading profit would do so if they factored in a charge for the cost of the capital invested in upgrading kitchens, roads, loos and the like to cater for the needs of the public. The most pertinent test would be to see what that capital would have done if invested in the stock market, as opposed to what has been achieved through all this activity and effort.

In short, there is much to be said for doing nothing. Those who have practised the 'do nothing' school of country-house and estate management have been among the most successful owners since the war. Sitting on their estates and shivering in front of log fires, they have seen their assets steadily increase in value and their incomes rise. Now, for the first time in perhaps a century, they can look at their future with a degree of equanimity and, just occasionally, give themselves a treat and turn on the central heating.

CHAPTER 3

The Big House – the Public Sector

The National Trust (NT) was founded in 1894 as a reaction to the danger presented by the growing urban sprawl of late-Victorian England; its aim was to secure beauty spots and other areas of the countryside to act – as one of the founders put it – as 'open-air sitting rooms for the poor'. Over a century later, it is the UK's largest private landowner and has a membership of over two million.

Although it accepted its first house, Barrington Court in Somerset, in 1907, and took over Montacute in 1931, it was an address by the Liberal peer Lord Lothian to the annual meeting of the National Trust in 1934 that started the ball rolling. He warned: 'Most of these [country houses] are now under sentence of death, and the axe which is destroying them is taxation, especially that form of taxation known as death duties . . . I do not think it an exaggeration,' he continued, 'that within a generation hardly one of these historic houses, save perhaps a few near London, will be lived in by the families who created them. Yet it is these 400 or 500 families who have for 300 or 400 years guided the fortune of the nation.'

There followed several years of difficult negotiations by the National Trust with the government of the day, but in 1937 Parliament passed an act which effectively enabled the National Trust to set up its country house scheme. By the end of the Second World War the National Trust had accumulated twenty-three houses and by 1950 forty-two; it now has over two hundred houses of various shapes and sizes, which are open to the public. These are not all, by any means, great houses or even country houses – for instance one of the more recent, and controversial,

CAPITAL REPAIRS – AVERAGE ANNUAL COST
(Long-term estimate, allowing for cyclical items)

Major works	Annual cost	Frequency (years)	Annual average
Structural repairs	£100,000	10	£10,000
Reroofing	£750,000	70	£10,700
Repointing	£700,000	25	£28,000
Joinery repairs (external)	£60,000	30	£2,000
Redecoration (external)	£25,000	5	£5,000
Rewiring (system)	£150,000	25	£6,000
Electrical mains	£30,000	40	£750
Renewal of boilers	£50,000	20	£2,500
Renewal of heating system	£30,000	30	£1,000
Plumbing services	£20,000	40	£500
Fire-detection systems	£10,000	15	£700
Security systems	£10,000	15	£700
Redecoration (internal)	£50,000	10	£5,000
Water mains	£75,000	40	£1,900
Drainage	£100,000	40	£2,500
Lightning conductor	£25,000	20	£1,250
Repairs to garden wall	£20,000	10	£2,000
Conservatory floor	£30,000	20	£1,500
Flat renovation	£60,000	15	£4,000
Restaurant/kitchen	£25,000	10	£2,500
Shop	£5,000	5	£1,000
Drives, paths, car parks	£75,000	10	£7,500
Renovation of cottage	£40,000	30	£1,300
Visitors facilities	£20,000	10	£2,000
TOTAL			£100,300
Add average annual minor works			£15,000
SUBTOTAL			£115,300
Add contingency @ 10%			£11,700
GRAND TOTAL			£127,000

acquisitions was John Lennon's terrace house in Liverpool – but just over a hundred of the National Trust's properties would probably fit the general criteria pertaining to a 'country house'.

The increase in National Trust ownership owed much to legislation passed by the post-war Labour government in response to the Gower Report, which finally allowed owners to do what Lord Lothian had urged in 1934: pass their houses and contents over to the Treasury in lieu of tax. The Treasury then made the property over to the National Trust. Initially this 'relief' was restricted to buildings and land but in 1953 the Conservative government extended it to cover contents.

Over the years, many owners concluded that the National Trust was the only option available to secure the survival of their property and its continuation as a residence for their family, albeit as tenants rather than owners. In some cases their judgement was probably correct, but in many others it was totally wrong, and their heirs rue the day their ancestral house, land, contents and heirlooms were given away so cavalierly. Today, the National Trust is a very different animal from the rather chaotic and amateurish organization depicted in Lees-Milne's famous diaries; whether it is more effective at its job, however, is a moot point. Some of the donor families, and many outside observers, would say it is not.

The modern National Trust is a hugely successful organization. With a membership of over two million, it is the largest private landowner in the country, with no lack of resources. The National Trust would, and does, strenuously deny this, pleading for money continually from the public, the government and that new 'heritage cash dispenser', the National Lottery.

This superabundance of resources is, of course, one of the reasons why a casual observer will note some salient differences when visiting a big house still in private hands compared with one managed and owned by the National Trust or English Heritage. Superficially, he will observe, the publicly owned properties look in rather better nick than the majority of those still privately owned. Both the National Trust and English Heritage have high standards, but then they also have deep pockets and do not suffer from the trauma of having large slices of their income and capital removed by the taxman at regular intervals.

It is often the case that the richer you are the more lavish and uncontrolled your expenditure, and it has to be said that the National Trust is no exception to this rule. It may be relevant in this context to insert here what the National Trust considers a reasonable annual budget for repairs to one of its houses. Admittedly the table on the facing page was drawn up in 1990. I expect the figures have been subject to considerable 'uplift' since then. The table, it must be remembered, does not refer to a true mega-house of Blenheim Palace, Burghley or Chatsworth proportions, but to an average-sized country house. It also, of course, refers solely to capital expenditure, not to the day-to-day running costs of staff wages, heating, electricity and minor maintenance.

I doubt if very many of the private owners of such properties spend a tithe of this amount per annum on their houses. This is hardly surprising when the National Trust was budgeting to spend, even in 1990, £12.7 million on this property over a hundred-year period. This certainly makes my proposal in the preceding chapter – that the government should grant owners of listed properties a depreciation allowance of £100 per square foot, to be amortized over a hundred-year period – seem pretty modest. Incidentally, I myself would not refuse the job of caretaker, with my flat being refurbished every fifteen years at a cost of £60,000. This is considerably more than my family have spent on redecorating our house over the last hundred years.

The budget in the table was drawn up by the National Trust to help it in construct something called the Chorley Formula, the purpose of which was to give the National Trust a means of calculating the size of the endowment needed before it took on any new houses. The organization had become increasingly concerned that in the past it had often accepted houses with an inadequate endowment and had 'lost' money as a result. It is perhaps not generally realized that the National Trust takes on a house only if it comes with a large enough chunk of land and money to cover upkeep costs.

The formula used by the National Trust to work out how much money it needs is extremely complicated, as you would expect, and is no doubt based on the old premise that 'bullshit baffles brains'. I set it out below in all its glory.

Annual property expenditure*		X
+ 20% (contingencies 12.5%, improvements 7.5%)		X
+ 20% management fee		X
TOTAL		X
Deduct annual property income:		
Rents (less one-third)	X	
Other income	X	X
Annual deficit		X
+ 50% uplift		X
Uplifted deficit		Y
Capitalization rate		Z%
ENDOWMENT REQUIRED		£Y x 100
		Z

Most of the headings are self-explanatory. The capitalization rate is taken after assessing the yield on dividend income on investments, so today it would probably be fair to put that in at 4 per cent. Anyway, I thought the inclusion of the formula would amuse those readers, with houses big or small, who, on a wet afternoon, wished to while away the time working out how big an endowment the National Trust would require to take over their property.

For a time it seemed that the advent of the Chorley Formula probably meant that no new houses would ever again be added to the NT property portfolio, as the endowment required was likely to be so large that few, if any, potential donors would be financially able to give the

* See table entitled 'Capital Repairs – Average Annual Cost' on page 55.

NT their houses. This state of affairs was graphically illustrated in 1992, when a black-and-white Tudor timber-framed house called Pitchford Hall came on the market. The National Trust offered to take over the house, but at a price: it wanted £11 million! Of this sum it generously proposed that £1 million should come from its own resources and the balance from the poor benighted taxpayer. In fairness, £2 million was going to be used to buy the house and contents from the owners, who had been hard hit by Lloyd's underwriting losses, but that still left a shortfall of £9 million. The National Trust justified its demand for such a large sum by revealing that £2.5 million was going to be spent putting the house to rights *à la* National Trust, and a further £500,000 on building visitor facilities, leaving a balance of £6 million to provide the inevitable endowment fund. Not surprisingly, the taxpayer balked at this generous offer and the house and contents were sold privately. I suspect they are now being very well cared for at no public expense.

The taxpayer, or rather, perhaps, the Lottery player, did not balk when a rather second division Victorian house called Tyntesfield was put on the market following the death of Lord Wraxall in 2001. He had decided to divide his inheritance among some twenty relations rather than leave the whole to the eminently suitable eldest son of his younger brother, so inevitably the family decided to sell up and split the cash. Of course the situation was now that the government, when confronted by the clamouring of the heritage lobby over some house or estate, no longer had to find the money out of tax but could direct the National Trust either to the Heritage Memorial Fund or to the National Lottery fund. This they did, and the cash, some £17.5 million, was coughed up by the said Heritage Memorial Fund, enabling the trust to purchase the house, contents and five hundred acres. This was, however, just the beginning. Through a public appeal, the trust had raised £1.5 million from 50,000 donors as well as with two anonymous donations totalling £5 million. Still, though, the trust demanded yet more money, so in steps the National Lottery fund and pledged that, in principle, they would contribute a further £20 million. Add all these sums together and the result is a figure of around £45 million, which the NT has insisted it needs to restore and run a moderate-sized Victorian house. Private owners can only gasp at the maths, the cheek, and the gullibility of both the public and the trustees of the Heritage Memorial Fund and National Lottery fund. Do people never stop and wonder how it is that some thousand private owners of houses, many of which are several times the size of Tyntesfield, manage to survive, and even in some cases prosper, on budgets that amount to less than a tithe of what the NT deems necessary? The lesson here is that people always believe what they read, especially if the writer is a professional of repute, even if logic and common sense forcefully suggest that the sums or statistics are a complete load of rubbish.

Incidentally, I expect most people will assume that the NT was keen to have Tyntesfield because it wished to preserve a wonderful, exuberant example of high Victorian gothic, complete with its 'time capsule' interior. How wrong they would be. The NT has a 'Tyntesfield Vision' and this is what it says:

> The purpose of the National Trust at Tyntesfield is to bring alive the ongoing conservation and public access though learning opportunities such as work placement, apprenticeships, events, guided tours, 'taster' sessions, volunteering over the coming years to name but a few! We hope that this will lead to the fulfilment of everyone involved whether it is personnel development, building new skills and confidence, becoming part of the history of Tyntesfield, or just having fun.

The execrable English aside, what does this mean?

The consequence of the Tyntesfield saga, in my view, will be that very few houses will be acquired by the NT in the future. I am not saying that no more houses will *ever* be added to the National Trust's portfolio, but I was struck by the deathly silence from them, and other paid-up members of the heritage lobby, when a premier-division house, Easton Neston, was put on the market, together with the surrounding estate, by Lord Hesketh. Not a squeak was heard from anyone. Even the NT seemed to have realized that it had so gorged itself on public (and private) money at Tyntesfield that if it had tried the same trick at Easton Neston it would have been laughed out of court. If public money is not available for new country houses to be acquired, then it is unlikely that private money, in the form of generous endowments, will be forthcoming either. Such is the arrogance and greed of the modern NT that its demands for money would be beyond the reach of any but the richest and most philanthropic owner. Gone are the days when impoverished aristocrats could turn to the National Trust *in extremis* and make over the house and park and a thousand acres or so of farmland in order to ensure the survival of their property. For today, if you have sufficient funds to endow your house you are – by definition – rich enough to afford to run it in complete luxury for your own selfish enjoyment.

In any event, few large country houses nowadays could be considered in danger of dereliction and eventual demolition, since rich men have recovered their appetite for conspicuous consumption. Buying and living in a great house is at the top of the conspicuous consumption pyramid. That this was not the case back in the glory days of the National Trust, just after the last war, goes without saying, and without doubt the job the organization did then was superb. But in those far-off days the National Trust was run by gentlemen amateurs; now we are subject to the formulas of the bullshit-baffles-brains variety, and the grip of the professional manager has tightened on even such a quintessential English institution.

In those halcyon days, owners who gifted their house to the National Trust often got, with the benefit of hindsight, very good deals indeed. The concept was simple. The nation preserved a historically important house and – usually – its contents, which it acquired for nothing. In return the owner and his family continued to live in the home of their ancestors. In 1994, an American, Paula Weideger, wrote the proverbial exposé book on the National Trust: *Gilding the Acorn: Behind the Façade of the National Trust*. She criticized many of the deals as being too 'generous to the owners'. But such criticism is misplaced, for several reasons. First, like all criticisms of past deals, it was made with the benefit of hindsight, and ignored the fact that if the National Trust made a bad deal then it is probably equally true that the heirs of the donor consider that their ancestor also made a bad deal. Second, if the families of the old owners had not continued to reside in the houses, then the National Trust would have had the expense of finding full-time caretakers. Last but by no means least, if you compute the capital value of the properties and works of art the National Trust received free of charge, the continued presence of the family seems a small price to have paid.

Inevitably, not all such arrangements have remained suitable to all parties. Those owners who gave their houses to the National Trust under the impression that they were dealing with gentlemen have now found, to their horror, that this is no longer the case. The result has been a certain amount of friction between donor families and the trust, which sometimes spills into the press and affords everyone a certain amount of amusement.

The most common cause of dissension seems to be the subject of taste. This is something most gentlemen feel they have in abundance, and they are therefore amazed when the National Trust spends a small fortune on getting some interior-design consultant down from London to advise on the colour of the paintwork. They are even more amazed when they see the result of this exercise, and sometimes vent their fury in print.

Friction is also caused by differing views concerning what a house *is*. An owner has no difficulty with a house being a place to live, but the National Trust sometimes views houses as 'time capsules' or, alternatively, as places in which to re-create the style of living contemporaneous with the period of the building. This, as often as not, leads to the banishment of any anachronistic object. The consequence is that, frequently, an air of sterility hangs over these houses. Indeed, the architect Clough Williams-Ellis summed up the National Trust's notion of a historic house as 'a museum in which are preserved, here and there, carefully selected and ticketed items of what England was'.

A classic instance, recorded by David Littlejohn in *The Fate of the English Country House* is the experience of Lord Scarsdale at Kedleston. In 1987, he wrote:

All I can say is that everything you have heard about their [the National Trust's] amateurishness, waste of money, lack of supervision of staff and contractors, purism, museumisation of the house, coupled with arrogance and lack of courtesy towards the 'donor family' (as they call us), has been repeated and suffered by us here! The National Trust makes it clear they regard us as some sort of thorn in their flesh which they propose rudely to ignore.

Later, in conversation with Littlejohn, Scarsdale outlined a veritable catalogue of complaints against the trust, casting doubt on their choice of colour schemes, deploring their removal of pictures and furniture from public rooms they considered 'out of keeping' with the house, and so on. A typical example concerned a stand of Wellingtonia redwoods, planted in 1852 to commemorate the death of the great duke. The National Trust wanted to cut them down – 'because they weren't here in 1760!' Such criticisms are not the sole preserve of Lord Scarsdale; they are echoed by many other 'donor families'. So what has gone wrong with the National Trust?

Undoubtedly, one of its problems lies in its success. Its sheer size has caused it to resemble some large corporation with a headquarters no longer able to control the operations in the field. Like a dinosaur, its body has outgrown its brain, and like many other flourishing organizations it has forgotten what made it successful in the first place. I have often noticed how companies that grow from nothing to become large and successful owe their success to brilliant, quirky individuals who, without any educational or professional qualifications, create highly prosperous businesses. What happens next? They announce that in future they will employ only graduates or MBAs, completely forgetting that the company reached its present level precisely because it did not employ such people.

As with large companies, so with the National Trust. The days of gentleman amateurs, such as James Lees-Milne, are over and the organization is stuffed with so-called experts. Experts are – almost by definition – arrogant and fanatical about what they see as their field of expertise; they are also surprisingly lacking in that vital component of human interaction – common sense.

The National Trust also suffers from the curse of purism that is presently manifesting itself throughout rural Britain. Kedleston is a typical victim of this disease: the experts want to turn it back into a 'pure' Adam house. To achieve their aim they plan to banish anything of a later date which might detract from the 'purity' of the design. This approach is fine for a museum, but country houses are not museums, they are – or, in the case of National Trust-owned properties, were – living, breathing, developing *homes.* That the development of a country house ceases the day the National Trust takes control is perhaps inevitable, but to try to turn the clock back and remove all traces of the couple of hundred years between a house being built and being given to the National Trust is arrogant and wrong-headed. After all, it is hardly likely that the original builder wanted to freeze, in perpetuity, his design and not allow future generations to improve on it or to hang their own portraits on the walls.

A further mistake made by the National Trust concerns the lengths to which it goes to 'preserve' items never intended to be 'preserved'. Threadbare curtains are conserved at great cost, without thought being given to whether (a) the original purchaser might – quite possibly – have made a gross mistake in the first place, (balls-ups in interior decorating surely not being a purely twentieth-century phenomenon), or (b) their survival is due solely to lack of funds on the part of previous owners. A classic instance of this was the £160,000 that the National Trust spent over eleven years restoring the king's bed at Knole; if I had been the lucky owner of that particular bed, I would have popped down to the Kings Road to an up-market fabric shop, bought some replacements and put the old hangings on the bonfire. An equally ludicrous example of this approach by National Trust has been the meticulous restoration of Uppark, which had been destroyed by fire. New wallpapers were painstakingly aged to replicate the ones they were replacing.

First prize for total stupidity in the restoration business, however, must go to English Heritage, which has spent £1 million on 'restoring' the ruin of Wigmore Castle on the Welsh Borders. It was once the home of the mighty Mortimers, the most famous of whom was lover to Edward II's wife and ended up being executed in a particularly revolting fashion – fair enough, in a way, as he had had Edward II killed by shoving a red-hot poker up his bottom. But I digress. English Heritage proposes carefully removing vegetation, such as ivy, from the walls, making them good, and then letting the ivy grow back! Keen 'conservationists' will be even more impressed to hear that when English Heritage removes grass and moss and suchlike from the ramparts and the tops of the walls to make essential repairs, every effort will be made to 'save' the same vegetation and to encourage it to grow back on the repaired part of the wall!

Needless to say, adopting such a 'purist' approach to the interiors of many houses, or, as in the case of Wigmore, the exteriors, has meant that the cost of managing them has got out of control. Just how out of control was shown on TV recently, when the National Trust proudly let the cameras in to see how it had managed to spend £10 million on restoring a lovely medium-sized moated manor house called Igathan Moat. Put simply, the obsession with detail, with preserving everything at any cost, seemed to me to be taken here to an unwarranted extreme. Is it really important to preserve structural items, such as beams and timbers, which have rotted? What is the point of it? Surely a beam is a beam; if it is cheaper to replace rather than preserve it, that is what should be done. It has certainly been done in every country house, castle, church and cathedral in the land up till now. The problem is that this new method of restoration is so enormously expensive that it soaks up all the limited funds available from such sources as grant money from English Heritage (which gave a large contribution to Ightham Moat), leaving less, if anything, for the private sector.

So whither the National Trust? In sixty years it has grown from a small group of enthusiasts living in virtual penury to one of the great pillars of the English establishment. It is a remarkable achievement by any standards but, as the City pages of the newspapers constantly remind us, it is, in some ways, easier to be successful when you are poor and struggling than when you are rich. The problems of success are real in business, and chief among their root causes is always that old favourite, arrogance: the belief that because the company you run is called Shell, Marks & Spencer, Sainsbury's or GEC – which have all suffered from this affliction in recent years – you must be right and above criticism. Just now there is a feeling among many that the National Trust is exhibiting exactly this symptom.

A classic instance of such arrogance was the furore over Avebury, the site of the famous stone circle. The trust acquired Avebury Manor and the surrounding land with the active help and support of local people, who were frightened that some unscrupulous developer would purchase the estate and try to commercialize the village and its prehistoric stone circle. What has been the result? The saviours are now the villains. The National Trust wants to build a 'visitors' centre' with 'an interpretation room'. In other words, they want to encourage more people to come to Avebury – the very thing the locals did not want to happen! The organization they put their trust in has effectively kicked them in the balls.

So what is the solution for the National Trust? Perhaps, to return to a business analogy, the NT should consider following the example of many large companies which have found themselves in a similar situation, and devolve power and responsibilities to subsidiaries, or in their case to the regions. Undoubtedly the main cause of the trust's current problems is its sheer monolithic size, and among the cognoscenti its performance is unfavourably contrasted with that of its sister – but independent and considerably financially poorer – organization, the National Trust for Scotland.

In any case the National Trust could make a start by changing its name for, although it is many things, one thing it is *not* is trustworthy. This unpalatable fact became apparent when the National Trust banned stag-hunting on its land on Exmoor, even though the donor of most of its acreage there had specifically expressed the wish that the sport should be allowed to continue on the land. By banning hunting, the National Trust demonstrated to all countrymen that it is not an organization that can be trusted any longer; it has thrown in its lot with all those other bodies whose sole aim seems to be the sterilization and 'Disneyfication' of the countryside. Many people expressed surprise at the National Trust's action, but if they had talked to the many poor sods who still live in houses which their fathers trustingly gave away to the trust they would have realized that the organization is a very different body today from what it was in the 1950s and 1960s.

The conflict between preservation and public access is not going to go away and we will come back to it later. Indeed, the two aims are too often incompatible, and one day the issue will need to be addressed not just by the National Trust but also by the National Parks and English Heritage.

CHAPTER 4

The Contents

If people only knew as much about painting
as I do they would never buy my pictures.

Sir Edwin Landseer (1802–73)

Big houses have contents. This fairly basic fact is, strangely, frequently
forgotten by people when they are buying a large house – let alone a
stately home. There is nothing more pitiful than wandering around one
with a new owner and seeing it virtually naked, stripped not only of the
good furniture, pictures and books but also of the clutter which gradually
accumulates over a few hundred years. Furnishing a big house from
scratch is an expensive business and the wise buyer should, mentally, add
at least a couple of million pounds on to the asking price to allow for it
before buying one.

The contents of big houses have played a large part in ensuring the
survival of many estates. Pictures and furniture acquired casually over the
centuries, with no particular aim in mind except to furnish the house,
have, to the delight of many owners, become objects of enormous value,
eagerly sought after by the new rich. As one of the aims of this book is to
give advice to owners and their heirs about how to survive and thrive, it is
time to write down one of the golden rules: Throw nothing away.
After all, one of the advantages of owning and living in a large house is
having plenty of 'space', so use it. Do not let your wife clean out the
house and throw away all that junk furniture your mother brought in the

1950s to furnish a couple of guest bedrooms. Actually, she has probably already done it, so 'bad luck', as now it is suddenly becoming collectable and therefore valuable. It is one of the invariable lessons of history: we hate what the previous generation (i.e. our mothers and grandmothers) loved. So we burn it on the fire, give it away, let it rot, or sell it for peanuts, only for our sons and grandsons to bemoan our arrant stupidity and short-sightedness as they proceed to do exactly the same with what we bought.

It would be fair to say that, without the acquisitive streak which, luckily, the eighteenth-century ancestors of most families appear to have possessed, the number of estates and large houses still in private hands today would be far fewer. It was also fortunate that this craze to collect, and beautify their houses, was mainly an eighteenth-century phenomenon, for that was a century when not only were art and good taste at their peak (it is hard to think of a single thing produced in the eighteenth century that is not beautiful) but also the fortunes of Britain's landed families were at their zenith. Indeed, the British golden guinea was so valuable abroad that those who had foolishly overspent their income in the UK repaired to the continent to live cheaply in luxury while allowing the rents at home to accumulate and pay off their debts. At the same time it was – conveniently – a period when the fortunes of Italian aristocrats were at an all-time low.

One other factor must be added: Latin. The study of classics – Latin and Greek – was *de rigueur* for anyone who had aspirations to being considered educated in the eighteenth century. (Not only then, of course; the author spent many useless and boring hours trying to master the languages at school, with a total lack of success, back in the 1960s.) The veneration accorded to Latin and all things classical led naturally to sending your boy on the Grand Tour to complete his education. And when in Rome, Florence or Venice the opportunity to buy art was an ever-present temptation. So perhaps Latin was not such a useless language to learn after all, as its popularity as a means of disciplining the minds of the young in the eighteenth century led, indirectly, to the accumulation of quantities of old master paintings in

Britain's country houses, which many owners have been happily living off for the last seventy-odd years.

Not that all Italian old masters were considered in the best taste. Many gentlemen considered that Italian art was inferior to the home-grown variety; witness this letter of Hon. John Byng, describing his visit to Tong Park in 1792:

> Every part of this magnificent house is covered by pictures from Christie's and other auctions of dying Saints, naked Venuses and drunkard bacchanals. Now why all this offensive show, disgusting to every English eye that has not been hardened in Italy? Surely the intentions of paintings should be to cheer the mind and restore your pleasures, to survey your ancestry with conscious esteem, to view the beauties of Nature, to restore the memory of famous horses and of faithful dogs; but why produce savage and indecent exhibitions before your children's eyes?

I think the Hon. John has a point. It must be healthier and more fun to have a picture of your wife or dog rather than yet another depiction of Saint Sebastian being filled with arrows or John the Baptist's head being brought into dinner on a platter. It has to be said, though, that Italian art did have one overriding advantage as far as the English aristocrat was concerned: the pictures were big, and if you were trying to cover the wall space of your vast new Palladian mansion this was a distinct advantage. Dutch paintings are glorious but they were, on the whole, produced for merchants and farmers living in quite modest houses and are therefore themselves mostly small and modest, hardly surprisingly when you read what John Evelyn, the seventeenth-century diarist, wrote when recalling his visit to Holland: 'The interior of Dutch houses is yet more rich than their outsides; not in hangings, but in pictures which the poorest there are furnished withal . . . It is an ordinary thing to find a common farmer lay out £2,000 to £3,000 on this commodity – their houses are full of pictures and they red them at their fairs at very great gain.' Some might wonder why, if the prosperous Dutch were such avid collectors and patrons of paintings and painters, their cousins across the North Sea were apparently not. Perhaps the clue to the answer lies in John Evelyn's diary entry: ' . . . yet more rich than their outsides; not in hangings, but in pictures . . . ' The British, it appears, continued to value 'hangings' – tapestries and cloths, often called arras in inventories – over paintings, which they deemed to be inferior. There was a certain logic to this preference in the days when the gentry and nobility travelled much between different homes, because 'hangings' could be rolled up and transported between abodes far more easily than painted canvases.

One of the principal myths about art and antiques is that they are a good investment. This is not always the case: art is a creature of fashion. At various times the *objets d'art* of certain periods and styles are in vogue and their prices rise to stratospheric levels, while, conversely, unfashionable forms of art are considerably undervalued. The valuation of art depends little on its quality but much on whether it is *à la mode* among those who have both the money and the desire to build up collections.

Examples of this abound. In the late nineteenth century, early English oak furniture was tremendously popular and, a little later, the price paid for eighteenth-century mezzotints and engravings of English portraits reached unprecedented levels, superb examples routinely selling, in the early twentieth century, for figures of around a thousand pounds or, in modern money, sixty thousand-plus. Today you could probably pick up similar-quality prints for roughly the same sum, in nominal terms, as they fetched then. To give another example, the composer Andrew Lloyd Webber always – even as a boy – admired and adored Victorian paintings. One day, he went to his mother to ask her if she would lend him £50 to buy a work by a Victorian artist called Alma Tadema. She refused and that painting is not in his superb collection but now languishes, worth millions, in a American museum. The lesson, however, is not just that Alma Tadema is now deemed collectable, but that in the 1950s he, and other Victorian artists, were hardly worth the cost of the canvases the pictures were painted on, despite having once been worth tens of thousands of pounds in their heyday. Victorian paintings and their roller-coaster ride in valuation terms over the last hundred and fifty years constitute a very good example of why you must follow the rule: THROW NOTHING AWAY.

When Britain's aristocrats found themselves on their uppers after the First World War, the fashionable things to buy were the very things they had most of: English eighteenth-century portraits and Italian old masters. As far as the buyers – rich Americans – were concerned, these were the greatest examples of world art and thus fetched staggering prices. Dealers, such as the notorious Duveen, made a fortune introducing rich Americans to impoverished – and sometimes not so impoverished – British aristocrats, who were only too willing to part with family portraits for what, at the time, seemed astronomical sums. It was a shrewd move on their part for, except in rare circumstances, eighteenth-century British portraits have fallen dramatically in value in real terms over the last sixty-odd years as the tastes of the mega-rich have turned to French Impressionists and Post-Impressionists.

The years since the war have seen an 'action replay' of the eighteenth century. Then it was the English 'milord' whose wealth staggered the continentals and the Italian aristocrats who were poor and eager to sell. Since the 1930s it has been rich Americans who have been able to buy from the impoverished descendants of these English and Scottish gentlemen. The excitement caused among British owners by the arrival of the 'wall of money' from America dedicated to buying art in the early twentieth century is hard to exaggerate. This extract from a letter written by my father, then a young officer in the army, to his mother in 1933 gives a flavour: 'I saw Symonds who asked if I had a Jourdains [*sic*] picture – I said I thought so but was not certain. He has got a rich Yank, Howard I. Young, who buys pictures for large sums, ten thousand pounds, etc. He said he wanted a Jourdains . . . He would like to bring H. I. Young over and show it to him . . . '

The readiness of the British to sell art was boosted by the fact that many of them had a large surplus of the stuff. As part of the aristocratic retrenchment caused by confiscatory taxation and depressed rental income, large town houses in London were being sold and demolished and replaced by office blocks, and subsidiary country houses were being closed down and leased to institutions or demolished. The result was that owners could sell off their 'surplus art' without actually denuding their principal residence.

Not that the sale of art from country houses was a new phenomenon. In previous centuries suddenly impoverished aristocrats had frequently sold off pictures and libraries. What was new was that now virtually every landowner felt he was poor and needed cash, so that every picture in the country was effectively for sale at the right price. Even the Duke of Westminster was persuaded to part with Gainsborough's 'Blue Boy' when offered £150,000 for it by Henry Huntington.

There are few owners who have not, over the last sixty or so years, yielded to the temptation to solve their financial problems by flogging the odd picture, piece of furniture or item of jewellery. Unfortunately, this does not always work. There is something about an overdraft that makes it very difficult to get rid of. I remember once when I was having lunch at my club, someone sat down and announced to all and sundry that he had finally persuaded his wife to part with the tiara; he had popped it at Christie's for a large sum, thus paying off the overdraft. We all congratulated him till a wise old bird at the end of the table said: 'I bet you've got the overdraft back now!' There was a moment's silence; then it was admitted that the overdraft had indeed mysteriously returned. Flush with riches, the couple had had an expensive holiday, he had bought a new car and a new suit, they had done up a couple of rooms, made over some money to some undeserving daughter and – hey presto – they were back to square one, but now they had no tiara left to sell.

This is the trouble with having 'windfall money' in the bank. Few landowners have ever, in their entire lives, had the luxury of a bulging bank account, so when it does finally bulge the temptation to go on a bit of a spending binge is hard to resist – as, incidentally, are the demands from your family to help them out now you have finally sold that picture, tiara or whatever.

As time went by, the export of art across the Atlantic from the UK was partially stemmed by a number of measures. First, in 1952, the government introduced what is known as the Waverley Formula.

When applied, this means that if a work of art is considered of 'national importance' an export licence can be denied for a 'reasonable time' to allow a British museum or art gallery the opportunity to collect sufficient money to match the price offered and thus 'save' the picture for the nation.

Another device employed is 'conditional exemption'. This may be invoked at the owner's death and means that the Treasury agrees not to charge death duties or, as they are known today, inheritance tax, on a work of art considered to be of 'museum quality' or to be a 'historically associated object'. The item then normally remains *in situ* on condition that it is available, at the very least, for public viewing on request.

A great number of families have made use of this exemption over the years and the *Register of Conditionally Exempt Works of Art* now consists of over sixteen thousand items. This vast amount of art must be worth at least an average of fifty thousand pounds per item, giving an overall value to the registered works of well over a billion pounds. Back in the early 1990s there was a bit of a row in Parliament about the fact that many of these 'exempt' works were tucked away in private houses not open to the public, and that few people knew about them, let alone how to gain access to them. Actually the critics were wrong, as the *Register* is freely available on request from the various museums and galleries that keep a copy. The critics also conveniently ignored the fact that only a fraction of the art owned by 'the nation' is on show at any one time. The basements of the National Gallery and the Tate, for instance, are simply stuffed with pictures for which there is no hanging space available. The government's own 'private' art collection, used to decorate the offices and residences of ministers of the crown, embassies, etc., accounts for another sizeable chunk of art owned by the public but, curiously, it is not available for the public to view.

Apart from public access, the main catch to conditional exemption comes if you ever sell the picture. First, you have to pay capital gains tax (CGT) on it (as you do with any high-value object you sell) but, in addition, you will be liable to pay death duties on what remains after CGT, at the rate prevailing when the object was exempted. For those poor sods whose father died at the wrong time, when death duties touched eighty per cent for estates over a million pounds in value, this effectively means they cannot ever sell them, as the 'dividend' would be prohibitively small.

A rough example: say your father died in 1953, when rates were at their height, and left an estate of well over a million pounds. In order to reduce the tax bill a picture worth £25,000 was accepted by the Treasury as conditionally exempt; now, a half-century later, you realize its value is a million pounds and you enquire whether it is worth selling. First you will pay CGT on the net figure, so your calculation will look something like this:

Hammer price	£1,000,000
Less cost of sale	(£100,000)
Less market value on 31/3/82	(£200,000)
So chargeable gain since 1982	£700,000
Less indexation allowance, say	(£150,000)
(*the value, for CGT has been indexed since 1982 to allow for inflation*)	
Leaving a gain for CGT of	£550,000
Less CGT payable at 40%	(£220,000)
Leaving a figure of	£330,000
Now pay death duties at 80% on what's left	(£264,000)
Residue left to spend – the princely sum of	£66,000

Actually, you would be extremely stupid to sell in the above circumstances. Conditional exemption lasts only for your lifetime; on your death, your heir has to reapply. If it is then granted again, the exemption will be at the then current rate of inheritance tax (at present forty per cent).

Gallingly, the responsibility for insuring and maintaining these objects – although, as the above calculation shows, they are effectively ninety-two per cent 'owned' by the Treasury – remains one hundred per cent the responsibility of their nominal 'owner'! This raises, for me, an interesting question. Suppose the object is stolen or destroyed in a fire; as you have been paying the premiums you pick up the sum insured, and as the object has been destroyed and not sold the state cannot claim its share. Of course, you would be subject to tax on the insurance payout – unless, that is, you bought something with the money to replace the object, which would then be totally yours if you ever had to sell it.

It is surely an anomaly that owners insure their works of art, and pay hefty premiums on them for their 'replacement value'; when so much of the market value, in the event of sale, is going to be taken by the government in the form of capital gains tax. Why, I wonder, should owners effectively insure the Treasury's interest in their works of art? After all, you may have a Van Dyck portrait of an ancestor valued at a million pounds; it is irreplaceable, so in the event of its being stolen or burned you cannot 'replace' it. Surely you should only be expected to insure your interest in the picture and, in the event of disaster, you should not be taxed on the insurance money, even if you decide to pocket the cash and not roll it over into a new work of art?

Another device often made use of by owners is 'heritage sales'. This is either the sale of an object to an 'approved body', like the National Trust or a museum, or to the Treasury in return for tax concessions. Such sales are conducted by private treaty. The advantage for an owner of such a transaction is that it is totally exempt from all capital taxes. As a result, although the 'approved bodies' take this into account when offering to buy, and the owner thus receives a significantly lower gross sum for his work of art, he may end up with a higher net figure than if he had sold through the auction houses and had to pay CGT and perhaps inheritance tax on the deal.

The first step in negotiating a private-treaty sale is that the seller and the 'approved body' have to come to an agreement on what the 'open market' price of the object would be. The next step is to calculate what the seller's tax liability would be if he sold on the open market at that price. The following example from Sotheby's *Management of Works of Art* will make the advantages clear:

Value of work of art	£100,000
Less CGT at 40% of, say, £20,000	(£8,000)
Leaving	£92,000
Less IHT at 40%	(£36,800)
Leaving	£55,200

So if the owner sold on the open market he would be left, after all capital taxation, with £55,200. If, on the other hand, he did a private-treaty sale he would be credited with a *douceur* worth twenty-five per cent of the CGT bill and twenty-five per cent of inheritance tax bill; in other words, his tax bill would be significantly reduced and, in the example above, he would receive an extra £11,200.

There is one further advantage of the system, which makes it particularly attractive to owners: the purchasing body may well decide to let the object remain *in situ,* if the house is open to the public and the object is considered to have important historical connections with the building. In other words, not only does the vendor pocket more cash, but he also gets – more often than not – continued guardianship of the work of art.

Such, then, is the theory. The problem comes with agreeing the initial open market valuation. The tax advantages on offer are of use only if the valuation is at the right price. If the two parties cannot agree to it, then an owner may still be substantially better off selling through an auction house and gambling that his advisers have got it right: that the price obtained is going to be vastly higher than what the museums were prepared to agree on. This, it must be said, has often been the case. The most spectacular example was the sale by the Duke of Devonshire of old-master drawings, which ended up fetching at auction several times the British Museum's estimate of what their 'market value'.

The calculations for selling an object in lieu of tax are exactly the same as for a heritage sale.

The consequence of all these measures is that the floodtide of sales has been somewhat stemmed.

The key to the valuation – in the case of a painting – is the identity of the painter. This is an obvious but often disregarded point. As an example of the importance of getting this right, take the case of the Duke of Devonshire, who settled part of his immense death-duty bill by giving a Rembrandt to the National Gallery. The joke was that some years later the experts decided it was not a Rembrandt after all, but by then the deal had been done.

Owners would do well to remember this as a cautionary tale. If you are thinking of selling something, it is as well to tout it round as many experts as possible in the search for the one who will give it the best attribution. Experts in art being no different from those in any other field, as often as not they will be in total disagreement. On the other hand, when valuing for probate, the last thing you want is for your things to be 'overvalued' because of optimistic attributions – unless, that is, you are planning to use the valuation as a base figure when asking the Treasury to accept the painting in lieu of taxes.

Country-house owners have been both the beneficiaries and the victims of the surge in art prices. It is true they can raise large sums of money by selling works of art but, at the same time, they are heavily taxed on inflated values if their father dies in possession of them. It is therefore a moot point as to whether an owner should be pleased or saddened at being informed that a picture which for years has been a source of enjoyment to him is now considered to be by, say, Van Dyck, and thus worth a million pounds – rather than being, as had previously been thought, just 'School of Van Dyck', and therefore worth only ten thousand pounds. It is the same picture; it is just that an 'expert' has now changed the attribution and, with it, the value. Now the poor owner has to consider the insurance and the security of it, and whether he can justify having a million pounds tied up in a canvas hanging on the wall. The answer, probably, is no, so up it goes to London for sale.

The real problem with works of art from an owner's viewpoint is that they are virtually valueless as a means of producing income, so any sensible owner will always sell a picture rather than a farm. After all, if you sell a picture for enough money, you can probably pay the debts off and have enough change left over to buy a replacement to hang in the empty space and, who knows, in fifty years' time that replacement picture may well be worth more than that which was sold off the wall in the first place, as the school of art it came from suddenly becomes flavour of the year in the art market.

The dribble of works of art from country houses will continue as long as inheritance tax is charged on them. The burden of inheritance tax will increase as works of art – on the whole – increase in value due to scarcity. In short, a vicious circle is created, with only one way of breaking it: the abolition of capital taxation on death.

CHAPTER 5

The Park and Gardens

Our England is a garden that is full of stately views,
Of borders, beds and shrubberies and lawns and avenues,
With statues on the terraces and peacocks strutting by;
But the Glory of the Garden lies in more than meets the eye.
RUDYARD KIPLING (1865–1936)
'The Glory of the Garden', 1911

The central and most visible sign of an estate may be the big house, but the first indication we have that we are in the vicinity of one is a striking change in the character of the landscape. Rolling fields are replaced by what look like the remains of some great forest, with ancient trees dotted over an expanse of verdant grassland. You know at once that you are passing by the park of some great house, and eagerly peer through the trees to try and catch a glimpse of the mansion itself.

I have two heroes as far as park and gardens are concerned: Capability Brown and the anonymous character who invented the weedkiller Round Up; let me explain.

Before Capability Brown arrived on the scene, most houses boasted elaborate gardens replicating, with their complicated parterres and formal, architect-designed layouts, the type perfected by Louis XIV's gardener, Le Notre. Everyone will be familiar with gardens of this sort; they are frequently depicted in the kind of seventeenth-century pictures of houses known as 'bird's eye views', and very attractive they must have been, too – provided, of course, you were a bird. Because it is a peculiarity of these grandiose designs that they can really only be appreciated by someone flying over them. From ground level they are just so many miles of gravel paths and clipped hedges. One is forced to the conclusion that garden-design experts in the seventeenth century were extremely clever salesmen; the plans of the garden they proposed – no doubt complete with the proverbial 'bird's eye view' – would have looked impressive on paper and the poor sucker of a client would have forgotten, in his enthusiasm, that he was not a bird. By the time he realized his mistake it would be too late; the garden would have been planted and the bills paid. Then his only option would have been to pretend he was a satisfied customer and to boast to his friends about his great gardens.

Capability Brown's novel concept was to realize his clients could not fly and to plan his gardens so as to dazzle from eye level. But his true genius, as far as we, the inheritors of his work, are concerned, was to abolish formal gardens. Instead, he replaced them with parks. Parks, moreover, which swept right up to the front of the house. The reason we bless his name so feelingly is that parks require little maintenance – the odd tree needs replacing, true, but on the whole animals mow the grass for nothing, so the park achieves the twin aims of making a house look grand while at the same time costing only a minimal amount to keep up. Brown's notion was not entirely original; many country houses already had deer parks, but these were not centred on the house and were often some distance away, located on a few hundred acres of poor land. Their role was twofold: as open-air larders and as gyms for our medieval and Tudor ancestors to exercise in. It was Brown's genius to see that by adding water, in the form of a lake, and perhaps a few architectural features of the sort that featured in the paintings of such popular seventeenth-century artists as Claude, Poussin and Salvator Rosa, a sort of Arcadian landscape could be created in England's green fields.

Not that these landscapes cost nothing to create. The eighteenth-century landed magnate was no different from a twenty-first-century multimillionaire in his desire for instant gratification. The Duke of Marlborough, for instance, demanded a lake and got one, but only at considerable expense, as Blenheim is built on porous soil. To ensure the lake did not leak, Brown had to import thousands of tons of clay to line it.

Brown, and the nurseries from whom he brought his stock, also developed 'instant trees' for the same purpose. In an account preserved at Petworth, Brown plants '40 Scotch Pine at 13 foot and upwards ditto 20 spruce'. He developed machines and techniques for moving far bigger trees than this, apparently successfully, but the whole meant that his client ended up forking out considerable sums for the aggrandizement of his seat. In 1774, for instance, Brown quoted the Earl of Scarborough £3,000 for 'improving' his landscape at Sandbeck in Yorkshire. I often wonder, though, when I cruise down a sweeping drive through rolling parkland, what Capability Brown would have created if he had had at his disposal the full range of modern earth-moving equipment. Would he still have restricted himself to working within the natural contours of the countryside, or would he have brought up rank upon rank of bright yellow monster machines and created great valleys and hills in the flat landscapes of much of England? The answer is that he would have gone for it and used them with a vengeance. On the other hand, if he had lived today he would have found his vision frustrated on every side. The Environment Agency would have refused him permission to build lakes or divert streams and his plans for rolling acres of verdant grassland enlivened with clumps of trees would have been politely turned down by the authorities as they would have entailed the removal of a few miles of useless hedge, now, alas, protected for evermore by the famed Hedgerow Act.

Many parks are now but a shadow of their former great selves. Our Edwardian and Victorian ancestors enjoyed them when they were at their peak, but perhaps assuming that trees lived for ever, they neglected to plant replacements. The result of their neglect, compounded by the ploughing up of parkland in the First and Second World Wars, was the virtual destruction of many fine landscapes. It is only in the last thirty-odd years that owners have begun to repair this damage, and it will – as ever with trees – be our grandsons and great-grandsons who reap the benefit. But what fun it is to plant and plan a park. Is there any greater art form than landscape gardening? A painter works with a poxy canvas of a few square feet while the landscaper has a canvas stretching from a few acres right up to one in excess of a thousand acres. And while a painter can see the result of his work at once, a landscaper has to visualize how his vistas, avenues, clumps and trees will mature and grow before arriving finally, in a hundred or so years' time, at their peak of glory and beauty. Are there rules for landscape gardening? I feel that this little ditty by William Shenstone is as good an *aide memoire* as any.

> Yon stream that wanders down the dale
> The spiral wood, the winding vale,
> The path which, wrought with hidden skill
> Slow twining scales yon distant hill
> With fir invested – all combine
> To recommend the waving line.

The need of estate owners to 'maximize income' has, sadly, led to parks becoming much smaller. As the home farm grew, covetous eyes were cast over vistas of 'unimproved' grassland, and all too often they were taken in hand to provide yet more arable acres. A cursory visit to many an estate will find the odd remaining grand tree standing forlornly in acres of golden wheat or dank brown plough, a sad reminder of what once was and could be again – if the owner could afford to forgo the income now being derived from what was his park.

One of the reasons the owner needs this income is that his wife insists on having a flower garden and a gardener to go with it. It was Humphrey Repton, the first person actually to call himself a landscape gardener, who restored the status of flowers in the garden by putting a formal terrace in front of his houses and planting them with beds of flowers. It was Repton too who promoted the concept of a conservatory attached to the house. He recommended that they be positioned by the library (then the most used room in the house). I wonder how many of the people who have made fortunes selling modern conservatories know this? Very few, I suspect, and even fewer of their clients.

The nineteenth century was the century of the Industrial Revolution, but the inventions of that period were to cause a similar revolution in gardening. Rich men – and not just *nouveaux riche* either – indulged in a veritable orgy of expenditure, to such an extent that the Duke of Devonshire had to sell off large swathes of land to pay debts accumulated by such extravagances as financing an expedition to India to search for as yet undiscovered orchids to populate his new orchid house. In 1884, a guest staying at Eaton Hall with the Duke of Westminster recorded that he employed fifty-six gardeners, and had over six miles of hot-water pipes, used to heat a vast number of glasshouses. The hot water was heated by coal, which arrived at the furnace via a branch railway line.

These great gardens were not just designed for producing exotic fruit, although eccentric peers liked to compete with each other in this department. It was Lord Leaconfield at Petworth who, taking a liking to bananas, decided to build himself a 'banana house'. Eventually the great day dawned when the butler, with great ceremony, produced the first fruit on a silver salver. Then he and the other servants watched nervously as Lord Leaconfield slowly peeled the banana and bit into it: 'Tastes just like any other bloody banana' was the verdict, and that was the end of the banana house.

Hot pipes and greenhouses also meant that a totally new concept in gardening was invented: bedding out. This form of gardening is now the preserve of the municipal authorities, particularly in seaside resorts, which compete to produce the most vulgar displays, but back in the mid-nineteenth century every large country house indulged in this practice. Their owners instructed their gardeners to dig up the lawn in front of the house and people it with the ubiquitous kidney-shaped beds to be filled up throughout the summer with bedded-out plants in bloom. The chief exponent of this fashion was the Rothschild family, who took it to such extremes that the fashion became known as *le style Rothschild.*

Most of this excess has been consigned to the dustbin of gardening history, but the dreaded 'flower garden' still survives in some form or other at most big houses, although now, where once 'bedding out' held sway, the herbaceous border reigns supreme. Personally, I put the survival and health of the modern flower garden down to the increasing influence of the female of the species, who likes colour and nice smells. I would suggest most houses would benefit from abolishing the flower garden and restoring the park; few wives, however, would agree to such a sensible course of action, so we are, I am afraid, stuck with flowers.

Which is where my second hero, the anonymous inventor of Round Up, comes in. This brilliant product makes gardening a pleasure. All you have to do is put a knapsack-sprayer on your back and wander round your flowerbeds zapping the weeds. No more boring hours of hoeing or hand-weeding for me. It is true that the occasional plant falls victim to the odd ill-aimed squirt, but that is surely a small price to pay, even if one's wife does not always agree.

Big houses invariably boast the remnants of a vegetable garden. This is usually a walled area of an acre or more. It is walled not just to keep small boys and other potential predators out, but also because a walled area on a south-facing slope is the equivalent, in climate terms, of moving your entire garden 250 miles south.

In the days before the advent of the ubiquitous superstore, the kitchen garden provided the household with vegetables and fruit which otherwise were difficult, or impossible, to get hold of. It is sad that my offspring have never experienced the sheer excitement and delight which a proper walled vegetable garden can give small children. The asparagus bed run to seed provided a 'jungle' environment to play in while the raspberry cage and the strawberry bed supplied feasting on a truly Roman scale. But the big thrill was the wall fruit. Were we to have peaches this year? And what of the nectarines, plums and greengages? My father was in command of this department principally because, as far as peaches were concerned, he was extraordinarily greedy. Every evening in late summer we small children would follow him as he inspected the crop and decided which peaches were ripe enough to pick. Now only the gnarled remnants of these trees survive against the cob wall of the grassed-down vegetable garden. The economics of employing a Mr McGregor to provide home-grown vegetables for the house no longer, alas, make sense. I suppose a modern Mr McGregor would cost around thirteen thousand pounds per annum, plus a rent-free cottage, and there is just no way that the average household could possibly eat enough produce to justify his employment in economic terms. This is sad, as a beautifully maintained walled vegetable garden is as important a part of a country house as old masters, libraries, gleaming silver and rolling open parkland, yet it is an aspect that has been sorely neglected, even by such owners as the National Trust. And yet the other day I wandered up to our old kitchen garden, cast an eye over the forlorn, knackered-looking fruit trees which had once been my father's pride and joy, and saw that the greengage trees were covered with more fruit than I can ever remember them having in my life. Why? Some freak of the weather, I suppose, because they have certainly not received any tender loving care for the best part of thirty years.

There is yet one more kind of garden: the pleasure ground or woodland garden. This is very much the legacy of our Victorian and Edwardian ancestors. By the middle of the nineteenth century, exotic plants were arriving on our shores, gathered by intrepid plant collectors from around the Empire, and many of them were found to flourish in this country, especially in the warm and wet west. Some introductions have proved to be 'invasive' and have created major environmental problems. Perhaps the most visible, as well as the most unwelcome, of these exotic colonisers is the rhododendron, which I will for ever associate with my prep school in Berkshire, not exactly the 'happiest days of my life'. We now know that actually this weed is not as alien or exotic as many people think, as it was a native in Ireland before the last Ice Age! No wonder then that it spreads so easily on wet and warm peaty soils, and no wonder that it is now such a curse in woodlands, where it was planted with the aim, one supposes, of giving ground cover to game birds or perhaps just for its purple flowers. So our Victorian and Edwardian ancestors indulged in this new craze for planting woodland gardens with rhododendrons, magnolias, camellias and other exotic shrubs, as well as specimen trees.

Such planting and management today is normally the preserve of the male of the house and can often be taken to excess. Many owners forget that the aim of a woodland garden should be to provide a pleasant walk and instead allow their walks to become the garden equivalent of an art gallery, with specimen after specimen planted in every available piece of open space. In short, they exhibit the classic symptoms of the mad collector. Sadly, they can never complete their collection, as plant breeders everywhere are busy developing new types of shrub faster than they can plant them. Walking through such gardens can induce claustrophobia, as one is perpetually hemmed in on every side by evergreen plants and never allowed a glimpse of a view. These owners forget that the primary aim of gardens should be to create something of beauty and interest and that a surfeit of anything is bad for you – even rhododendrons.

Paradoxically, I expect future generations will get a lot of good healthy exercise from cutting down and ripping out the shrubs that are now being planted, just as I, today, when I feel in need of exercise, reach for my saw and go and tackle some overgrown laurel or rhododendron. For it has to be said that gardens, both of the flower and woodland variety, serve a valuable purpose. The *nouveaux riches* have their indoor gyms to work off the surplus flab and keep themselves fit, but the gentry have their gardens and shrubberies.

CHAPTER 6

The Land

They love their land because it is their own,
And scorn to give aught other reason why;
Would shake hands with a king upon his throne,
And think it kindness to his majesty.

FITZ-GREENE HALLECK (1790–1867)
'New England Character', 1829

If the country house and surrounding park are the heart of an estate, then land is surely its blood. Without land a house loses its purpose and becomes just a rich – or perhaps poor – man's plaything. As in France, where *châteaux* stand in a few acres of lawn and garden shorn, by a combination of revolutions and the application of inheritance laws, of the once vast estates which originally were their *raisons d'être*. Their owners live and work in Paris, coming back to the *châteaux* only for holidays. How different in Britain, where most owners live in their houses as their forebears did, managing the estate, running the house and playing an active role in the locality.

So important is this link between the house and its land that it is simply impossible to understand the one without knowledge of the other. When agriculture was booming and rents rising, that was the time the landowner could, and more often than not did, indulge his penchant for 'improving' his estates. When the dark shadow of depression and heavy tax burdens fell on the countryside then the squire battened down the hatches and tried, as best he could, to survive. Those who did not, went under.

As we have seen, as early as the fifteenth century an Italian was remarking on the propensity of English merchants to put their ill-gotten gains into land, and the reason for this was clear. Land not only gave social prestige; it was also safe. Having built up a fortune by speculating in the medieval equivalent of financial derivatives, our man wanted to ensure that his money was not lost. With few alternative investments available to him, land was his obvious choice. It provided an income while at the same time affording him status. To quote the words Trollope put into the mouth of Archdeacon Grantley: 'Land gives so much more than rent. It gives one position and influence and political power, to say nothing of game.' It also provided the new owner's sons with an opportunity to matriculate as gentlemen and to shake the polluting dust of trade from their shoes and join the nobility.

The desire to own land was thus, in medieval times, driven partly by economic considerations and partly by the social ambitions of the buyer for his family. Exactly the same factors are normally uppermost in the mind of the modern buyer. As far as land goes nothing ever really changes, but there is surely another abstract factor involved in its ownership. The right to call something *mine*, the right to be king over one's own acres, however rough and dull they may appear to an outsider, is something town-bred people cannot understand. They change houses so often (every seven years on average) that they have no time to put down roots or to develop pride in their locality. It was this pride that caused the Earl de Warrene of Surrey, when summoned before the king's justices in 1278 to show by what right or warrant he held his property, to produce dramatically a rusty sword in court, crying, 'Here is my warrant ! My ancestors came with William the Bastard and won their lands with this sword. With this I will defend them against all usurpers!'

Land remained a good investment right up to the start of the great agricultural depression in 1873, although, like all investments, it had its ups and downs. By the late nineteenth century many alternative forms of investment vehicles had arisen, but none had quite the same cachet as land. The most common form of alternative investment was lending to the government. Kings, of course, had borrowed money from rich subjects throughout history, but in earlier times it had hardly been a 'risk-free' investment (for the lender, that is), as rulers had an irritating habit of, at best, reneging on their debts or, at worst, actually killing the people who had lent them money – as the Order of Templars found out when Pope Clement V abolished them in 1312 and burned a large number at the stake, or the Jews of England, who were summarily expelled in 1290 by Edward I.

The financial scandal of the South Sea Bubble in 1720, which burned a lot of landowners' fingers, convinced them once again that there were only two safe investments: land and government stock. This dictum held good for many years. Land that in 1725 had been worth twenty-four years' purchase rose to thirty years' purchase by 1800 and peaked at forty years' purchase in the 1860s. Taking the rent roll and working out the number of years it was going to take, at current rents, to earn back the capital was the accepted method of valuing land back in those days. Doing the same sum today and assuming a rent of £60 per acre, we come up with a value, for tenanted land, of £2,400 per acre at forty years' purchase.

Land is no longer a single market, but rather a three-tier market. Land with vacant possession is valued more highly, for instance, than land with a pre-1976 tenant (whose heirs have the right of inheritance). In addition, it must be remembered that back in the eighteenth and nineteenth centuries (and indeed right up to the late 1960s) farmhouses were not greatly valued – it was the land that was important. Now, especially with small farms in scenic landscapes within easy reach of London, it is, more often than not, the house which is sought after and the land regarded as an incidental amenity rather than an essential income-producing business opportunity. In 1997, farms let on the open market were routinely making over £100 per acre and, in certain cases, up to £150 an acre, which would give us a price for land, at forty years' purchase, of around £4,000 or £6,000 an acre. Land that attracted such rents, however, was more likely to be fetching £3,500 an acre or, to use the old-fashioned method of valuation, between thirty and thirty-five years' purchase – still some way off its late-nineteenth-century peak. In fact, since reliable records began in the late eighteenth century, land has fluctuated between – in modern terms – £1,200 and £4,000 an acre. In essence, then, land prices in 1997 were near their peak. This is hardly surprising, as farmers had just experienced 'seven fat years' and, as usual, were spending the money in anticipation of the 'fat years' continuing. They did not and, as I write in 2004, they still have not returned. Whether you regard land as being a good investment depends on what you consider the purpose of investment to be. If the aim of your investment strategy is to preserve the value of your money while at the same time producing a small income and perhaps giving you a lot of fun, then land has been a pretty good investment in (most of) the past and is likely to remain so in the future.

Land has another characteristic, however, which makes it ideal as a means of storing wealth: it is difficult to sell. Stocks and shares can be flogged by making a simple telephone call, but the decision to sell land is just the first step in a long, tortuous – and often painful – process. It has another major drawback or virtue: it is public. You can gaily flog your entire portfolio of investments and none of your neighbours or friends will be any the wiser, but as soon as you put a farm or estate on the market your financial situation becomes public knowledge and a subject of gossip. So land is the last thing anyone likes to sell and many owners cling to the last remnants in comparative poverty, hoping against hope for some windfall legacy from a distant relation to save them. Strangely enough, this often happens, and the family fortunes are temporarily restored.

Those who doubt this analysis should consider whether or not there are any descendants of rich merchant families of the fourteenth or fifteenth centuries still surviving on the remnants of what were, then, vast fortunes. The answer is that there is none – unless their ancestor invested in land. Conversely, there are several hundred landowning families who can trace their current prosperity back to those times and – in some cases – beyond. Such a record would make you think that, logically, businessmen and bankers would be beating a path to landowners' doors to find out what the magic ingredient is for such a successful long-running track record. Sadly they do not, perhaps knowing the answer would be highly unpalatable to them, since the basic constituents of the formula for long commercial life are a commitment to long-term investing and forswearing short-term greed, values few – if any – in the City these days could contemplate.

The value of land is no different from any other commodity: its price reflects its ability to produce income. I say that even though I know there is the caveat, going all the way back to what that Italian merchant wrote back in the fifteenth century, that people will buy land for the social position it gives them and for the recreational opportunities it offers, not just for its income producing qualities. The price of land will always be underwritten by these factors, as well as an Englishman's instinctive desire to carve out his own kingdom, however small or scruffy it may be, and play God on it.

It has been land's food-producing role that has understandably attracted the attention of kings and governments for much of history. The provision of food is, after all, essential to our existence. In 1672, and again in 1688, Parliament passed the Corn Bounty Acts, designed to discourage imports and boost exports, measures aimed at stabilizing the price of corn at around forty-eight shillings a quarter or approximately £10.65 a ton. That should give us pause: £10.65 for a ton of wheat in 1688 would be the equivalent of around £1,192 a ton today! A quarter (consisting of eight bushels) was the normal unit of measure used up until the 1920s for marketing corn. To complicate matters still further, it was a measure of volume rather than of weight, although approximately four quarters do equal a ton.

The price of wheat was to fluctuate wildly as time went by, depending from year to year on whether or not the harvest was good and if we were at war and with whom. In the year of Malplaquet (1709) the price reached seventy-five shillings a quarter, but by 1881 – when, we are taught, cheap wheat from America had virtually destroyed English agriculture – it was still forty-eight shillings a quarter – £10.65 a ton – or exactly the same as it had been in 1688. The trouble was that a pound in 1881 was worth only half a 1688 pound and costs had risen enormously over the previous two hundred years while yields were still pathetically low by modern standards – eighteen hundredweight an acre being the norm as against three or four tons today.

The golden period for agriculture was perhaps 1790 to 1815, when the Napoleonic Wars made imports difficult, and sometimes impossible, at a time when the urban population was expanding rapidly and needed to be fed. Over the twenty-five-year period of the wars, rents increased by between a hundred and two hundred per cent as the price of wheat rocketed; in 1812, it reached 122 shillings a quarter. Landowners and farmers invested heavily in new buildings, enclosures and drainage, and much land that had always been pasture was brought under the plough.

In 1808, *Vancouver's Survey of Agriculture in Devon* reported that the value of accommodation land in the neighbourhoods of large towns had become very high: 'near the docks in Plymouth there is land now rented from £12 to £16 an acre . . . ' The same source later states: '£1,200 guineas was recently paid for four acres of pasture land lying under the Church walls of Ashburton.' These are enormous prices, especially when you apply a multiplier of about forty to get to some semblance of 'modern' values. The high value given to accommodation land outside big ports and towns, however, can be understood when we take into account the fact that such land fulfilled the role of larder and fridge for the urban population.

Inevitably the boom ended with the final defeat of Napoleon in 1815. The reason for the slump had little to do – this time – with cheap imports, as the Corn Laws, passed in 1815, forbade the sale of imported corn on the home market unless the price of wheat exceeded eighty shillings a quarter; this price level, as a matter of interest, was not reached until over a hundred years later, in 1920. The fall in prices had more to do with improved arable techniques producing higher yields, the expansion in the arable acreage caused by the sky-high prices wheat had fetched during the wars, and a series of good harvests; all these factors conspired to bring about a crash in prices from which the market was not to recover until around 1837 – a period of recession, oddly, roughly as long as the preceding boom. It is true that the effect was patchy, with many farmers on the light land continuing to make reasonable profits while naturally those farming marginal arable land suffered most. During these bad years, landowners found themselves having to reduce rents by between ten and twenty per cent. The net impact on landowners' incomes was relieved by the fact that, with the end of the wars, taxation levels fell and severe deflation set in, reducing wage costs, etc. Those who were worst hit were, as usual, those who had borrowed heavily towards the end of the boom to invest either in improvements or in a grandiose new country house.

This propensity farmers and landowners have for overspending in the good years, thus causing the bad years – when they inevitably come – to be far worse than they need be, is repeated so often that one is forced to the conclusion that God, in his infinite wisdom, has programmed man's brain with a self-destruct device to stop individuals from getting too rich. Sadly, it is a fact that no one ever learns from history, or from anything else for that matter. The best business advice for landowners may be found in the Bible, in the Book of Genesis, where Joseph is called to interpret Pharaoh's dream, described as follows:

'And, behold, there came up out of the river seven kine [cattle], fat fleshed and well favoured; and they fed in a meadow.

'And, behold, seven other kine came up after them, poor and ill favoured and lean fleshed, such as I never saw in all the land of Egypt for badness.

'And the lean and ill-favoured kine did eat up the first seven fat kine.

'And when they had eaten them up, it could not be known that they had eaten them; but they were still ill favoured, as at the beginning. So I awoke.'

Joseph interpreted Pharaoh's dream thus:

'The seven good kine are seven years . . . and the seven thin and ill-favoured kine that came up after them are seven years.

'Behold there come seven years of great plenty throughout all the land of Egypt.

'And there shall arise after them seven years of famine; and all the plenty shall be forgotten in the land of Egypt; and famine shall consume the land.'

Pharaoh was so impressed by Joseph's interpretation that he immediately made him the ancient Egyptian equivalent of prime minister and put him in charge of arranging the storage of one-fifth of the harvest during the good years to provide for the lean times ahead.

Time after time we go through agricultural booms, and time after time we make the same mistake: spending the surplus on frivolous things during the good years so we have no reserves when the bad years come. Not that landowners are unique in this regard; every business sector acts in the same way.

In any event, come 1835 things began to improve; as an illustration of the roller-coaster nature of the market which then developed, the following are figures for the price of a quarter of wheat in Salisbury market:

November	1835	1836	1837	1838
Price per quarter	36s.	60s.	58s.	72s.

It was the dramatic rise in corn prices that caused the pressure from the urban masses for the repeal of the Corn Laws, which eventually happened in 1846. Initially, this had little effect on prices, due to a mixture of bad harvests and European revolutions, but in 1850 England was flooded with cheap European grain and the price of wheat dived to 40s. a quarter. This was to be a low point; prices gradually recovered and over the next thirty years only once touched 40s. a quarter again, in 1864. Sir Herbert Maxwell, in his book *Evening Memories*, had this to say about these halcyon (for farmers and landowners) days:

> The competition for farms was very keen, causing rents to keep rising far beyond what was thought possible when Peel abolished the Corn Laws. Lavish outlay on land improvement, an opulent home farm, a

stable full of good horses – the whole atmosphere of the establish-ment, despite my father's grumbles about shortage of cash, gave one the impression the good times had come to stay, and that it was safe and sober for a country gentleman to live well up to, even a trifle over, his income.

The good times, though, were about to end.

In 1873 the full horror of falling corn prices once again arrived to hit farmers and landowners, but this time it was to be no flash in the pan. Low prices had arrived and they were going to stay for a long time. The great agricultural depression had begun. This was caused by a combina-tion of events and mechanical advances, which brought disaster to farmers and landowners. These included the opening up of the prairies in North America, the expansion of the railway network there, improve-ments in harvesting technology and faster and bigger ships able to ply the North Atlantic route. All these factors together led to an avalanche of cheap corn pouring into the UK market, causing enormous distress and economic hardship among farmers.

The following extract from Sir John Fortescue's memoirs, *Author and Curator*, gives a flavour of the crisis that afflicted agriculture, especially the arable areas, by 1890.

My father owned in Lincolnshire an estate which had brought him, in good years, a gross income of £7,000 to £8,000 a year. It was all of it reclaimed land, arable; but corn brought no price, the tenants had thrown up their farms, and my father was fain to take them in hand himself. I went through the accounts with him: and we found that instead of a net profit of £4,000 to £5,000 they showed a dead loss of over £2,000. Yet he did not repine. Land once reclaimed – he said – must never be allowed to go back.

In 1895, Oscar Wilde could put these immortal words into the mouth of Lady Bracknell in *The Importance of Being Earnest* and bring the house down: 'Between the duties expected of one in one's lifetime and the duties extracted from one after one's death, land has ceased to be either a profit or a pleasure. It gives one position, and prevents one from keeping it up. That is all that can be said about land.'

As income from land collapsed, so did the values. In 1897 an article in the *Economist* stated: 'No security was ever relied on with more implicit faith and few have lately been found more sadly wanting, than English land.' Land prices collapsed from an average of £51 per acre (£2,193 in today's terms) to a low point in 1930 of £28 per acre (£1,344).

By now it was clear that the political map of the United Kingdom had changed: power had switched to the towns. Not even a sympathetic Conservative government could do anything to alleviate the crisis. By 1899, the *Estates Gazette* could observe: 'This country appears to care little for the position of land . . . Unquestionably, politicians mould their conduct on the wishes of the towns rather than on the country.' Meanwhile, Lord Ernle, in his *English Farming*, wrote:

The legislature was powerless to provide any substantial help. Food was, so to speak, the currency in which foreign nations paid for English manufactured goods, and its cheapness was an undoubted blessing to the wage-earning community. Thrown on their own resources, agriculturalists fought the unequal contest with courage and tenacity. But as time went on, the stress told more and more heavily. Manufacturing populations seemed to seek food markets everywhere except at home. Enterprise gradually weakened; landlords lost their ability to help, farmers their recuperative powers. Prolonged depression checked costly improvements. Drainage was practically discontinued. Both owners and occupiers were engaged in the task of making both ends meet on vanishing incomes. Land deteriorated in condition; less labour was employed; less stock was kept; bills for cake and fertilisers were reduced. The counties which suffered most were the corn-growing districts in which high farming had won its most signal triumphs.

Initially the depression was restricted to the corn-growing areas of the UK: by 1900 the acreage under corn had dropped from eight million acres to six million, a fall of twenty-five per cent. Livestock farmers, however, did not escape for long as during the 1890s ships began arriving with frozen meat from the colonies, causing even this sector to be plunged into recession.

This was not, of course, the first agricultural depression. As we have seen, farming had suffered before, most recently at the end of the Napoleonic Wars between 1815 and 1824, but unlike previous recessions in the farming industry this one was to last a very long time indeed.

It seemed the attack on land was not to be limited to a collapse in food prices. From the valleys of Wales came a man with a silver tongue and a loathing for landowners: Lloyd George. He was to wage a long-running war on landowners until the advent of the First World War diverted his energies to other avenues.

It was a Conservative government that, bowing to pressure from the middle classes about a so-called monopoly of land, commissioned what is sometimes called 'the New Domesday' but was officially called *A Return of Owners of Land.* It was compiled between 1874 and 1876, and although the operation was incompetently carried out – in stark contrast to William the Conqueror's effort some eight hundred years previously – it was to provide much ammunition to the increasingly vocal anti-landowner lobby. It found that 25 per cent of the British Isles was owned by 1,200 people while 66.14 per cent of the total land area was owned by 10,911 people, who individually owned land in excess of a thousand acres each. Naturally this percentage varied considerably over the country. In Scotland, for instance the percentage held by landowners was over 92 per cent, while in England it was only 56 per cent. It is interesting to note that in France, at about the same time, there were only around a thousand estates with more than a thousand acres, such had been the ravages of revolution and the Code Napoléon.

These returns were published in four large volumes, which an enterprising gentleman named John Bateman edited, producing an invaluable reference work called *The Great Landowners of Great Britain and Ireland.* His book concentrated on those landowners with three thousand acres or more who were in receipt of an income in excess of three thousand pounds. He did deign, however, to include details of some estates and incomes that fell just below this category.

It was then as common a misapprehension, among the mass of the public, as it is today that a landowner is rich. To a true landowner, of course, the value of his property is of interest only when he is speaking to his bank manager. Otherwise it is an irritant. Foolish people talk in terms of so and so being worth millions because he happens to own two thousand acres of land, and technically this is the case, but he is only as rich as his net income until he sells his land, and as the true landowner has no intention of doing this he does not regard himself as rich. Bateman tackled this subject by drawing up an imaginary annual profit-and-loss account for a squire with a 3,500-acre estate and a income of £5,000. He called his typical £5,000-a-year squire John Steadyman, of Wearywork Hall, Cidershire.

This left our worthy squire the magnificent annual sum of £1,032 to live on which, if we convert the sum to modern money, converts into £58,816 of 'spending' money left over – not a huge sum, especially as Bateman has not made any allowance in his putative budget for wages of staff. Perhaps in a time when a skilled farm worker received thirteen shillings a week and live-in domestics considerably less, he did not feel the sums were financially relevant, but I would have thought, at the least, the wage bill at Wearywork Hall would have been in the region of another £250 a year, or £11,250 in modern money, which would reduce his disposable income to £47,566 in today's coin. How, though, does Squire Steadyman's financial state compare with that of his great-great-grandson?

Like his forebear, he too is called John and still resides at Wearywork Hall. By a mixture of financial astuteness, native cunning and a great deal of luck (for instance his grandfather, Colonel John Steadyman was killed in action in 1942, thus allowing his father, then a young subaltern, to inherit the estate without paying any death duties. His father was also fortuitously wounded in the closing stages of the same conflict, enabling his doctor to attribute his death, at the ripe old age of eighty-two, to 'war wounds', with similar benefit for his heir. The

Steadyman estate has, almost uniquely, remained at the same size.

So, as you can see, the net disposable income of the estate is, in modern money, virtually the same today as it was 130-odd years ago! Now I would hazard an educated guess that very few – if any – landowners would have bet on that result, as most of us consider that our ancestors in the nineteenth century where living 'high on the hog'. Of course, both the 1876 budget for Wearywork Hall and my imaginary one for 2004 are

	1876 values	Converted to today's values
INCOME FROM RENTS	£5,000	£226,126
Deduct: value in the rate books put upon mansion, grounds, etc.	£220	£9,900
Deduct: also value put on cottages lived in rent-free by old retainers	£30	£1,350
Leaving: a clear rent roll of	£4,750	£214,876
EXPENSES – *now deduct as under*:		
His late father's two maiden sisters, Jane and Esther, who each have a rent charge of £180 per annum (N.B. both these old ladies seem immortal)	£360	£16,200
His mother, Lady Louisa Steadyman, a rent charge of	£700	£31,500
His sisters, Louisa, Mariam and Eva (all plain) each £150 p.a.	£450	£20,250
His brother, Wildbore Steadyman, who was paid off and emigrated but almost annually comes down	£50	£2,250
Mortgage on Sloppyside Farm and Hungry Hill (started when his father contested the county) – interest	£650	£29,250
Ditto on Wearywork End (started when his one pretty sister married Sir Short Shortt Bt and was paid off – interest	£150	£6,750
His managing estate agent, Mr Harrable – salary	£150	£6,750

open to criticism and debate. Looking at my estate accounts for the same period, I see my poor indebted ancestor was able to squeeze a rent roll of only about £2,200 from his tenantry from an estate roughly the same size as Wearywork Hall.

Bateman was writing at the time when the great agricultural depression was only just beginning to bite. Over the next fifty years landowners' net disposable incomes were to plummet by up to ninety per cent as a glance

	1876 values	Converted to today's values
Continued		
Keep of horse for ditto, £35 and house for ditto, £45	£80	£3,200
Average of lawyers' bills	£60	£2,700
Average cost of farm repairs	£350	£15,750
Draining tiles furnished gratis to the tenants	£40	£1,800
Repairs to the family mansion	£70	£3,150
Voluntary church rate, pensions, local charities, etc. (N.B. If Mr S is a Roman Catholic, which I do not think he is, a private chaplain, chapel, school, etc. would increase this to at least £225)	£175	£7,875
Subscription to county (Liberal or Tory) registration fund	£10	£450
Ditto to the Cidershire Foxhounds (£25) and Boggymore Harriers (£5)	£30	£1,350
Ditto to the Diocesan	£25	£1,125
Other county subscriptions – hospitals, flower shows, races, etc.	£35	£1,575
Returned 15 per cent of rents in 'hard times' averaging perhaps one year in five (would that we could say so now, 1882)	£150	£6,750
Loss on occasional bankrupt tenant	£30	£1,350
Arrears of rent, say annually £300, loss of interest thereon at 5 per cent	£15	£675
Income tax at 4*d* in the pound on rents paid and unpaid	£83	£3,735
Insurance on all buildings	£55	£2,475
TOTAL OUTGOINGS	£3,718	£166,910

at the table on the next page will show (figures in brackets represent rents adjusted to modern-day values).

Average gross rent per acre		
1872	1938	1946
34s. 6d	25s. 6d	27s. 6d
(£77.40)	(£60.90)	(£35.60)

So between 1872 and 1946 gross rents fell by some twenty-five per cent in nominal terms, but by over fifty per cent in actual value. That, though, is only part of the story. Mr Bateman's Squire Steadyman paid only 4d in the pound, or less than two per cent of his gross income in income tax. His descendant in 1946 would have paid more like eighty per cent on his net income. At the same time, wages for workers, such as gardeners, gamekeepers, building workers, foresters and domestic servants, had increased enormously. In 1873 the average farmworker in England received 13s. a week; by 1914 this had risen to 25s. a week and

INCOME FROM RENTS	£413,000
Now deduct those expenses that are tax-allowable	
Land agency fees plus costs of running the 'estate office'*	£60,000
Legal bills*	£5,000
Accountant bills*	£5,000
Insurance on estate buildings/cottages and liabilities*	£10,000
Repairs to property*	£100,000
£300,000 loan taken out to pay Lloyd's losses (which J. Steadyman had foolishly joined, believing that there was such a thing as money without risk) at 5 per cent	£15,000
£300,000 working estate overdraft at 6 per cent	£18,000
Tax-deductible staff wages, say	£20,000
Total tax-allowable expenses	£233,000

by 1920 it peaked at 42*s.* a week, before falling as farming went back into recession. By 1948, although wages for farmworkers had reached £5 a week, not only had the gross income of landowners remained static but their outgoings in the form of staff wages had multiplied alarmingly. To add to their woes, few of the estate tasks had yet been mechanized – for instance, gamekeepers, foresters, gardeners, carpenters, masons and the like still worked in virtually the same manner as their grandfathers had done in the nineteenth century. The Industrial Revolution had, as yet, hardly encroached at all on the working practices of the average estate workforce.

Rents did not begin to exceed the 1870 levels in nominal terms till the late 1960s, and only now – in 2004 – are they remotely comparable to 1870 when the ravages of inflation are taken into account.

Looking at such figures, it is hardly to be wondered at that so many landowners elected to call it a day and sell up between 1910 and 1979. The wonder is that there are any decent-sized estates left at all. That there are some can be explained by a number of factors.

Leaving a balance of	£180,000
on which tax is due, say	£65,000
Leaving a balance to spend of	£115,000
Now deduct	
Allowance to aged mother, who lives in a cottage on the estate	£15,000
Contribution to the education of grandson	£15,000
Mansion house repairs	£15,000
Heat, light and electricity	£15,000
Motor cars – an old Land Rover and a not so old saloon car – running costs and depreciation	£5,000
Indoor staff – two ancient dailies who know every nook and cranny	£5,000
Water rates and council tax	£3,000
Total	£73,000
Leaving him with a balance of spending money per annum of	£42,000

Some large landowners were the descendants of those parvenus businessmen of the late nineteenth century who had kept their business empires together and were thus able to continue to subsidize their country estates out of business profits. Other landowners had such a large acreage to start with that they were able to carry out a long-term policy of selling outlying areas to raise capital to pay for running expenses, without destroying the heart of their estate. Still others had secondary estates and, due to the passing of the Settled Land Act of 1882, were now able to break the entails and sell them off. There were also a few landowners lucky enough to have sizeable chunks of urban property, and still others could sell off works of art.

The ones who suffered most were, of course, Bateman's Squire Steadyman and his ilk. They did not have the advantages of their noble kinsmen's vast acreages or valuable art collections or urban property portfolios and had always relied totally on the income from their estates. For them Armageddon loomed. That any survived at all was a minor miracle, due in the main to that old-fashioned virtue we have mentioned before: guts – the refusal to surrender to the inevitable, the sheer determination to survive.

During the First World War, the government, alarmed by the success of the U-boat campaign and anxious to encourage the expansion of the wheat acreage, brought in the 1917 Corn Protection Act which enabled – for a short period – bumper profits to be made by tenant farmers, though little of this prosperity filtered up to the landowner. In 1921, the Corn Protection Act was abolished and farmers and landowners were once again at the mercy of free world prices; wheat prices almost immediately dropped by fifty per cent and by 1931 wheat had fallen to 24s. 8d a quarter – the lowest price recorded (except for a brief period in 1894–95) in a history of agricultural statistics going back as far as 1780! As at this time the cost of growing and harvesting an acre of wheat was estimated at around £8 an acre (compared with an average today of around £240 per acre), average yields being about thirty hundredweight, it can be seen that farming in the 1930s was indeed *in extremis*. The government finally woke up to the disaster and in 1932 brought in the

Wheat Act which effectively marked the end of an era. Except for the brief period of 1917–21, for almost a hundred years, from the abolition of the Corn Laws in 1846 to 1932, British agriculture had survived, and at times prospered, without any form of protection from free world markets.

The Wheat Act was the beginning of the British system of subsidizing farming that went by the name of deficiency payments and was, together with marketing boards for specific products, to provide the template for all forms of UK subsidization until Britain entered the Common Market. One of the reasons why the general public was willing to accept some form of agricultural protection in the 1930s was that food from retailing outlets no longer reflected the cost of the basic raw material; for instance, between 1924 and 1931 the price of wheat halved, yet a loaf of bread only fell from 8*d* to 7*d* over the same time.

The Wheat Act forced all farmers to register their wheat acreage and guaranteed them a price of 45*s*. a quarter (the average cost of production being estimated at 40*s*. a quarter), which you may note was exactly three shillings less than the price which King William III had attempted to stabilize wheat at in 1688. The farmer was to be paid the difference between the average price of home-grown wheat and the price for which the miller could have bought the wheat on the world market (the 'deficiency' price) on all wheat of a millable quality delivered to the miller. In order to protect itself from farmers switching into wheat in large numbers, however, the government set a ceiling on the amount of wheat it would pay out on at six million quarters.

So the period between the wars was a rough one for both farmers and landowners. It was an especially tough time for those farmers who, encouraged by the large profits they had made during the First World War, had borrowed money and bought their own farms from landowners eager to sell in the immediate aftermath of the conflict. Although landowners also suffered during this depression, they were at least not subjected to the various forms of land nationalization and expropriation which, after 1918, were inflicted on most continental landowners. The new countries carved out of the carcasses of the old German Reich, the

Austro-Hungarian Empire and the Russian Empire embarked on an orgy of land reform aimed at reducing or eliminating large private estates and filling up the land with smallholders. In Romania, individual ownership of more than a hundred hectares in mountain districts and two hundred hectares elsewhere was forbidden. In Czechoslovakia about one-third of the total land area changed hands, while in Estonia all the properties of the great landowners were seized. In Poland expropriation and subdivision were initially limited to the land of specific owners, such as the Church and members of the previous reigning families, and all land which was 'badly managed', but ultimately all private ownership of more than four hundred hectares of land was outlawed. Similar stories could be told of virtually every country in Europe. Not that there was not much chance of carrying out a similar programme in the UK; there was talk about it, but it never happened. The consequences of this massive pan-European agricultural revolution are still with us today, although of course the aftermath of the Second World War brought about the 'collectivization' of many of these small-holdings in Eastern Europe.

CHAPTER 7

Land – since the War

'We are the masters now.'
HARTLEY SHAWCROSS (1902–2003)
Speech in the House of Commons, 1946

The end of the war in Europe brought with it the breaking up of the coalition and a general election, with the result that Churchill was booted out of office; for the first time, a Labour government returned with a massive majority. The initial reaction of many landowners was that the end was nigh and many of those who were soldiers made sure that they brought back with them their service revolver, plus a useful supply of ammunition, just in case the situation degenerated into outright communist revolution. The new Labour government was one bent on carrying out radical reforms: it believed totally in the principle of public ownership and, if that was for the moment impractical, then public control and direction of every aspect of every major strategic business. For although the shooting war was over, the new government soon discovered that it was fighting a financial war every bit, in its way, as serious. Its ambitious programme of social reform needed money, and money was in short supply. Vast debts to America had been incurred to help win the war and these now had to be repaid. Britain was, in effect, broke but it still had vast commitments overseas which it could not easily disengage from and, at the same time, an enthusiastic electorate wanted to be rewarded for winning the war with all the goodies they had been promised.

Looking back, it may seem strange that as shipbuilding, railways, road transport, coal and the steel industry were nationalized one after the other, landownership was – comparatively speaking – left alone.

There were a number of reasons for the government's relatively benign attitude to landowners. To begin with, they needed land to be farmed with the maximum efficiency and productivity. Farmers had proved during the war that, given the right incentives, they could achieve 'miracles' of production. Back in 1939 only twelve per cent of the flour used in the UK was home-produced; by 1945 this had risen to forty-four per cent while during the same period milk production had increased by 69 million gallons to 1,188 million gallons. Forced to keep rationing in place by the need to save precious foreign exchange, the Labour Party decided to work with the farmers and landowners rather than against them. Now began the great age of agricultural progress. In order to achieve the aim of increasing agricultural production the Ministry of Agriculture developed two weapons: prices and grants. The prices farmers were to receive for their produce were to be set annually and were designed, naturally, to encourage them to increase their production to the maximum extent. This was called the deficiency payment system and worked by the government refunding to the farmer the difference between the agreed price for a product and the world price. So, for example, if the price the government had agreed to pay farmers for a ton of wheat was £30 but the world market price was only £20, then, initially, the farmer would receive only the world price of £20 a ton but would then get a cheque from the ministry to make up the 'deficiency'. Farmers thus got a subsidized price for their product, but the public got cheap food. The second weapon in the quiver of the Ministry of Agriculture and Fisheries was grants. These were given to farmers and landowners for carrying out capital improvements that would help them boost production.

Farmers and landowners responded with enthusiasm to these twin incentives. Hedgerows were ripped out in their thousands. Orchards were grubbed up. Drainage systems were installed in fields, marsh and 'wetland' and small 'uneconomic' holdings amalgamated. Actually, farmers and landowners had little option but to respond enthusiastically to the new regime's agricultural policy for, to quote from the 1947 edition of *Rural Estate Management* by Charles Walmsley:

The State directs the farming policy of the country through its County Executive Agricultural Committees in conjunction with its land commissioners and advisory staff, and has the power to dispossess a farmer or landowner who fails to comply with its orders or is deemed to be unworthy of his trust or inefficient in his practice. The utilization of land is controlled by the Ministry of Town and Country Planning, and the housing of rural workers by the Ministry of Health.

Reading this, you may well come to the conclusion that the Labour government had no need to go through the expensive and controversial business of actually nationalizing land, since they effectively had total control of all land anyway, but without the burden and cost that nationalization would have entailed.

Labour's agricultural policy was, unlike most of its initiatives, a success. The farmers responded and continued to respond to these incentives, right up to Britain's entry into the EEC in 1973, with vim and vigour. Production soared, foreign exchange was saved and the public was suitably grateful. All this was soon to change, but it is ironic that, when we look at newspaper coverage of agriculture today, we often read of farmers being castigated for carrying out a policy that only a generation ago they were being urged to follow. It may be of some comfort to the farming community to realize that this is a characteristic British reaction to success. Anyone who has ever served in the armed forces is well aware of it, as Kipling wrote so perceptively:

For it's Tommy this, an' Tommy that, an', 'Chuck him out, the brute!'
But it's 'Saviour of 'is country' when the guns begin to shoot.

A typical example of the sort of press comment that farmers today have to put up with is this extract from an article in the *Daily Mail* by the highly respected columnist Andrew Alexander, on 20 January 1998:

If there is one body of men to whom we should not entrust the care of the countryside, it is the farmers. Their record over the past fifty years or so has been appalling. If they see a hedgerow they want to uproot it. If they have trees in their fields, especially mature trees with sizeable roots, they want to cut them down. If it were not for shooting and the woodland required for it the countryside would have been even more desolated.

Of course, in the dash for modernization and increased production mistakes were made – no one would deny that. Some land was brought into production at a totally unacceptable cost – both economically and environmentally – but back in the late 1940s and early 1950s cost was not an issue and the word 'environment' had yet to feature in our everyday language; feeding the population and saving foreign exchange were the chief priorities. A good example of wrong thinking during this period was the programme of wholesale grant-funded drainage schemes carried out throughout the country on wetlands. The result has been disastrous, not only for the environment but also in purely economic terms. Drainage schemes on wetlands meant that rain, instead of soaking into the natural sponge of the soil, ran off at once into rivers. Towns and villages that had never known floods in history now found themselves on the receiving end of them, and hundreds of millions of pounds had to be spent on flood defences. At the same time, rivers that had once been fed by the water seeping gently out of the wetlands over a long period became discoloured spate rivers, carrying tons of silt down to the estuaries. Valuable salmon rivers were wrecked.

Conservationists and the like should not despair, however, about many of the 'improvements' carried out by farmers over the last fifty years. Most are easily reversible and many of the bogs and much of the marginal land drained in the last fifty years will, in all probability, revert to their old state as farming on such terrain ceases to be profitable. Indeed, any person who cares to take a spade into a field and dig a trench will discover that over the last few hundred years generation after generation of farmers have had a crack at draining a field during the good times, only to allow it to revert when the bad times come.

The vast dispersal of so much land since 1910 has, of course, fundamentally altered the English countryside. The removal of land from the ownership of a small group of – on the whole – benign landowners, who took pride in their ancestral acres, and their replacement by men who – also on the whole – viewed land purely as a means of making money, has caused much of the damage to the English landscape that people bemoan today. It is one of the ironies of life that those who complain most about factory farming, the proliferation of unsightly developments, the despoiling of our villages are, more often than not, the same people who raise a glass of elderflower champagne to their lips to toast the demise of yet another old family that has been forced finally to sell the family estate. It is a truism that if you admire a piece of unspoilt landscape or a village not ruined by unsympathetic development, nine times out of ten you will find it is either owned by a private estate, or once was and is now owned by the National Trust.

The horrors of taxation, and especially the taxation bias against what was deemed to be unearned income, resulted in many landowners deciding, during the late 1950s and early 1960s, that to survive they must get their hands dirty and work. Looking around in a desultory fashion at the opportunities open to them, many latched on to the natural choice: farming. Farming his own land had numerous attractions for a landowner, so when a tenant died or retired, landowners started taking the land back in hand.

Initially this worked well. The tax regime was not geared to cater for farmers who had other sources of income beside their in-hand farms, and landowners discovered to their delight that they were in a heads-I-win-tails-you-lose scenario as far as the taxman was concerned. Losses on the home farm could be set off against other income, so even if they were to lose money the taxman effectively gave them back over ninety per cent of their losses; if they made money, they paid tax at an earned-income rate.

No one likes losing money, even if someone else picks up ninety per cent of the losses, but landowners discovered that many expenses which, while technically allowable against tax, had in the old days been paid out of net income, could now be put through the farm accounts. Gardeners and gamekeepers, for instance, metamorphosed into farmworkers, drives became farm roads and were done up accordingly, cars became farm vehicles, and so on; the result was favourable to the landowner who took land in hand.

This happy turn of events lasted till the late 1960s when an unsporting Labour government insisted that farms should show a profit at least once every five years to justify their tax advantages. This proved not to be too arduous for all but the least efficient home farms – although there were quite a large number of these, many of their owners finding, to their surprise, that it was more difficult than they thought to make money out of farming. The reason for this gradually dawned on them – though it is fair to say it still has not dawned on everyone – that gentlemen make bad farmers. Many gentlemen had already taken this fact on board and had effectively subcontracted their farming to a character called a farm manager. The problem with this approach was at once apparent: the farm manager needed to be paid. If the home farm was not of sufficient size, all the profits went to pay the farm manager's salary. Even if there were excess profits in the odd year, landowners found the farm manager always had a good idea of how to spend them, so very little ready cash ever seemed to end up in their pockets. In short, they had forgotten – if they had ever been taught – the ditty:

> He who by the plough would thrive,
> Himself must either hold or drive.

The biased tax treatment on earned – as opposed to unearned – income, however, was such that landowners who had become involved in farming eagerly took every farm in hand when it became vacant; it was, in short, the only way they could see to survive. Perhaps they also believed what their farm managers and professional advisers told them *ad infinitum*; the larger the farm, the greater the profits would be, due to a mysterious concept called 'economies of scale'. The result has been that the percentage of land farmed by tenants has continued to fall inexorably and is now hovering just above twenty per cent of the total agricultural acreage in the country – down from over ninety per cent in 1900.

The arrival of Mrs Thatcher in 10 Downing Street heralded a dramatic change in taxation policies. As the rate of tax fell and the bias against unearned income disappeared, making losses in farming became rather less attractive. When the marginal rate of tax is over ninety per cent, losing a few thousand is frankly no big deal, but when it falls to forty per cent even the stupidest landowner can see that there is a problem.

Future agricultural historians will look on the years of the Conservative government, 1979–97, as one of the boom times in agriculture; this – it is true – owed much to the entry of the UK into the Common Market and the Common Agricultural Policy (CAP), of which more later, but it also saw the emergence of a new creature on the agricultural scene: the contract farmer.

Landowners with loss-making farms had a problem: what to do with them. They were loath to re-let them – partly perhaps from pride, but also because although income-tax differentials between earned and unearned income had disappeared, there was still a substantial bias against let land in the form of capital taxes, namely death duties. In addition, re-letting would mean putting a tenant in, and since 1976, due to what can probably be described as one of the stupidest bills ever passed by Parliament, tenants had been given the right to pass their farms on to their sons. This bill, proudly backed by the National Farmers Union (NFU) – the leadership of which is not particularly well known for having large reserves of grey matter at the best of times, but in this instance conclusively proved it was entirely vacant in the top storey – effectively managed, at a stroke, totally to destroy the market in new farms for tenants, thus adding greater impetus to the formation of larger and larger farming units and making it virtually impossible for young men of limited means to get into farming on their own account.

Fortunately for landowners, there was a solution: contract farming. Actually, there were two alternative solutions to hand, one being that landowners learn how to farm. It is one of life's little mysteries that contract and tenant farmers can pay rent or equivalent sums to land-owners and still make a decent living out of the land, but that once the landowner himself takes control the profits disappear into a morass of red ink. Entering into a contract farming arrangement, however, was the approved solution for understandable reasons: it required a lot less effort and yielded a more likely positive rate of return. Contract farming was the brainchild of lawyers and land agents working together over the years to develop a way in which landowners could effectively 'let' their farm without granting an agricultural tenancy; in other words, it gave landowners many of the benefits of tenanted land with none of the drawbacks.

Thus a contract farmer enters into what is effectively a partnership agreement with the landowner. In return for the landowner providing the capital – in the form of land – the contract farmer guarantees to pay him a fixed sum, called the 'rent equivalent', of, say, £80 per acre, and also a share of the profits. This is truly blissful arrangement for the landowner: he gets all the advantages of having a tenant, yet none of the hassle. His contract is for a set period of years. He gets a regular income. He keeps his working-farmer status for purposes of taxation. He gets a decent slice of the action when profits are good and he does not have to worry about tenants' rights and all the other minor problems that bedevil the average landowner, or wonder, if he is farming in hand, by how much his farm manager is ripping him off.

The contractor benefits enormously as well. He can achieve huge economies of scale, which, with farm machinery getting bigger and more expensive, he needs, and because (usually) he is a genuinely efficient farmer, he will produce handsome profits not only for himself but also for the landowner.

The result has been yet another radical alteration in the British countryside. Houses once lived in by tenant farmers are now redundant and are sold off to weekenders or, if near enough to big cities, executives of banks and the like, who commute into work. The number of jobs on the land plummet as the contractor achieves the promised economies of scale which allow him to pay the landowner his 'rent equivalent' and share of the profits. As a rough rule of thumb, a fifteen-hundred-acre arable farm might give a living to two families: those of the owner and a farmworker. At the other end of the scale, that same fifteen hundred acres could today support up to five tenant farms, each probably providing a livelihood for on average one and a half families – perhaps more in a livestock-farming area. It is ironic that one of the primary reasons for the demise of the tenant farmer can be laid at the feet of the one organization that was supposed to represent him: the NFU.

But then, sadly, the NFU has often exhibited all the faults associated with traditional trade unionism in the UK in being over-concerned about achieving short-term benefits for existing members rather than acting for the long-term health of the industry. Such short-term attitudes, combined with a fear of offending any farming member, have undoubtedly contributed to the fall from grace of the farming industry in the eyes of the general public over the last thirty years.

It is fair to say, however, that the NFU at last woke up to the stupidity of its old policy and gave its support to a new form of tenancy called a farm business tenancy; this allows a landlord to let his farm on whatever terms can be agreed between himself and a willing tenant. The result has been that a little more land has been made available for letting – but its probable effect will not be to raise the level of land at present farmed by tenants to much above its present level, but rather to act as a brake on the total demise of the tenanted sector. The much-vaunted farm business tenancy, incidentally, is virtually identical in form to the tenancy agreements devised by our Tudor ancestors in the late sixteenth century. So much for progress.

I suppose it is yet another minor miracle of the British countryside that any tenant farmers still exist at all, bearing in mind the best efforts of successive governments and the NFU to destroy the sector. Many commentators would argue that their continued existence is down to idle and unenterprising landowners. This is an argument I find difficult to refute. Certainly no commercially run business would have tolerated the continuation of tenants, especially when the value of the attractive farmhouses in which they live rent-free went through the roof back in the 1980s. And yet many landowners, to general amazement, continue to take a rather less than commercial view of their estates and re-let farms as and when they become vacant. Perhaps they see their estate not so much as a vehicle to be driven to its economic limits but rather one to be nurtured and allowed – providing it will still get you from A to B – to chug along quietly in the slow lane.

Even the owner of the most traditionally run estate, however, has since the war been amalgamating holdings and investing in new farm buildings on his tenanted farms. For the sad fact is that small tenanted farms are uneconomic for a landowner and, in the most part, uneconomic for the tenant. To understand this it is necessary to remember that – to all intents and purposes – the tenant lives rent-free in the farmhouse. Imagine two farms of a hundred acres each equipped with a spacious traditional farmhouse. Both are paying a rent of £50 per acre or £5,000 a year. Then one gives up; the landowner amalgamates the two farms and, in this simplified model, still gets £50 per acre rent for the two hundred acres but now lets the redundant farmhouse on an assured shorthold tenancy for £12,000 per year. In other words the landowner has, by amalgamating the land with another holding, more than doubled his rent.

Actually, it is arguable if a tenant or farmer any longer needs to live on a farm. Many tenants themselves rent additional land 'off farm', for which they are often – strangely – prepared to pay a far higher rent than for the land in the immediate vicinity of their farmhouse. We shall have to see how the letting of land under the new Farm Business Tenancy Act develops, but my guess is that landowners are going to be less and less likely to 'chuck in the house for nothing' when discussing rental terms with prospective tenants in the future.

Not that the tenant system could have been dismantled overnight anyway, even if landowners had wished it. Tenant farmers, depending on what date they took up their tenancy, have many legal rights, not least, in the case of those with pre-1976 tenancies, that of inheritance.

The changes that have taken place have not gone unnoticed by commentators on land-management techniques and forms of tenure, and contract farmers and the like receive considerable flak from environmentalists and conservationists. These groups talk of moving back to 'sustainable' farming, by which, ironically, they mean the opposite of what they say. For farming has done what for generations people demanded: provided ever cheaper food for the urban masses. A ton of wheat in 2004 sold for around £60; back in 1881 it sold for £10.65 a ton. In modern money this is over £457 per ton. If that is not sustainable farming, I don't know what is. One wonders what some of today's critics of farming would have to say if the price of wheat had kept pace with inflation and was now around £700 a ton! I suspect they might find their weekly shopping expedition to Sainsbury's a rather bigger financial burden than it is at present. They would be urging that every last square foot of land be brought into production. For it is only because farming today worldwide is so efficient that the urban population can give rein to its conservationist instincts. If the price of wheat were ever to rise significantly, the knock-on effect on the price of food in the shops would cause an uproar. In other words, low food prices, the consequence of efficient food production, are good for conservation.

It is true to say, however, that the farming industry, as it is presently run and financed, is not sustainable in the long term. No industry which produces more than there is demand to satisfy can continue to operate in the same way for long. This is common sense. The problem with food production is a simple one: there is only so much food you can cram into your stomach during a day; *ergo* constant increases in production by farmers need to be matched by increases in population. With the population of Europe showing no sign of expanding, we need new markets to sell the surplus to if the farming industry is to remain 'sustainable'; or we need profits, and therefore land prices, to fall to such a level that large areas of farmland are taken out of production and put to some other profitable use because they are uneconomic. This does not necessarily mean that these areas have to be taken out of farming *per se*; it could mean that farmland that has been intensively farmed reverts to being extensively farmed so that production per acre falls. This is exactly what happened during the great agricultural depression: the corn acreage shrank by around forty per cent as marginal corn-growing land reverted to grassland. If, though, you want to see what can happen to land when agricultural economics suddenly – for whatever reason – suffer a periodic radical change of course and there is no safety net provided for farmers, then you should visit New England. Ideally, you should time your trip to coincide with the fall, that three-week period when the forests of New England suddenly change colour and blaze forth in such a variety of red, orange and yellow that even Turner would have been momentarily stunned. As you admire the view, try to picture the same landscape a hundred years ago, when it would have been very different. Then it would have been mainly open hillside, green fields divided by stone walls with dairy cows feeding on the lush grass and attractive white-painted clapboard farmhouses dotting the landscape. All that is now gone. The farmers abandoned their holdings and left, heading west when the railways came and made their farms uneconomic. The forests then recolonised the farmland. It is an interesting experience to view New England. I came to the conclusion that, although the fall is visually one of the wonders of the natural world, on the whole, the landscape of New England would be much improved if most of those farms were still in existence and not buried beneath towering thickets of red oak and sweet gum.

There is one inescapable fact, confirmed by our short overview of the history of land ownership. Landowning has always been about money. There appears to be some vague idea buried in the minds of many of those who pontificate on the environment that past owners of land somehow did not bother about the sordid subject of making cash, but were happy to live in a sort of Arcadian society where country gentlemen in palatial seats co-existed with happy and contented peasantry.

The desire of landowners to manage their land for maximum efficiency and to improve their estates is not new, but is as old as civilization and – contrary to what the environmentalist would have you believe – there is not one acre of land in the United Kingdom that has not been affected by man's desire to extract money from the earth. We have already seen from entries in the Domesday Book of 1086 that our Norman ancestors were competent improvers. Agricultural improvement is like a craze; throughout history it goes in and out of fashion. For instance, the late sixteenth and early seventeenth centuries witnessed great agricultural improvement: landowners started to drain the fens and marshes and enclose land. There was strenuous opposition to this from those who feared that the resulting efficiencies would cause widespread depopulation and hardship in rural areas – which of course is what happened. Periods of improvement tend to coincide with times when the price of agricultural produce is high and landowners' expenditure is rising, causing them to look at barren and unproductive acres with a gleam in their eye and wonder how to bring that land into production.

Not that every farmer and landowner in history has been an 'improver'. Improving land is capital-intensive and the profits are in the future while the costs are borne today. Many landowners, both past and present, would sympathize with the view of the eighteenth-century academic who, urged to spend money on improving college lands for posterity, retorted: 'We are always talking of doing for posterity, I would fain see posterity do something for us.'

But then farmers and landowners are no different from any other businessmen. There are the conservative ones, husbanding scarce resources, and the risk-takers, borrowing money, expanding, modernizing and dreaming not of survival but of enormous riches in the future. Since the war, of course, the retail sector of the UK has changed radically. We might bemoan the standardization of the high streets of our market towns by chains of building societies and chemists and the concerted and continuing attack made on small grocers, butchers and the like by 'out of town' monster supermarkets, but, like it or loathe it, it is progress of a sort, and leads to cheaper food and other products for the sainted consumer. Farming is no different. Like other businesses, it benefits from economies of scale and, as with other businesses, the people who run it are fighting to survive in a competitive world.

The chief cause for criticism of farming is that, over the last fifty years, its modernization has been funded by enormous taxpayers' subsidies in one form or another. The universal assumption seems to be that without such dollops of public money being spent on it we would today have a very different farming industry, one more in keeping with what the 'public' would like to see.

In one way this view is correct: we would indeed have a very different farming industry. History teaches us that low prices and tight margins in any industry encourage amalgamations and suchlike. In other words, a Britain without a subsidized farming sector would probably be a Britain with even fewer farmers than at present and an even more 'industrialized' farming sector. If you doubt this diagnosis, look at what has happened to the retail sector since the abolition in 1964 of retail price maintenance.

Subsidies, for all their faults (which are many), have acted as a brake on the 'industrialization' of farming – not as a spur, as often asserted. Nevertheless, the trend towards larger farms is one set to continue. In 1950, Britain had some 550,000 farmers who employed around a million farmworkers; today, there are only some 220,000 farmers, ten per cent of whom produce around fifty per cent of the total food consumption of the country. These figures may horrify some, but my guess is that, without the cushion of subsidies, the number of UK farmers would have fallen even more steeply.

The provision of subsidies has been seized upon by certain pressure groups. The ramblers, for instance, see it as a justification for their demand for 'public access' or the 'right to roam'. They argue that because farmers have been in receipt of so much public money in the form of subsidies then the taxpayer should have the 'right' to walk over their land. This argument is patently flawed. Few industries have not been in receipt of some form of government subsidy over the years – the railways, the car industry, the steel industry, shipbuilding, electronics, aerospace, textiles, tourism, have all had their fair share of handouts, and many of these subsidies are still running today. The railways still get a large annual sum, as does virtually every major factory investment. If every business which had ever received a government subsidy was, retrospectively, forced to provide public access, then there would not be one square foot of the United Kingdom from which walkers could be excluded. For instance, many of the ramblers probably live in houses bought with mortgages subsidized via mortgage interest tax relief, or have had their roofs insulated with the help of a grant. So, taking their argument to its logical conclusion, this fact would allow anybody to walk in and inspect every nook and cranny of their property whenever they felt like it. It would also be grossly unfair and inequitable to alter the conditions of grants and subsidies retrospectively. It could be argued, though, that if the government ever wanted to, it could make grants and subsidies in the future conditional on public access – and, indeed, there are schemes where this is actually the case.

Contrary to the opinion of many conservationists, not all farm improvements are bad for wildlife. It is one of the ironies of country life that yesterday's farm improvement is all too often today's wildlife habitat. No more classic example exists of this than that of hedgerows. Recently an Act of Parliament was passed to protect hedgerows. It is worth recalling, however, that the majority of them are of comparatively recent origin. The great age of enclosures was the nineteenth century. Prior to 1845, enclosures required a special Act of Parliament, which was extremely expensive. The Enclosure Acts of 1801 and 1836 simplified the procedure, but it was not until 1845 that the requirement for an Act of Parliament to allow the enclosure of land was finally abolished. Until that date, most of the land in the Midlands was virtually open country. Hedgerows were then planted as agricultural improvements; now they are protected as wildlife habitats.

Popular mythology has it that the 'enclosing of the commons' was some kind of 'theft' by the landowners and is something landowners should feel ashamed of. Actually, the opposite is the case, since a glance at the few remaining commons will show that 'everyone's responsibility is no one's responsibility'. So when you view Northumbrian moorland devoid of heather but covered in dull white grass you are seeing the result of common agricultural practice which can be paraphrased as: 'If I don't rip the arse out this land then some other bugger will, so it might as well be me.' This is why so much of the uplands of England and Wales are either covered in bracken or white grasses, neither of which provide anything like the environmental benefits that heather does. It is also easy now, when we live in a land of plenty, to forget that in the seventeenth, eighteenth and nineteenth centuries food (and its price) was of vital importance. A bad harvest and a large rise in the price of wheat could and did – in France – lead to revolution and the guillotine. If wholesale enclosure, with the accompanying enormous increases in the productivity of land, was the price required to ensure that this did not happen in Britain, then it seemed to nearly everyone to be a very small price to pay.

Of course, some parts of England were enclosed much earlier. Of Devon, J. A. Venn, in *The Foundations of Agricultural Economics* (1933), wrote:

> The average field is some four or five acres in extent, instead of ten or twenty found elsewhere in England, and there is no doubt that such parcels of land form serious obstacles to efficient arable farming. Calculations have been made that show the direct loss of space from excessively wide banks and hedges alone amounts to some 6% of the farming area, and, if the further loss caused by shade is included, this figure may be increased to anything from 10%–20%. Added to this is the handicap entailed by use . . . of abnormally small instruments, and the sheer inability to introduce certain types of machinery into them . . .

In view of this, it is little to be wondered at that so many hedgerows were removed – once again, the wonder is that so many were not. Today, I suspect more hedgerows are being planted than are being grubbed up, but sadly no one seems interested in this good news. This is not surprising, as we all know that good news does not sell newspapers and it is far more fun – for a journalist – to announce, in banner headlines, 'farmers grub up two thousand miles of hedgerows a year', even though such figures are not based on anything other than guesswork. Actually, even if the figure of two thousand miles were correct, it is not a large amount in the scheme of things. For example, on my own three-thousand-acre estate I have over one hundred miles of hedgerow and woodland edge, and three thousand acres is less than five square miles of land.

But the point everyone should remember is that from the most barren Scottish hillside to the seemingly unspoilt downs of southern England, all stand witness to man's efforts to make money out of them.

There is no wood or stream or hill in this country of ours that has not been worked for profit at some time in its history. The ignorant who bemoan modern farming and forestry methods forget, conveniently, that at one time the Highlands of Scotland were covered in trees and that England was devoid of hedgerows. Today, landowners are castigated both for planting trees on hillsides and for removing hedgerows, when they could logically argue that by so doing they were returning the land to a similar state in which it existed in, say, the tenth century.

CHAPTER 8

The Common Agricultural Policy

'I loathe abroad, nothing would induce me to live
there . . . and, as for foreigners, they are all the same
and they all make me sick.'

Uncle Matthew, in NANCY MITFORD'S
The Pursuit of Love, 1945

The very words Common Agricultural Policy (CAP) are enough to send
the most insomniac among us to sleep. But no book on the British
countryside can avoid mentioning a policy which has had such a far-
reaching effect on the structure of rural Britain and on the incomes
of farmers and landowners and, incidentally, their popularity, since the
UK joined the then EEC in 1973. Love it or loathe it, the CAP has
been the dominant factor affecting agriculture in rural Britain over the
last thirty years. This being the case, a basic knowledge of it, and its
background, is essential.

The reason for the existence of the CAP is simple and in America
they have a good phrase to describe it: pork-barrel politics. Back in
1962, when the CAP was effectively born, West Germany and France
had, respectively, twenty and forty per cent of their population involved
in farming. That twenty per cent in Germany, was an extremely
important segment of the electorate; about ninety per cent of them
were Catholics and routinely voted Christian Democrat and, at the
time the CAP was being put together, this was the party in power.

Germany also had a history of agricultural protectionism stretching
right back to the days of Bismarck, who had introduced tariffs to protect

German farmers in the nineteenth century. The result was that German farms were small and chronically inefficient – as indeed most of them still are. In the 1950s, only one-fifth of one per cent of German farms were larger than a hundred hectares! So the Germans were very happy to go along with the French, even though it would be German money which, by and large, was going to pay for most of the subsidies including those that were going to be gobbled up by all those French farmers. It was not until 1967 that the CAP was actually up and running as negotiations between the various EEC countries had been long and tortuous, since each fought for its own interests. The eventual result was, predictably, an economic shambles.

The method of subsidy decided on by the EEC was guaranteed prices. In simplistic terms, the CAP guaranteed the price of all farmers' production, but the cost would not, as in Britain under the deficiency payment system, be borne by the taxpayer – instead it would be passed on to the consumer in higher prices. This was, on the face of it, a clever move, as it made the cost of subsidizing farmers (it was hoped) virtually invisible. When the UK joined in 1973, the rise in the cost of food to the British consumer came as a bit of a shock but, as the powers that be had anticipated, the British housewife soon became accustomed to the higher prices and forgot who was responsible for them and how cheap food could have been if the CAP had not existed. If the housewife forgot however, others did not and in 1991 the National Consumer Council (NCC) published a paper estimating that the CAP was costing each and every person in the UK an additional £110 a year in higher food prices, not to mention another £59 a year in higher taxes, bringing the grand total cost of the CAP for a family of four to £680 a year.

	UK wholesale	World market
Butter – price per 250g	47p	19p
Beef (topside) – price per kg	178p	112p
Sugar – price per kg	37p	12p
		Source: NCC 1991

It is one of the great puzzles of life that if a government were to propose putting VAT on food it would probably lose the next election, which is why chancellors do not tax food, yet food *has* been taxed and taxed heavily for thirty-odd years without the public apparently minding at all, let alone protesting. When Margaret Thatcher proposed a poll tax, however, protesters took to the streets in their thousands, yet there has never been one violent protest about the 'poll tax' on food. Truly it could be said that the extra cost of food under the CAP was the first successful 'stealth tax'.

The hope of originators of the CAP – that the cost of it would be met mainly by the consumer – was soon demonstrated to be way off the mark, as unfortunately what they had forgotten was that if you guaranteed prices then production would inexorably rise. As an illustration, between 1965 and 1991 consumption of food in the UK increased by 0.1 per cent per annum, while production rose by nearly 2 per cent per annum. The UK was not unique in this respect. Throughout the history of the CAP, demand has been rising significantly more slowly than production has. The predictable result was the arrival on the scene of beef and butter mountains, wine lakes and so on. Initially these 'surplus' foods were sold into intervention and stored at great cost to the EU, who hoped that a series of bad harvests or some other act of God would allow them to be unloaded back on the market some time in the future. When God proved unco-operative, the great brains of the then EEC decided to sell them on the world market and so invented export subsidies.

In effect, the EEC paid exporters the difference between the intervention price in Europe and the world market price in order to enable exporters to flog the stuff outside the Common Market. Needless to say, this did not exactly endear the EEC to other exporting nations, who saw the world price fall because of the quantities of EEC-subsidized grain flooding the open market. Nor did it endear the EEC to farmers in Third World countries, who saw the price of their produce plummet as shiploads of EEC grain arrived in their ports at bargain-basement prices.

All these actions caused the cost of running the EEC to escalate out of control and produced the absurd result that an industry, agriculture, which accounted for only around two per cent of the total GDP of the European Union, took fifty per cent of the total EEC budget.

The real irony of the CAP, however, was that it had the reverse result to that which had originally been intended. Instead of keeping people on the land by ensuring that farmers had enough income not only to live but also to pay their farm labourers, the EEC discovered that the ungrateful peasants were taking the money and with it buying a tractor and sacking the labourer, who then emigrated to the nearby town. So the drift from the land to the towns was not halted by the CAP, but rather accelerated, much to the benefit of the middle-class Brits, who suddenly found that large areas of rural France were dotted with delightful abandoned farmhouses, barns and cottages, all going for the proverbial song. As the farmers of France and Germany busied themselves spending their subsidy money on modernizing their farms and getting rid of old Gaston, few of them paused for thought and considered that by replacing Gaston with a tractor, and selling his old cottage to that gullible English couple, they just may have been helping eventually to destroy the system that was now making them rich. Today, agriculture represents around two per cent of the GDP of France and only one per cent of Germany's, and no longer do forty per cent of Frenchmen earn their living from agriculture. Now the figure is less than four per cent and dwindling. Such a seismic change in the employment situation of the average Frenchman has inevitably attracted the attention of politicians, who have suddenly realized that the 'farm vote' is no longer quite so essential as it once was. Not that any French politician is ever going to ignore the 'farm vote' completely, as their counterparts across the Channel feel free to do, for what French farmers may have lost in numbers they have more than made up for with their love of violent protest and lawlessness, which the so-called forces of law and order in France seem powerless to do anything about, especially if the farmer's anger is directed at English lorries bringing lambs into France.

With the waning of the 'farming vote', married with heavy international pressure to reform a system that was seriously distorting the world free market in agricultural produce, Brussels finally decided to 'reform' the CAP, and the first slow and tortuous steps were taken. These were the MacSharry reforms, which first saw the light of day in 1991 and, eventually, in much-watered-down form, were implemented. The main target was the arable farmer. In simplistic terms, support prices for grain were to be cut by twenty-nine per cent over three years, with farmers offered acreage payments (arable area aid), provided they placed at least fifteen per cent of their grain-growing area in set-aside. This represented a major change of direction for the CAP: a departure from subsidies aimed at encouraging production and a swing to subsidies on acreage, regardless of the level of production.

The MacSharry reforms were to herald a major boom in farming incomes, and once again proved, if proof were needed, that long-term plans made by bureaucrats are almost always fatally flawed. MacSharry and his team had not considered the unthinkable: that world grain prices would, or could, actually rise! So farmers in the golden years of 1994, 1995 and 1996 watched in amazement as the world price for wheat soared to in excess of £120 per ton by mid-1996, as opposed to the price the EU had assumed for wheat when it set the subsidies for 1996, of £88 per ton. At the same time, the devaluation of the pound caused by Black Monday resulted in the compensatory payments to farmers in the UK, which had been set in ecus, rising considerably, so instead of receiving a forecast £86 per acre of arable area aid, they got about £110 an acre. Hardly surprising, then, that farmers rejoiced and, as ever with farmers when the good times arrive, rushed out and started spending money on more land and machinery – saving for a rainy day not being an attribute possessed by most of them. So farmland prices soared into the stratosphere, as did rents on new farm business tenancies.

Come 1997, the gathering storm broke. Prices of wheat went into free fall ending up at around £75 per ton; the pound strengthened dramatically against European currencies, and suddenly the smile was wiped off the face of the agricultural community.

One wonders if future historians will not take 1997 as the start of a

Great Fulford lit up by floodlights for a dance in 1960. Good lighting, as all girls will tell you, can flatter, and even the scruffiest house can be turned into a veritable fairytale castle – if only for one night.

The Last Day in the Old Home – what every owner of a 'Big House' strives to avoid happening. Though, everything considered, the gentleman happily toasting the future with his bemused eldest son looks rather cheerful.

Cocks only – Lord Lonsdale shooting with three guns at Lowther Castle. Many Edwardian landowners indulged themselves to excess – to the extent that they left little, if anything, in reserve for their descendants.

Many happy hours can be spent going through old trunks and boxes in attics in the hope of finding something valuable to sell at auction.

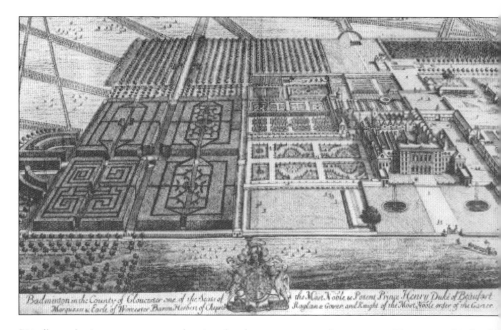

'Bird's-eye' views were popular in the late seventeenth century. From on high the spectacle is pleasing when at ground level things can look quite uninspiring: miles of straight gravel paths, flanked by neatly clipped hedges. Not only are they tedious to walk round but they are, of course, also expensive to maintain.

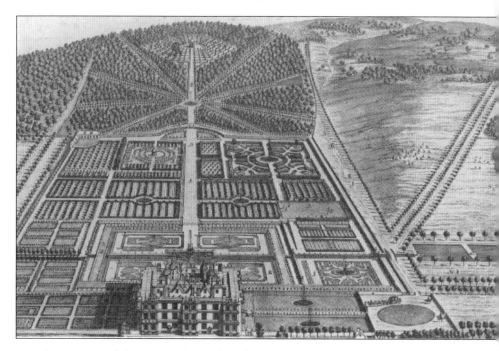

Longleat – one of the great Elizabethan houses built by one of the *nouveaux riches* of the time. Sadly, today's *nouveaux riches* are restricted by planning laws from giving free expression to their innate vulgarity and desire to show off: a problem that their Tudor and Jacobean or even Edwardian predecessors did not have to contend with.

The family. My great-grandfather, grandfather and father on parade – together with assorted aunts and uncles – for a formal photograph to celebrate the coronation of Edward VII. Children are the biggest investment anyone can make in the future; it s strange why so many people today seem to neglect them in favour of so-called rewarding' employment.

Above: My father helping in the garden in the early 1900s. Gardening is the country gentleman's equivalent of the investment banker's indoor gym.

Left: An early attempt at DIY. I do not look overly happy and the slope of the ladder would, I am sure, horrify the health and safety fascists. On the whole though, I adhere to the dictum laid down by Hilaire Belloc:

Lord Finchley tried to mend the
                    Electric Light
Himself. It struck him dead: And
                    serve him right!
It is the business of the wealthy man
To give employment to the artisan.

The courtyard at Great Fulford undergoing restoration. Some of these windows had been blocked up to avoid paying Window Tax in the late eighteenth century, and remained blocked up for some one hundred and fifty years after the tax was abolished. Old houses are rather like over-made-up old tarts: scrape off the make-up and the real age of the building is revealed.

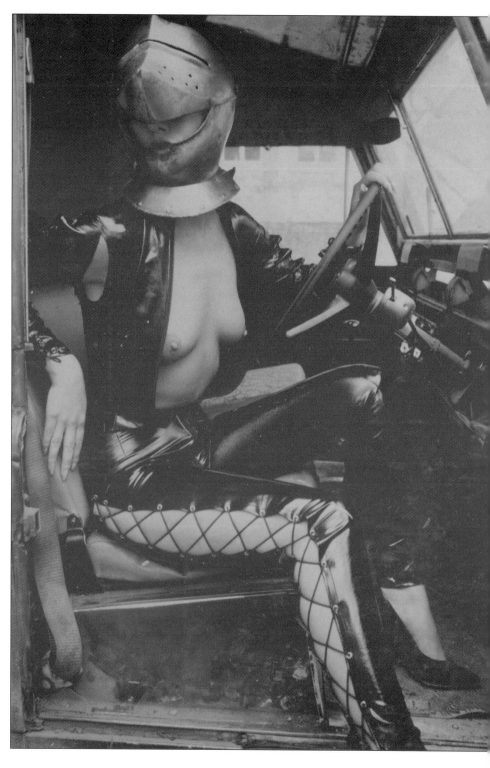

Diversification need not be dull. Glamour photography is one of the areas o diversification providing both profit and amusement that I have explored.

new long period of agricultural depression. I hope not, but certainly the last seven years have proved tough for farmers and, to find a comparable period, you need to go back to before the last war. This depression in farming circles is compounded by the new wave of reforms, which are coming into force in 2005. In effect, these reforms will finish off the old CAP. No more 'production-based' subsidies will be paid; instead, all subsidies will be on an 'area basis'. What this means is that technically farmers will be 'paid to look after the country'. In broad terms the average farmer will receive an annual payment of around £90 per acre and that will be that. If he chooses to run his sheep and beef animals on his land, so be it – it is up to him – but, when he comes to sell them, he will get only what the market pays. In return for this payment he has to keep the land in a fit state for agriculture. In other words, he cannot just lie in bed and let his acres revert to scrub waste, as they quickly would. Or at least he cannot lie in bed every day of the year, as he still needs to trim those hedges and top off the grass in order to get his £90 per acre.

I expect there are some readers already frothing at the mouth at the thought of farmers getting paid for doing nothing although, as I have pointed out, this is not strictly what will happen. Let me tackle this 'subsidy' argument head on. The total amount of subsidy dished out to British farmers in any one year is around £2.2 billion, and averages £5,000 per British farmer (not every farmer being a corn baron in East Anglia). This is not too far adrift of the total subsidy (licence fee) received every year by the BBC (£2.5 billion) or the total subsidy (legal aid) received by the legal profession (£1.9 billion), not to mention the annual subsidy to run the London buses of £650 million, or the estimated subsidy on London Underground of one pound per passenger, while the cost of keeping the Scots happy (or, more accurately, just a little less miserable) is a whacking great £25 billion per annum, or £11,000 per head!

If you are still irate about farming subsidies as you read this, sitting in your subsidized bus on your way to work in London, looking forward to your evening out at the subsidized opera and wondering whether you might not pop in over lunch to see the subsidized art exhibition at the

National Gallery, it just might occur to you that you are, perhaps, a bit of a hypocrite.

Actually, when you get to the opera, please spare a moment to work out why your tickets are so expensive. It is simple: it is because opera is subsidized. Not just opera in London, of course, but every major opera house all round the world. So what does every opera house in the world do with its subsidy? Why, it gives it to the top performers like Pavarotti. In other words, all the subsidy given by every nation or city to its opera house ends up in the pockets of the top performers, as the rival opera houses bid against each other with the subsidy for their favours. Ridiculous, isn't it?

The other thing critics of farmers' subsidies ought to remember is that the EU is not alone in subsidizing its farmers. Throughout the world, with the almost sole exception of New Zealand, developed and developing nations subsidize, in one form or other, their farmers. The great USA, that zealous apostle of free trade, is itself is one of the greatest villains when it comes to subsidizing its farmers, while Japan has taken the art to such a high level that their farmers have become so rich that many use helicopters to plant their rice, thus keeping their feet dry. The tragedy of worldwide subsidies is that the primary reason why European farmers need help is that American farmers are subsidized. In other words, if America stopped subsidizing its farmers, vast areas of the prairies would revert to being open grassland, as they would become uneconomic to farm. Consumers, though, should be aware that the result of all countries giving up subsidizing their farmers would probably, conversely, mean higher food prices; it would certainly mean a roller-coaster ride in food prices as farmers went in and out of production as the prices of different products rose and fell.

I am a committed 'free trader' and I believe that in a subsidy-free world UK agriculture would be extremely competitive. Sadly that world does not exist and, as long as it does not, then British farmers deserve protection from unfair competition from countries such as Australia and the USA.

All this talk of subsidies for farmers is a bit of a misnomer, for not every farmer gets the benefit of the subsidy, as subsidies benefit only those in possession at the time they are introduced. This, incidentally, does not just apply to farming subsidies but to all subsidies. So when, until it was finally abolished in the mid-1990s, there used to be a thing called mortgage interest tax relief (MIRA), it did not actually benefit the people whom it was meant to benefit (first-time buyers); it made everyone who could get a mortgage that little bit 'richer', so they could all afford a bigger mortgage. All MIRA did was push up the price of houses for the benefit of those who actually already owned them, not exactly quite what was intended.

As it was with houses, so it is with farming subsidies. Long-term subsidies have a major economic drawback: they become capitalized in the price of land. Let me explain. The price of agricultural land is intrinsically linked to the potential income it generates. It is true that over the last thirty-five years various apparently intelligent people have invested in land because, as Mark Twain said, 'God isn't making it anymore'. They assumed for this reason that the price of land would rise, regardless of its profitability. Most of these people bought on behalf of City institutions and the like – as did Jim Slater, the City financier who, in 1973, told his agent to go out and buy land, and when asked by his agent when he should stop, said: 'When you reach the sea.' Actually, Slater and his City friends in the pension fund and life insurance business made a drastic miscalculation when they decided to add agricultural land to their portfolio: they brought the wrong type of land. They went for the highest-quality arable farmland which, almost by definition, tends to be flat, boring countryside. This was all very well when the prices of wheat and other agricultural produce was in the ascendant, but when the CAP began to be reformed in the early 1990s and those reforms began to bite, with a drop in prices, the investment began to look not so hot. Flat East Anglian 'bread basket' land has little appeal for the new City buyer, who is not an institution but an individual who has made his millions and is looking instead for something scenic and probably something he can turn into a half decent shoot, in other words Grade 2 and Grade 3 land in the west of Britain.

Even so, and taking into account the large increase in 'lifestyle' buyers of land from the City, on the whole the price of land continues to demonstrates that the largest factor in making up its price is its potential for producing income. So high subsidies are transposed into higher rents and higher land prices. In other words, it can be argued, someone who buys a farm at today's inflated land prices receives no benefit at all from farm subsidies, as the price he pays for his land reflects the value of the current level of subsidies. For example, let us assume that the value of a bare acre of land today is £2,500. We know that under the extremely complex CAP reforms the occupier of that land will receive a sum of £90 per acre in subsidy. We also know that not all that £90 is straight 'profit', as he will have to keep the land in agricultural condition to receive it but let us say that the cost of doing this is only £40 an acre, so we are left with a potential profit of £50 an acre. Now if you put £1,000 on deposit at the bank you might get four per cent, so to receive an 'equivalent income' I would need to deposit, say, £1,200 with the bank. In other words the 'capital value' of the subsidy to the farmer is £1,200 per acre, meaning that the 'true' value of an acre without the subsidy is not £2,500 but only £1,300.

As with so many things in life, the 'law of unintended consequences' came into play with the CAP. When Britain joined the EEC the farming community saw a land ahead flowing with milk and honey. What they did not take into account was what all their gorging on all that milk and honey would do to their public image.

Back in the 1940s and right up to the early 1970s, farmers were hailed as the heroes of British industry. Newspapers ran leading articles praising farmers for achieving higher and higher productivity and contrasting the abject performance of British industry with the brilliant efforts of British agriculture. All this changed with the arrival of the CAP. Farmers suddenly became villains instead of heroes and found themselves held up as heavily feather-bedded scroungers – always with their hands out asking for more money and, when they got the money, using it to destroy yet more of the unique environment of the British countryside. I am not saying I agreed with that image, but that is how farmers were perceived by the vast majority of the public until recently. Things are now, I think, beginning to change. The ongoing reform of the CAP has removed many of the abuses in the system, the guaranteed price regime has pretty well gone and the foot and mouth crisis introduced the British public to the fact that not all farmers were grain barons greedily exploiting the CAP and destroying important 'ecological sites' along the way, but that a large number were livestock farmers scraping a living from some pretty inhospitable terrain. Also, the British press have identified a new villain – the supermarkets – and if they are now the villains, who then are the victims? Why, the two hundred-odd thousand farmers who have found themselves at the mercy of the four major supermarket groups controlling over seventy per cent of the retail market for food in the UK and who are abusing their monopolistic position big time by squeezing supplier prices to the limit, notably in the dairy industry.

As we approach 2005 and the new non-production-based regime of subsidies, a *frisson* is running down the spine of all British farmers. How will they cope? What will happen to prices in this new era? It is, after all, over seventy years since farmers had to cope with living and working in a totally free market, the only difference being that today's farmers will have the option of not producing food and letting the land lie fallow while waiting for prices to turn in their favour, still getting paid a basic subsidy. In short, the financial prospects of Britain's farmers do not look great but, if I were a betting man, I would put my money on many of the descendants of today's farmers still farming their ancestors' land when the likes of Tesco, Sainsbury's and Asda are just a footnote in retailing history.

CHAPTER 9

The Woodlands and Forestry

Trees are an excrescence upon earth provided
by God for the payment of debts.

SAMUEL PEPYS (1633–1703)

We live at a time when short-term investments are everyone's ideal. People are keen to make a quick buck and then either retire or move on to the next enterprise. Forestry, however, is the ultimate long-term investment. I am now cutting down oak trees my ancestor planted to provide the timber to build ships in which some day to beat the French. Sadly, ships are today made of steel and the French are now a protected species.

Such is the long-term nature of the investment. It is also a good example of how, quite often, the markets for which the timber was intended have entirely disappeared by the time the trees are ready to cut. When that happens many owners give up and woods become neglected. Many estates have hundreds of acres of neglected broad-leaved woods and are at a loss to know what to do with them. It is one of the major failures of British forestry policy since the war that no serious effort has been made to tackle this problem. Actually, this is not quite fair, as until recently the solution was to fell them and replant with conifers. Now the chances of getting permission to do this are on a par with getting an iced drink in the middle of the desert. So while on the one hand government forbids you to carry out the only economic solution for neglected woods, on the other it offers no alternative solution.

This is a pity, as there is value in most timber; the trick is getting it out. The concentration, over much of the last fifty years, on softwood production has meant that the marketing and selling of the UK's hardwoods has received little attention. In short, what is required is a national body to carry out research and development in timber products and then to sell those products to the architects and builders who are its end users. Instead, we have money being thrown around in penny packets at various worthy local initiatives run, on the whole, by enthusiastic environmentalists who know little about the business of timber or the art of marketing.

But let us leave the contentious subject of neglected broadleaved woodland for a moment and look at the history of forestry over the last half-century or so.

The average estate will have a mixed bag of woodland depending on previous owners' views on forestry. Estate owners after the Second World War fell broadly into two categories: those who believed forestry could be the way to the promised land of making estates pay and building up a large capital sum, and those who despaired about the whole thing and either did nothing or leased their woods to the Forestry Commission on 999 year leases.

Most estate woods were ravaged during the First World War, when the demand for timber soared (all those duckboards needed in the trenches, not to mention pit props for mines, huts for troops, wooden chassis for vehicles, aircraft frames, etc.) and the government found to its dismay that UK timber resources were negligible. Landowners everywhere were forced to sell their trees to the nation and approximately 500,000 acres of woodland, fifteen per cent of all Britain's woodlands, were clear felled. After the war only a few landowners had the resources, the foresight or the energy to replant their decimated woodland. Any good broadleaved woodland left after 1918 was, in all likelihood, felled during the Second World War. The result of all this devastation was not only that the forests were wrecked but also that the industry that existed to process and market the hardwoods grown was also doomed as, come 1945, there was little good raw material left for it to handle.

The lack of a major hardwood industry in the UK today is a direct result of the toll extracted from Britain's forests during two world wars, and the lesson for politicians and environmentalists is that a forestry industry is like a huge oil tanker: it needs ten miles of sea-room to stop. The economic consequences of decisions made today about forestry may not become apparent until a hundred years have passed.

The forests we see today owe much to the policies enacted by the Labour government of 1945–50. At the end of the Second World War a new generation of owners returned from the fighting to find that once again their woods had been devastated, but this time the Government had a plan. The plan was something called 'dedication' and was brought into being by the Forestry Act of 1947. This was a carrot and stick act. The Government had decided that 'the rehabilitation of woodlands must proceed with both certainty and rapidity' and that if an owner 'is so prepared and can give satisfactory assurances he is deserving of financial assistance from the state' but, *'where no satisfactory assurances are forthcoming within a stated period the state should acquire the land'.* Those landowners who accepted the carrot entered into a 'dedication' scheme. In return for a raft of grants and assistance, they agreed to manage their woods according to an approved plan of operations, which aimed to maximize the productive potential of the woodland. Those owners who did not take the carrot, however, were offered another option: lease the land to the Forestry Commission and let it plant and manage the land in return for an annual rent (not normally – sadly for the heirs of the owners – adjustable for inflation) on a 999-year lease. That they agreed to these terms seems silly to us but at the time the best advice was lease to the FC or face the prospect of your land being nationalized, and many chose the lease option.

Those who did not do this and took the 'dedication' route often became fanatical foresters. Trees became the 'in thing' in landowning circles, and agèd woodland workers, who for years had done little except sweep the drives, trim the laurel and provide firewood for the house, found themselves put to work planting, weeding, beating up and brashing new plantations. For some it must have been a severe shock to the system, for others a new lease of life.

Apart from the advent of grants, a further incentive was that woods managed with the long-term aim of being a commercial enterprise could be assessed under schedule D for income tax purposes – in effect, this meant that all expenditure on such woods could be set against other income for tax purposes. At a time of high marginal tax rates the attractions were obvious. Technically, of course, although woods could benefit from schedule D in the growing stage, once they were felled and produced income, profits would be taxed. However, as on change of ownership the new owner could opt to switch from schedule D to schedule B – which meant that expenditure could not be set against other income for tax purposes but that profits were tax-free – this was not a problem. Trees, even coniferous ones, take at least twenty-five years from the time of planting to the time when they begin to produce profits in the form of thinnings, so if the original owner had not died in the period, he could transfer the ownership of the plantations, as they came into profit, into his son's name, and his son could elect for a change of schedule.

There was one other significant advantage, taxwise, to woodlands: they did not attract death duties. It would have been ludicrous if they had. How could death duties, or inheritance tax as it is now called, be levied on a crop which, in the form of coniferous timber, takes roughly fifty years to mature, and for species such as oak, over one hundred and twenty years? If death duties had been levied, the result would have been the wholesale destruction of the very woods the government was so anxious for landowners to plant, as their heirs would have been forced to fell semi-mature woods to pay the tax.

This last benefit of woods was not lost on some of the more astute landowners. Several estates saved themselves a fortune in death duties when doctors told some agèd peer that he had only six months to live and he went on the spending spree to end all spending sprees, buying up forests the length and breadth of the country. The system was relatively easy and especially beneficial if he borrowed the money to do it. Say he borrowed £100,000 to buy woods; that £100,000 would count as a debit item on his heir's eventual death-duty bill, while the assets it had bought – the forests – would have been tax-free and could be sold to pay the tax bill on the rest of the estate.

Thus a renaissance in estate forestry occurred, fuelled by a mixture of grants and tax relief. It is worth reflecting that today, in 2004, fifty-six years after that Act of Parliament, the trees it inspired are only now being cut. Of course, most owners have throughout history planted trees to provide future profits for their descendants, forestry being the ultimate in long-term investment planning. Samuel Pepys's description of trees as provided by God 'for the payment of debts' was not so wide of the mark. Trees are indeed a useful way of storing cash for that rainy day.

There are those, however, for whom it is a matter of jam tomorrow, jam yesterday, but never jam today. Many woodland owners have given up waiting for the promised profits from their fathers' forestry efforts to enrich them and have become disillusioned by the whole business, repeating *ad nauseam* when you ask them about their woods, on which their father lavished so much time and attention: 'Oh, there is no money in forestry.'

This negative attitude is in part due to the removal of schedule D tax relief on forestry in the 1986 budget. Once again a privilege had been granted by government to landowners. Once again grubby little ac-countants moved in and with – it must be said – the active support of private forestry companies, began abusing that privilege. The final straw was when the wholesale planting up of the 'flow country' in the far north of Scotland began in the 1980s. I have been up there, and a less hospitable place to plant trees it would be hard to find, but that did not matter; what mattered were the tax advantages of planting them for the accountants' clients. Predictably the greed of the few caused the privilege for the many to be lost.

The removal of these tax breaks came as a blow to those with traditional estate woodlands. Following their practice in farming the home farm, many landowners had found it conveniently easy, for tax purposes, to put part of the gamekeepers' and gardeners' salaries down against expenditure on woods. The sudden realization that every pound they spent on their trees was now a pound out of taxed income gave them a rude shock from which most, eighteen years later, have still not recovered.

Of course, the reason they do not make profits today is relatively easy to spot. Landowners and their advisers have, like the dodo, failed to move with the times. In the bad old days before Mrs Thatcher, top rates of income tax regularly exceeded ninety per cent and in 1979 were at ninety-eight per cent. Expenditure on woodlands, therefore, was not a big issue for a high-rate taxpayer, as the taxman effectively picked up more than ninety per cent of the bill. Landowners became lazy and forest management companies became rich as there was little incentive for woodland owners to scrutinize their expenses in relation to the woodland account. Now, with no tax relief on expenses but tax-free profits to be had on woodland income, there is every reason for a landowner to take a greater interest in the management of his wood-lands – but few do, preferring instead to cry into their soup and ceaselessly moan, 'There's no money in trees.' Which is true if you insist on paying large sums to outside managers to do the work for you. After all, qualified foresters have to be paid and paid well, so who pays them? Why, the landowner – who is then disgusted with the small amount of money he receives for the timber his father planted fifty years ago.

The solution is obvious: learn to do most of the management tasks in your own woods yourself. That this simple remedy has failed to register in the minds of so many owners is, I am afraid, not flattering to the overall intelligence of the average owner.

To illustrate the point let us look at a coniferous plantation of fifteen years' standing, coming up to what is called the 'first thinning stage'. The purpose of thinning woods is quite simple. Initially more trees are planted than required for a final crop; close proximity encourages them to grow fast, to suppress the undergrowth beneath them and to self-prune. Unless we wish to end up with a rubbishy crop of softwood in fifty years' time (like most of the Forestry Commission plantations, of which more later), we need to thin them out at regular intervals to give them space to put on girth as well as height. This is an expensive process. The product from first and second thinnings goes normally for pulp or chipboard, and the price paid is unlikely to be much better than £20 a ton delivered in. Now if you employ a professional forestry management company to do the work for you they will charge at least £30 per hour to mark up your timber and in some cases up to £80 an hour, a commission of five per cent normally on the total value of the sale, plus supervisory fees, etc. As the costs to the landowner of the professional come out of net income, it follows that if he is paying someone £80 an hour it is the equivalent of at least £120 gross, and I very much doubt if many landowners have ever been paid £120 per hour in their lives to do anything. In other words, if they got off their arses and went on a few days' training they might find to their amazement that there actually was jam today in their woods. Their attitude is all the more difficult to understand as many of them are not only woodland owners but also working farmers. As such they should realize that their view of forestry as an investment is akin to a farmer looking at a field of winter wheat in March and moaning: 'There is no money in wheat.' Nor is there till the crop is ripe and safely harvested and in the barn. In other words, trees will produce substantial profits only when they are mature and ready for cutting. But the farming analogy does not just stop here. A farmer knows that once he has sown his field of wheat the work has only just begun. There is much to be done to the land between planting and harvesting it if he is going to maximize his profit and produce a high-yielding, quality crop. Yet the same man will often assume that a tree – once planted – can be left alone to look after itself, and will not need any money or time spent on any aftercare. The result is that his descendants will be left with a worthless, messy wood fit only for firewood.

The removal of the schedule D tax relief in the 1986 budget was forced by a ground swell of public opinion, carefully orchestrated in the press, against the planting of alien species of coniferous trees, especially in parts of the far north of Scotland. In fairness much of the press criticism was justified; a lot of the planting taking place was not good forestry and was being carried out solely as a tax-avoidance scheme.

The reasons for the fall from grace, in the public's eyes, of the government-sponsored 'dash for growth' in forestry is, as ever, simple:

the aforementioned muscling-in of canny accountants and their undeserving clients on grants aimed at private landowners to help them solve
a problem. Schedule D tax relief had been a privilege granted to the
forestry industry, but when privileges are granted they can, and will be
removed if they are abused.

Actually, it is doubtful if most of said canny accountant's clients will
ever get much benefit from their forestry investment. As usual, the men
who will certainly have made money will be the accountant who advised
his client in the first place, the agent who sold the land and the
management company which has been looking after it. The humble
investor comes, as so often in 'alternative investment' schemes, a long
way down the pecking order. The figures, of course, would have looked
good and persuasive on paper, but because the client knew nothing
about forestry, he was often a chicken ripe for the plucking.

One forestry expert reckons that twenty-five per cent of the forestry
in Scotland is valueless, because it will cost more to fell and extract the
trees than they are ever going to be worth. This is not surprising if you
think about it. Any fool can walk over a hill and plant it up with
thousands of seedlings, but when those trees mature you need to get
enormous great timber lorries and harvesting machinery into the same
plantation. It is only then that the awful truth dawns. The roads are too
narrow, the bridges are not built to sufficient standard to take heavy
timber lorries or, perhaps, there is no access at all to the plantations. In
summary a lot of the plantations in Scotland were planted with the
same lack of foresight evinced by the legendary man who built a yacht in
the back garden of his house only to realize when he had completed it,
that the only way he could ever get it out was by knocking down the
house.

Commercial forestry – by which I mean actually growing trees with
the eventual aim of making a profit out of them – has, as we have said,
like commercial farming, received a bad press in recent years. The
mainstay of the forestry industry are the so-called exotic species, i.e.
coniferous trees. These, with a rotation period of only forty to fifty years,
give a good return on investment, if managed properly. The many

environmental lobbies, however, have managed to persuade the vast majority of the population that coniferous trees are a *bad thing*. In a way, the public's receptiveness to this idea is understandable. Much of the upland planting was not only, as has been said, badly sited from an economic point of view, but was grossly badly sited from a scenic point of view as well. Square- and oblong-shaped spruce plantations on otherwise bare hillsides are not, to say the least, pretty or attractive. Neither, though, are the town and city centres or the tower blocks and shopping centres that were being built at around the same time. The inept planting and landscaping of forest plantations in the 1950s, 1960s and 1970s were just symptoms of a national malaise in the appreciation of beauty, which manifested itself wherever man was active. Planners, architects, foresters, farmers and governments of all political colours were apparently obsessed by a creed of brutalism, perhaps best summed up in the erection of the National Theatre on the banks of the Thames. Forestry, however, has one enormous advantage over such concrete brutalism: you can cut trees down and you can easily reshape the boundaries of plantations. Much work on this has been done over the last twenty years and more will be done in the future, but sadly once a industry has, in army parlance, 'lost its name', it takes an awful lot of work to get it back.

It may also be that we are being slightly unfair to all those planners and futurists who produced both the tower blocks in the towns and the square plantations on the open hills. Back in the 1950s the planting up of the barren hill land of the uplands of Britain was seen as a major economic tool in the regeneration of British uplands. Tens of thousands of jobs were going to be created, both in the sawmills and pulp mills that were going to be built to handle the produce from the forests, and in the tens of thousands of positions for people required to work in the actual woods themselves. In the late 1950s for instance, the Forestry Commission suddenly realized it had a major problem on its hands. It had planted the largest man-made forest in Europe at Kielder on the Scottish border, but there was no town big enough to house the estimated ten thousand workers required to work in it when it came into production around the turn of the century. What to do? The problem was so large that there was only one thing to do: nothing. The result? The Forestry Commission now directly employs some seventy men to look after the whole of the enormous Kielder Forest. What is the lesson to be learned from this? It is one that I will come back to again and again. Do not, if you can help it, make long-term decisions based on current assumptions.

The result of the 'dash for growth' in the forest industry is that the industry made a lot of mistakes and is today, perhaps unfairly, judged by the public on the basis of its mistakes rather than its successes. So while the words 'woods' and 'woodland' produce a 'warm' feeling with the public, the words 'forestry' and 'timber' raise the average punter's blood pressure. This is sad, as my suspicions are that he is not comparing like with like. In other words, when he is shown a newly planted spruce plantation and then asked whether he prefers that to a mature oak wood, his answer is obvious. Strangely, if you take a rabid, but uneducated (as most are) environmentalist into a mature softwood plantation, which has been well managed, the trees thinned and pruned and now, at fifty years-plus, soaring a hundred feet up in the air, and ask him if he likes what he sees, he will wax lyrical with enthusiasm and be amazed when you tell him that these are the dreaded coniferous trees.

Today's government, ever ready to bend its policy to the voice that shouts loudest in its ear, has a forestry policy which, if it were not so pathetic and disastrously wrong, would be downright risible. On the one hand, it has announced – to the usual fanfare of publicity – that it wants to double woodland cover in England over the next fifty years. On the other, it has structured the grant system in such a way that nearly all areas that are being planted are 'amenity' woods, acres of hardwoods which, in all likelihood, will never be of any economic value whatsoever but will at least guarantee a gross oversupply of firewood in fifty to a hundred years' time.

This is sad, because the UK does have the foundations of a first-class forestry industry. Currently some thirty-five thousand people are producing high-quality timber using modern and extremely efficient timber-processing methods. All this is at present being put at risk for short-term political gain which, as timber is a long-term industry, is rather unfortunate and not a little depressing.

Forestry has become a political hot potato and, at present, the environmental lobby have the high ground; ignorance is triumphing over experience. Perhaps the most flagrant example of ignorance is the introduction of tree preservation orders (TPOs). They are, as any woodland owner knows, a contradiction in terms; you cannot 'preserve trees'; you can, of course, prolong their lives till they are completely useless, rotten and then cost a small fortune to fell, but you cannot prolong their lives for ever. The result of TPOs is that a woodland owner stops carrying out any management of those trees to be preserved, since there is no longer anything he can do – they have been effectively 'nationalized'. So what will happen when the big wind next blows and they fall down? Why, nothing – the landowner has no money to clear up the damage and replant and no incentive to do either. Many environmentalists would welcome this approach to forest management and enthusiastically point to the amazing natural regeneration that occurred in some woods after the great storm of 1987. That this did happen in some woodland is true, but not all woods react in the same way; soil is critical as far as natural regeneration is concerned. If your wood is on 'greensand', then as soon as a tree falls or is felled and light reaches the forest floor, seedlings will spring up everywhere. If, on the other hand, you are on heavy clay, the only result is likely to be a covering of bramble which will quickly stifle virtually any regeneration.

TPOs are, frankly, selfish short-term solutions. What are needed are species preservation orders, which would allow landowners to fell trees provided they replanted with the same species, thus enabling our grandchildren to enjoy the same sight of large mature broadleaved trees as we do today. This is merely common sense, but common sense is in short supply in the environmental lobby.

The truth of the matter is that all the woodlands in the UK exist for one of two reasons. They were either planted and maintained for field sports, or for making money. Often, because the economic reason for the existence of woods has long disappeared, they are assumed to be the remnants of some ancient forest and are designated 'ancient woodlands' and surrounded by a plethora of regulations. Classic instances of this are the steep river-valley banks of Devon, clothed in stunted oak coppice – now virtually valueless as timber, but back in the eighteenth century a highly remunerative source of income for landowners. Then they were grown on a twenty-year rotation for bark for the tanning industry. Marshall's *Rural Economy* states: 'Formerly, within living memory, four or five pounds an acre was reckoned a good price for wood of the middle quality and twenty years' growth. Within the last ten years, or less time, ten pounds an acre was esteemed a good price for such wood. Now [1794] it is worth fifteen pounds an acre.'

The result of slapping TPOs and other such orders on these woods is that management by the owners ceases. The canopy closes in and the woods – instead of being a living, breathing diverse, natural environment, with some areas clear felled, other areas in the brushwood stage and some areas mature – become one large monoculture, supporting only one form of wildlife.

The current state of regulation and restriction on the forestry industry by the government via the Forestry Authority is bad enough, but at least it is carried out by qualified foresters at the government's expense. Now, a new group has arrived on the scene determined to impose its own agenda on woodland owners and yet another layer of costs and bureaucracy. I refer to those paragons of good conservation and the environment, the supermarkets and retailers, such as Sainsbury's, B&Q and WHSmith, who, with some forty-odd other companies, have joined together to form something called the ''95 Group' under the aegis of the Forestry Stewardship Council (FSC), itself a spin-off of the Worldwide Fund for Nature (WWF). The group's stated aim was that by the year 2000 all wood and wood by-products (such as paper) sold in their stores would come from 'certified' forests. The reasons for the foundation of the FSC was presumably to help stop the exploitation and destruction of tropical rainforests, an aim which few of us would quarrel with. The FSC, however, has got rather carried away and is now seeking to impose those standards on UK woods – and not just standards; for, if their aim is implemented, woodland owners will be subject to a whole raft of bureaucratic forms and professional fees to be paid to the proverbial 'environmental' storm-troopers who will carry out the certification process.

Before I go into this whole question of certification in a bit more detail – and I promise you all a good laugh, so bear with me – let us just consider what qualifications companies such as Sainsbury's, B&Q and WHSmith have to lecture woodland owners on conservation. Just have a little think for a second. Do they perhaps sell PVC? Or soft-porn books and magazines? Non-returnable bottles? Tin cans? Junk food? Surely not, for these companies must be whiter than white to have taken the stance they have regarding forestry. So what is their stance? The best way to find out is to look at the 'ten principles' of the FSC. Most of them are, on the face of it, totally innocuous and cannot in any way, one would have thought, apply to private forestry in the UK. After all, what the FSC is trying to stop is the wholesale 'rape and pillaging' of the world's rainforests for private profit by unscrupulous logging companies.

Well, that was all pretty boring, wasn't it? I suppose you are wondering why I felt it was important to quote, in full, all ten principles? (See table on facing page.) A number of reasons spring to mind.

First, like it or not, this is the way the countryside is going – what is being tried on the forest industry today will, in one guise or another, be tried on the farming community tomorrow.

Second, it strikes me as a perfect example of the sort of meaningless gibberish that those of us in the country have to put up with now from urban-based pressure groups who have no idea what they are talking about.

Third, those reading it will be wondering what all the fuss is about, as clearly these ten principles do not apply to forestry in the UK – or only if you really stretch a point on one or two of the principles. If you are thinking this you are perfectly right, but completely wrong. Or rather, the FSC thinks you are wrong and wants all owners of productive woodlands in the UK to jump through the hoop of applying for certification status.

1 **Compliance with laws and FSC principles**
Forest management shall respect all applicable laws of the country in which they occur, and international treaties and agreements to which the country is a signatory, and comply with all FSC principles and criteria.

2 **Tenure and use rights and responsibilities**
Long-term tenure and use rights to the land and forest resources shall be clearly defined, documented and legally established.

3 **Indigenous peoples' rights**
The legal and customary rights of indigenous peoples to own, use and manage their lands, territories and resources shall be recognised and respected.

4 **Community relations and workers' rights**
Forest-management operations shall maintain or enhance the long-term social and economic wellbeing of forest workers and local communities.

5 **Benefits from the forest**
Forest-management operations shall encourage the efficient use of the forest's multiple products and services to ensure economic viability and a wide range of environmental and social benefits.

6 **Environmental impact**
Forest management shall conserve biological diversity and its associated values, water resources, soils and unique and fragile eco-systems and landscapes, and, by so doing, maintain the ecological functions and integrity of the forest.

7 **Management plan**
A management plan – appropriate to the scale and intensity of the operations – shall be written, implemented and kept up to date. The long-term objectives of management and the means of achieving them shall be clearly stated.

8 **Monitoring and Assessment**
Monitoring shall be conducted – appropriate to the scale and assessment of forest management – to assess the condition of the forest, yields of forest products, chain of custody, management activities and their social and environmental impact.

9 **Maintenance of natural forests**
Primary forests, well-developed secondary forests and sites of major environmental, social or cultural significance shall be conserved. Such areas shall not be replaced by tree plantations or other land use.

10 **Plantations**
(Draft principle for plantations, not yet ratified by FSC membership.) Plantations should be planned and managed in accordance with principles 1–9 above, and the following criteria. Such plantations can and should complement natural forests and the surrounding eco-systems, provide community benefits and contribute to the world's demand for forest products.

Fourth, just cast your mind back to the great and good of British retailing and wonder how they would match up if such standards were required of them by, say, a Retailers' Stewardship Council (RSC). Just run through those ten principles and place the word 'retailer' where 'forest management' now stands. Amusing, isn't it? Or perhaps you don't find it amusing at all and think that most of the members of the '95 Group must be a complete load of hypocrites.

Fifth, you may, like me, have got quite excited about principle number 3, the one about indigenous peoples' rights. I expect you thought you might qualify under that heading? Well, so did I, but sadly apparently not. Being indigenous is apparently a *Catch-22* designation. You can be considered to belong to this privileged group only if you live in an 'indigenous' manner – i.e. as a primitive person. So, presumably, once the native people make enough money out of their forests, because of their indigenous status, to start buying modern goods they then lose this coveted title. It does strike me that this is something to keep a watching brief on. With any luck the UK government, or perhaps the EEC, will one day sign some ridiculous document promising to respect 'the legal and customary rights of indigenous people', safe in the knowledge that they do not have any, and then we can take them to court and get the meaning of the word indigenous re-defined. Who knows, we might win. After all, many landowners' families have lived on the same spot for five hundred years or more and if this does not make them 'indigenous' I don't know what does.

Certification is 'voluntary', and there is nothing to stop a woodland owner not joining, but he may have severe difficulties in marketing his timber if he does not join. Why? Because the '95 Group made a commitment to buy timber products and by-products only from forests which are certified by the year 2000. Actually that proved to be a 'commitment too far' – it looked good on paper and sounded great as a soundbite but like many 'sounds good' pronouncements it was, is, and has proved totally impractical.

To understand why, take the case of WHSmith. If they actually go down this route it means that every item of paper they sell must be either recycled or come from a certified forest. So the publisher of a soft-porn magazine, for example, which relies on WHSmith for a large percentage of its sales, would have to ensure that the paper it uses all comes from such a source. *Ergo* pulp mills will be forced to buy only from certified forests because the buyers of the end product insist on it.

You may by now be thinking, 'This certification thing is going to cost a fortune to run and administer' – if so, you are correct. Then you may be wondering, 'Who is going to pay for all this?' One guess is all you are allowed, I am afraid. The retailer, do I hear? – wrong, bottom of the class! No, the entire cost will inevitably fall on the woodland owner. Already managers at some chipboard and pulp mills are having to spend time and money checking the forest origins of their raw materials at the behest of some of the '95 Group. The result is that they are having to take that cost and pass it back to the woodland owner.

So how do you get your forest certified? By spending lots of money, how else? Whom do I pay that money to? Why, who else but with approved FSC certifiers, and they don't come cheap! Expect to pay £450 a day for one of these boys – and, as you will need at least two visits before you get the necessary certificate, and as on one of these visits two of these creatures will have to be present, and as, in addition, you will be subject to a further visit at least every year and, after six years, you will have to go through the whole tedious process again, it will not be cheap.

To the surprise of the unholy alliance of environmentalists and retailers who foisted 'certification' on the UK forest industry, it has to date been a pretty big failure and virtually ignored by private growers. Woodland owners have, in effect, gone on strike and refused to cower before this arrogant and ill-informed group. The result is that some radical changes are in the offing to try and make certification more attractive to private growers, so a small victory may yet emerge for common sense and equity over the bullying of unaccountable super-markets and environmentalists.

But let us end on a bullish note – and I *am* bullish about the long-term prospects for commercial forestry. There are several reasons for this. For a start, most of my fellow landowners are depressed about

forestry and, as history convincingly demonstrates, my fellow landowners' ability to guess the future correctly is non-existent. A friend of mine,
Sir Benjamin Slade, once had a stockbroker who was infallible, his
advice always bloody awful; if he said the market, or a share, was going
down it always went up and vice versa. So it is with landowners. Their
prognosis of what the future holds is nearly always wrong, so if you do
the opposite you have a very good chance of getting the future right.

But there are also good fundamental reasons for thinking that the
next fifty years might hold extremely attractive returns in commercial
forestry. The price of any product is decided by supply and demand.
The demand for timber has remained constant since the 1960s at 0.67
cubic metres of timber and timber by-products per head of the world
population per annum. The world population, however, is expanding
and, over the next forty years, will increase by about 900 million people
per decade. *Ergo* the world demand for timber in forty years' time will be
around 2.4 billion cubic metres larger than it is today, or about sixty-five
per cent greater.

And this is not the whole story. People in developed economies
consume a greater amount of wood than those in undeveloped countries. In the UK consumption is currently 0.9 cubic metres per head per
annum, about fifty per cent greater than the world average. Now, over
the next thirty years China, India and other South-East Asian countries
will achieve developed status, causing their consumption of timber to
rise considerably. In other words, I anticipate that world demand for
wood will more than double over the next thirty years.

So if demand is going to be strong and rising, what about supply?
Timber is what my economist friends call an elastic commodity. In other
words, as its price rises so consumers, and end users, switch to alternative
raw materials. For instance, it competes in manufacturing with other
substitute raw materials such as plastics and steel; as a fuel, with oil, coal
and gas; and with recycled material for paper and board production.
Also, as the price of timber goes up, so formerly uneconomic forests
suddenly become profitable to fell, thus increasing supply. These factors
all act as a break on the cost of timber spiralling out of control.

I think it is fair to say, however, that if the economies of Asia do continue to expand at their current rate, then many competing raw materials will enjoy similar price rises to that of timber. As for recycling, if timber prices rise, then this will become more and more attractive and some timber substitutes – such as straw and hemp in paper – may become economic crops; but it must be doubtful whether they can have more than a dampening effect on overall price rises.

The other question mark is over supply. If prices rise, it will undoubtedly encourage the exploitation of the vast untapped reserves of timber within the old Soviet Union. This is a potential problem, but it is one of success – i.e. the rise in price has happened. In addition, serious questions have to be raised about the cost, both on economic and environmental grounds, of the successful harvesting of much of these reserves of timber. A lot will depend on how the Russian economy develops over the next few decades. If – a big if – they can raise themselves out of their current vodka-soaked corruption, then the threat of unplanned exploitation of the Siberian forests decreases. Another bearish factor is the development of fast-growing types of trees for the industrial timber market. Trees such as radiata pine and varieties of eucalyptus can grow at phenomenal rates, producing some fifty-five tons of timber per year per hectare of land. In warm and wet lands, such as parts of South America, industrial forestry using these species is being conducted on a grand scale. The timber produced though is just that: industrial. In the UK we have to aim at a different market: that of quality, not industrial-grade timber. It is a tragedy of the last fifty-odd years of UK forestry that so much effort has gone into doing the opposite: producing an 'industrial' product.

In summary, then, trees are good news and will become even better news financially. Those who plant and nurture commercial forests today will reap substantial benefits in years to come.

CHAPTER 10

Forestry – the State Sector

With some two and a half million acres of land, the Forestry Commission is not only easily Britain's biggest landowner but is also probably its least loved. This is not entirely fair, but when was public opinion ever fair? To understand the Forestry Commission (FC) of today, why it has such an enormous landholding and why it is so unloved, you have to understand its history.

The Forestry Commission was born out of the Forestry Act 1919, which was the then government's response to the wholesale cutting of virtually the entire mature timber reserves of the nation during the Great War. The act itself was the result of a report issued in 1918. The key findings of that report should help the uninitiated to understand better why Britain 'went for growth' in planting coniferous timber.

The report highlighted the problems during the war, stating:

> Dependence on imported timber has proved a serious handicap in the conduct of the war . . . the area of land utilized for rough grazing but capable of growing first-class coniferous timber . . . is not less than three and probably more than five million acres. Two million acres could be planted without decreasing the supply of home produced meat by more than 0.7% and if so used would ultimately afford employment to at least ten times the number of men now engaged on that area.

By the start of the Second World War the FC had managed to acquire and plant only around 500,000 acres, however and once again the woods and forest of the UK were stripped to provide Britain's needs. Come the end of the war and the election of the Labour government, the powers that be were convinced that, if there was a problem, then the way to solve it was to produce a 'national plan' and have it administered and enforced by a 'national' body. This concept is now so discredited that people may find it difficult to understand how intelligent men – and there were some highly intelligent men in that first Labour administration – could fall for it, but the reason for their conviction in the rightness of 'national' planning makes sense if you recall that we had just won a titanic struggle with Germany by deploying, successfully, national planning and national management in virtually every facet of life and industry.

So a 'national' forest plan was produced with the stated aim of having at least 5,000,000 acres of productive forestry in the UK. In order to reach this target as quickly as possible the plan envisaged a two-pronged attack. First, as we saw in the last chapter, the act contained a 'carrot and stick' approach for the private sector: either replant and manage your woods properly or the state will, if necessary, take them into public ownership. That this 'stick' was never used does not matter; most people thought it would be and one way out of the quandary was to lease your woods to the FC and let them get on with the job of managing them. In this way the FC estate expanded rapidly in England, but it has to be said that the result is not very satisfactory, from a modern forest management point of view, since much of the English FC estate is scattered in penny packets across the length and breadth of the country and badly needs rationalizing.

Apart from taking in hand and managing private woods, the FC also embarked on a policy of buying up vast areas of upland Britain with the aim of planting them with productive coniferous forests. Today (2004), looking at a currently depressed timber market, it is difficult for many people to understand the thinking that has resulted in so much of our uplands being covered with Sitka spruce. But the foresters of the late 1940s and 1950s believed what they were doing was in the national interest, vital to the long-term prosperity and security of the country. They pursued the aim of achieving a national productive forest of 5,000,000 acres with an enthusiasm bordering on fanaticism. One ex-FC employee of my acquaintance remembers organizing chains of men to bring soil in buckets up a steep hillside in north Wales so that he could plant the ubiquitous Sitka in the scree! This attitude is not so extraordinary when you remember that the FC comprised men who had either fought in the war or who had very recent memories of it. They knew also that, because of the war, Britain had massive foreign debts (oddly most people seem to believe the Americans gave us all those tanks and aircraft free – they did not; we bought them, and the debts incurred had to be paid back) and that every pound of foreign exchange saved by producing home-grown timber was of great importance. They knew all these things because they were the 'certainties' of the day. They could not envisage a time, fifty years on, when the value of the pound would not be of central interest, when the balance of trade figures would not hit the headlines, when the deep coal mine industry would virtually have ceased to exist. If they got things wrong it is no shame to them but it would be arrogant of us to assume they *did* get things wrong and we have got things right. The certainties of today are, I would suggest, just as vulnerable to change over the next fifty years as their certainties were. Who knows? We may yet live to be grateful for all that Sitka spruce.

Forestry is, as I have continually emphasized, a long-term business. The FC woods and forests that you see are the progeny of the great burst of evangelical zeal which embraced all those involved in forestry from the mid-1940s to around the mid-1980s. Then doubts began to set in. As the doubts slowly transformed themselves into certainties, the morale of the FC began to wane. Now no one would deny that the FC made many mistakes during those forty-odd years of unrestricted expansion, but this does not mean that everything they did or accomplished was bad. The modern FC is a different animal, with different aims from those of its forebear. Today, the buzzwords are 'sustainability', 'consultation', 'environment', 'continuous cover', 'regeneration', 'native species' and so on and so forth.

Again let us be fair. The FC is a government agency, and as such its aims reflect those of the government, and governments of all political colours have asked only two things of the FC for the last twenty-odd years. First, do not cause any controversy if you can possibly avoid it, and second, do not cost us any money. The FC has done quite well according to the first requirement. It has embraced 'political correctness' and the new religion of environmentalism full on and has 'engaged' with every 'stakeholder' group it could possibly identify. The result has been a satisfying reduction in bad press. On the second front, however, its performance has not been so hot. Beset by falling timber prices, the 'commercial' arm of the FC, Forest Enterprise, has lost serious money. In actual fact it is doubtful whether FE has ever made a proper trading profit in its entire existence. For years trading losses were disguised by that old trick favoured by accountants: revaluing assets (i.e. existing plantations) and announcing a paper profit. For instance, in their 1992 accounts, Forestry Enterprise had an operating loss of £21.1 million, but managed to change this into a profit of £60.9 million by using this discreditable accounting method! Chickens have now come home to roost, as with falling timber prices plantations can no longer be re-valued upwards. Instead, FE now has the reverse problem of actually writing down its assets and has consequently recorded a horrendous loss in 2002/03 of £352 million. Even when you strip out the loss accruing because of 'Mickey Mouse' accountancy practices, you are still left with significant annual trading losses, currently running at around £20 per acre.

Considering the Forestry Commission has been assiduously planting trees since the 1920s and consequently has many plantations maturing and being felled, this result is frankly pathetic and contrasts appallingly with the record of the private sector. While there is no central body of data for the profit and loss accounts of all private forestry operations, the estate agents Savills annually publish financial data covering some 750,000 acres of privately owned land, of which some 75,000 acres are woodland. According to the Savills Estate Benchmarking Survey, while Forest Enterprise was losing £20 an acre the average estate was losing £7.50 an acre. Such a discrepancy will not surprise any modern-day economist, since the thinking that led to the foundation of the FC and to its enormous post-war expansion has now been entirely discredited and the FC is an almost lone remnant of that great era of national planning and national ownership.

The 'dash for growth' policy of the old FC has produced successes and failures. One success must be that the FC now has a dominant position within the UK market, supplying around forty per cent of the total of UK timber production. A principal failure, however, is that, as a result, the reputation of British timber is highly influenced by what comes out of Forestry Commission plantations; sadly, that reputation is that the UK grows rubbish. This is not surprising, as rubbish is what the Forestry Commission specializes in growing. This has little to do with the type of species planted, but a lot to do with how the plantations are managed.

The vast majority of the Forestry Commission plantations are managed on a low-input system. In other words, once a wood is planted, very little further investment will be made in managing that wood until the day it is felled. This form of management, which I call industrial forestry or 'plant-and-forget forestry', results in a low-quality crop of small saw logs after forty or fifty years.

This management regime can be contrasted with that undertaken by many traditional landowners. Their trees are rigorously thinned as they get older to allow their girths to expand and side branches are pruned off; the aim is to produce big, high-quality saw logs over a fifty-year-plus period and attract a premium price for the eventual product.

Sadly, the Forestry Commission management system is dominant in British forests and the result is not only that UK timber is widely regarded as low-quality, but an even more worrying side effect has been the universally bad press that coniferous plantations receive in the media from environmental pressure groups. They wax critical about 'dead coniferous forests', but there is no reason why coniferous forests should be 'dead' from an environmental angle if they are thinned and managed properly. It is only when they are left, in a 'plant-and-forget' management system, that eventually, as the trees mature, the canopy closes over and all vegetation underneath dies.

In fairness, it has to be admitted that in many of the places the Forestry Commission has planted, 'plant and forget' was probably the best management solution for the site. If you thin high upland plantations of shallow-rooted conifers, you risk letting the wind into the forest and having the whole lot blown down. The criticism is that the Forestry Commission also applied such management techniques to areas of lowland forestry, where the risk of wind-blow is minimal.

It is perhaps not surprising that an organization dedicated to producing large amounts of industrial timber should have no interest in marketing. There is no senior executive with either Forestry Enterprise or the Forestry Commission with this responsibility. Perhaps I should make clear that by marketing I do not mean the selling of trees; what I mean is the development of markets for the timber produced. In other words, working with other parts of the industry to promote timber products and to research and develop ways that timber can be used on higher-value products, thus boosting the price you receive for the primary product.

One of the inherent problems with UK forestry is the absence of any large timber-owning company with the financial clout to promote the use of timber and to research ways to substitute timber economically for less environmentally friendly materials. This is a role the Forestry Commission could – and should – have taken on. Its failure to do so is a sad reflection on its management over the last seventy-five years. So the forest industry looks on helplessly as rival products, which are often environmentally unfriendly, such as steel, PVC, plastics, concrete and the like, are assiduously promoted by their manufacturers and win more and more of the market share from traditional wood products. A typical example is the explosion in PVC windows over the last few years at the expense of traditional wooden ones. Who among us has not winced at seeing these excrescences despoiling some period house, or any house for that matter? Yet the fault lies with the British timber industry, which for years palmed off low-quality softwood windows, liable to rot, on an unsuspecting public. It is therefore hardly surprising that a market was lost; even though the lesson has now been learned and timber windows are as good as – if not better than – PVC ones, the advantage can never be regained.

But it is the Forestry Commission's regulatory role which most concerns private woodland owners. Worrying 'racist' tendencies are surfacing. The new obsession in conservation circles – as far as trees are concerned – is racial purity of seed source. For many it is now not enough that a landowner plants an oak tree; it must be an oak tree grown from an acorn from a 'native tree'. As for planting trees such as beech or sweet chestnut, both of which have been cultivated in this country for at least two thousand years, these are now condemned as 'not native species'. Conservationists sometimes sound remarkably like Adolf Hitler at the Nuremberg rally. The eventual aim of many conservationists is that all future broad-leaf planting will be from a 'native seed source'.

Actually, this is scientific and historical nonsense. For centuries, landowners have travelled widely and a three-hundred-year-old oak tree is likely to be the result of a keen seventeenth-century forester (and there were many of them, as conservationists would know if they ever bothered to read Evelyn's seventeenth-century classic, *Sylva*) seeing a fine stand of oak on his travels and filling his pockets with acorns to sow on his estate on his return.

If the conservation lobby has its way, in the not-too-distant future landowners will be forced to plant trees only from local native seed sources, regardless of the quality of the source from which the seeds come. There are a host of problems inherent in such a policy. For a start, our ancestors in the eighteenth century were growing oak for purposes very different from ours. Then, heavily branched oaks were especially valuable, as the great boughs were ideal for shipbuilding; equally, coppice oak, as we have already seen, was grown specifically to provide bark for tanning. Now those industries have disappeared and the value of oak is in planking or veneers, for which tall, straight, clean trees are required. Are landowners to be forced to plant a genetic type of oak for which there will be no future market? As the conservation lobby is so strong that few people seem to have the guts to stand up to it, the answer is probably yes.

The modern FC is now divided up into three sub-conservancies, looking after the forestry in Scotland, Wales and England, while in

England itself decision-making about forestry management and policies looks likely to be devolved to the nine regions of England. As I wrote earlier, most of the ills we criticize the FC for today are the result of work done and decisions made when most of the current management of the FC were only children. Experience teaches us that there is only one certainty in forestry: there are no certainties. Those who seek to impose extreme environmental-fascist policies on the woodland-owning community should remember that they will undoubtedly look as stupid and idiotic in fifty years' time as that enthusiastic FC employee planting up slopes of scree with Sitka spruce does to our eyes fifty years on.

CHAPTER 11

Diversification

'Here's the rule for bargains: "Do other men,
for they would do you." That's the true business
precept.'

CHARLES DICKENS (1812–70)
Barnaby Rudge, 1840

Diversification is the buzzword whizzing around landowning circles at
the moment. In the opinion of many of the best professional brains in
the business, diversification is a way of making all those high-value, low-
yielding assets sweat a bit. It is, in short, the Holy Grail of modern estate
management. Nevertheless, landowners should beware and remember
what happened to King Arthur and the Knights of the Round Table
when they left Camelot and went off on the quest for the Holy Grail.
The result was the break-up of the Round Table, civil war and the
collapse of King Arthur's kingdom. Holy Grails are, in short, dangerous
things to look for and best left well alone.

Actually diversification is not a new game. Landowners have always
indulged in it, some on a spectacular scale – like the Duke of
Bridgewater, who was responsible for building most of the canal network
in the latter part of the eighteenth century. Tragically the entrepreneurial
streak in landowners was effectively snuffed out, between 1900 and
1980, by the burden of excessive capital and income taxes, which forced
landowners to think about only one thing: survival. One of the side
effects of the punitive taxation regime was the removal of virtually all
liquid capital out of the country and into the coffers of the Treasury. It

would be interesting to work out how much money was transferred by capital taxation from the countryside for the benefit of the towns between 1900 and 1980. One thing is sure: the financial vendetta against landowners removed from them the wherewithal to carry out any entrepreneurial activities. It could be argued that even if that money had been left with the landowners not all of it would have been invested on their estates. This is true, but on the whole landowners do have a tendency to invest profits made elsewhere back in their estates. In any event, the punitive tax regime succeeded in destroying the historic source of rural venture capital, and much of the blame for the present dearth of rurally-based businesses and the current high level of rural unemployment can be laid at the door of Lloyd George and his successors.

Diversification nowadays is like a war with lots of battle honours on offer. Some estates have avoided it altogether, but most have probably tried one or two of the following: deer farming, golf courses, commercial shooting, angora goats, llamas, ostriches, Christmas trees, paint-ball games, car rallying, sawmills, farm shops, pick-your-own, fishing lakes, corporate entertainment, conference centres, snail farming, crayfish, membership of Lloyd's (perhaps the most classic case of diversification) and so on *ad infinitum*. Not all of these are ill-advised and certainly some have made some people very good money, most, it must be said, for the character who persuaded you into the 'diversification' project in the first place and either pocketed his fee or commission, or sold you some extremely expensive breeding stock.

As with opening the house to the public, so with diversification: it requires capital outlay. That capital might well be better employed in the stock market than in some new craze; diversification is a fashion-conscious business and at various times over the last twenty years all the activities in the paragraph above have been flavour of the month. The problem is that if you set up some nice profitable fishing lakes there is no guarantee that your neighbour, being on the thick side, will not decide to do the same, thus splitting the market and driving you both into loss. The inability of most landowners to understand the basic economic rules of supply and demand is one of the serious shortcomings behind the failure of so many diversification projects.

Landowners tempted to dip their toe into the waters of diversification should remember that the penalty for failure can be the loss of the whole estate, as Lord Brocket has found at Brocket Hall. Sir Charles Wolseley also discovered this harsh truth at Wolseley Hall, where an ill-thought-out venture into gardens brought to an end the family's one-thousand-year tenure of their estate, while the Phillips family were forced to sell the palatial Luton Hoo after investing in a speculative property venture in the late 1980s boom with disastrous results. More recently, Lord Hesketh's decision to sell his marvellous house Easton Neston, and the accompanying estate, must in part be attributable to his business ventures. Though these are all high-profile cases, there are, sadly, many smaller estates and houses that have had to be sold in recent years due to their owner's desire to be 'seen to be doing something', his urge to try his hand in the glamorous world of business. Too late comes the revelation that business is not glamorous at all, that most people in it are crooks, and that the persuasive cash-flow forecast that looked so optimistic on the computer screen and promised immense riches was fatally flawed.

But if one should beware of professional experts who charge one fees, how much more dangerous are one's friends, who, for a reason that totally escapes me, consider themselves qualified to advise you on every aspect of estate management although they themselves live in London and know nothing whatever about the subject. It is one of the oddities of life that if you live in a large house everyone feels they have a right to give you advice. The fact that their expertise is minimal is not a problem to them. Personally I feel it may be because they somehow resent the fact that you are leading what seems to them an idle existence in the country while they are having to get up at seven o'clock in the morning to get into some ghastly office in the City. In any event, when they come as guests their stay is often peppered with such remarks as: 'Why don't you . . . ?' or, 'If I were you I would . . . ' or, 'Surely you could do . . . ' ending with, 'Oh, you are so unenterprising.'

Well, they are probably right, but the problem with being enterprising is that there is a downside as well as an upside. The upside is that you might make quite a lot of money and be able to afford to do all the things the experts think you should do to stop the house falling down, while the downside is called losing buckets of money, which you cannot afford, and eventually being forced to put that advertisement in *Country Life*.

You may happen to have a bucket of money. That ten-acre building plot on the outskirts of your neighbouring town might just have come good and you are now the proud possessor of that rarity, a healthy bank account. The temptation to do something 'constructive' with this windfall is all too great. If you are foolish you will consult your professional advisers. Perhaps one should not be too hard on them, poor sods; it can't be a lot of fun being a professional adviser to an impoverished estate. It is a lot more fun when there is half a million pounds or more sloshing around seeking a home. Inevitably their advice will be that you 'plough it back' into the estate. So what aspect do you 'plough it back' into?

Even if you do live within London's magic circle, or have, like some houses in the Midlands, twenty-five million people living within an hour's drive, it is a moot point whether the return on capital you might achieve by 'diversification' is really worth the effort. Before you succumb to the blandishments of your advisers, please remember that an average business investment ought to provide a minimum return of twenty per cent, but a diversification needs to produce a lot more. Why? Because you can't sell it. An ordinary business can invariably, even if it is loss-making, be flogged, but the old stable block converted at enormous expense into offices, for which suddenly there is no demand, is a white elephant. If you sell it, you create a no-go area right next door to your house – so what can you do with it?

As for 'the latest craze', ignore it. Little is lost in waiting to see if there really is going to be gold in golf courses (there isn't) or if angora goats produce golden fleeces (they don't) but a lot is risked by jumping on a bandwagon too quickly.

If you are still determined to risk all on a venture, try and minimize your risk by making it a joint venture. Get an experienced partner to put up the capital and run the project, and in return give him a generous lease at a generous rent. Remember that landowners have got rich in the past doing exactly this: letting someone else take the risk and taking the majority of their profit in thirty or forty years when a profitable and well-run business falls neatly into their, or their son's, lap.

A significant difference between a landowner and a public company is that a landowner can (and should) take the long view, while a company needs to satisfy the short-term ambitions of its shareholders and is therefore less interested in acquiring expensive freeholds and more interested in developing quick short-term profits at minimal cost. Always remember this when dealing with companies; to them a seventy-five-year lease is as good as a freehold, so give them the lease for the same money they would have paid for the freehold and leave a nice little bonus for your grandson.

The main point to remember is that you have a good reason for going into diversification – it is that you have not got enough money to satisfy your everyday needs and those of your house. Fair enough. But please consider that the reason your finances are in such a parlous state in the first place may be because you are a lousy businessman. The greatest gift a landowner can have is a knowledge of his own weaknesses.

If you are still determined to be a businessman, then so be it, but why do it on your own estate? Why not start a business up in the local town or elsewhere?

When the siren voices whisper the phrase 'plough it back' into your ear, on the whole you will be wiser, and richer in the long run, if you plough it into the stock or bond market instead. Not *only* will you be richer, but you will also find that life is a lot less hectic and you have more time to enjoy your estate, which come to think about it is what estates are meant to be for: to be enjoyed.

Talking about 'enjoying your estate' reminds me of one other form of 'diversification' popular among the more intelligent younger members of the landowning fraternity: working in London. Not that there is anything wrong with working in London *per se*, as London provides today, as it always has done, a contrasting environment for the budding landowner to work and play in until the time comes to move back to his roots and take over the running of the family estate. Not only that, but many members of the landed aristocracy have proved to be adept at making large sums of money in the City and have, with the resulting cash, rejuvenated their estates. The cost of living in London, however, is horrendous, as is the cost of being an absentee landowner, and many of those who do work in London have not really 'run the numbers' on how much 'net' money they are actually making by sweating away there instead of, say, doing nothing in the country. So I will endeavour to do it for them.

Our hero is forty years old, married with two children aged five and seven, and works in banking in London, going down to his family estate, some 200 miles away, at weekends. Comparing his 'running costs' with his opposite number who has chosen to give up London and look after his estate, we come up with something like this.

	London banker – *Country squire*

School fees: £7,500 each for 'smarty pants'
    London day school – Zero as they go
    to the village primary school
	£15,000 – £0

Au pair – Not needed, got wife	£7,500 – £0

Travel weekends (wife takes children down
    after school Friday and you take train) –
    Not needed
	£10,000 – £0

Taxis in London at £180 per week – Not needed	£10,000 – £0

Restaurants and other entertainment
    at £400 per week (the wife likes a lunch) –
    Not needed
	£20,000 – £0

Clothes for you – new suit, shirts, shoes etc. – Not needed	£2,500 – £0
Clothes for her (being optimistic) – Not needed	£3,500 – £0
Membership of 'sports' club / Not needed	£1,500 – £0
Total	£70,000 – £0

In other words, if our hero just gave up London and moved to the country, did nothing and lay in bed of a morning reading a good book it would be the equivalent of earning a salary in London of in excess of £100,000 a year and that, as you see, assumes, for London, a fairly frugal existence and a wife who is quite economical. But that is only, as they say, one side of the coin. The other side is the extra expense he incurs by not being on the premises. He will discover this cost only when he actually returns and takes up full-time residence in the country but he will certainly be surprised at how many people were 'taking a drink' out of the estate with relatively little effort while he was labouring in London. If we are generous and estimate this 'extra cost' at, say, a further £40,000 per annum, we now see that the net cost of his decision to keep working in London is £110,000 a year, to earn which he needs a salary of around £160,000. In other words, unless you are really a big player, earning over £250,000 a year, you are kidding yourself if you think you are benefiting your inheritance by working in London rather than returning to your ancestral acres and relaxing and, yes, actually enjoying them.

CHAPTER 12

The City

'If God had not meant them to be sheared
He would not have made them sheep.'

ELI WALLACH
in *The Magnificent Seven*, 1960)

It is not that long ago that landed gentlemen regarded the City, and the people who worked in it, with a jaundiced eye. There was something not quite right about stockbroking and the other arcane financial trades carried on within the Square Mile, although an exception was often made of banking, partly because, one suspects, so many landowners were either descended from bankers or were still involved in the family bank in some form or other. This attitude to the City was well described by H. Rider Haggard in his classic novel of rural England during the agricultural depression, *Colonel Quaritch V.C.*, when writing of the banking anti-hero, Edward Cossey:

Goldsmiths two centuries ago, then bankers from generation to generation, money bees seeking for wealth and counting it from decade to decade, till at last gold became to them what honour is to nobler stock – the pervading principle and the clink of the guinea and the rustling of the bank note stirred their blood as the clank of armed men and the sound of the flapping banner with its three golden hawks flaming in the sun, was wont to set the hearts of the race of Boissey, of Dofferleigh and of de la Molle, beating to that tune to which England marched on to win the World.

Great stuff, and even truer today, at a guess, than it was then.

Circumstances have caused this old attitude perforce to change, in public anyway, as landowners and their sons have joined in the unseemly 'gold rush' and headed for the City in the hope of striking it rich Klondyke-style. For today it seems that that old legend of the streets of London being paved with gold is not that far from being true – if you are a partner of Goldman Sachs or one of the other major investment banks. Oddly, many of the scions of landowning families have found that they have a knack for the business of making money and have done rather well in the rarefied atmosphere of high finance. Several estates and great houses have, in recent years, been saved by the highly profitable antics of the son and heir in the City. Not all ventures into the City have been successful, however: if some landowners have profited and some estates and houses been saved, then others have been destroyed or impoverished by disastrous investment in the Lloyd's insurance market.

The Lloyd's disaster is a long story, but one that will bear relating – briefly – as there are so many lessons to be learned from it.

Lloyd's is a market. A market is purely that – a place where people do business; in the case of Lloyd's this business is insurance. The role of Lloyd's was simply to provide the roof over the heads of the underwriters and loosely to regulate their activities. Lloyd's, though, was a privileged institution. Over the years successive governments had cosseted it and given the traders (names) tax breaks in order to encourage them to write international insurance business. The reason was simple. In those long-forgotten days of fixed exchange rates the strength, or more often the weakness, of the pound was a matter of profound concern to every government, and Lloyd's consistently produced, year in year out (with the odd exception), substantial foreign currency earnings, which helped to bolster the pound.

The workings of the insurance industry are very simple. The client pays the underwriters a premium and in return, if you have one, they pay your claim. The skill of the underwriter is to ensure that he rates the premium at a sufficient level to ensure that he makes a profit on the transaction. There is, however, another side to the business: what to do with the premiums once they have been paid. They are invested and, if everything goes according to plan, by the time the claims come in, the premiums will have produced sufficient capital growth to pay for a large percentage of them.

Turning the clock back to the 1950s and the 1960s, we have seen that landowners were crippled by exorbitant tax rates, which approached, and sometimes exceeded, a hundred per cent of their income – how did so many of them survive? One of the answers was Lloyd's.

Lloyd's worked, and still partly does, by encouraging people with large assets to become 'names' and write insurance business on one or more underwriting syndicates. The concept is simple. An underwriter is limited in the amount of premium he can write by the amount of security he can show the regulators. The normal multiple is that for every one pound of security he can write two pounds of premium income. Somewhere in the not-so-dim-and-distant past someone in Lloyd's realized that landowners had lots of assets (security) but little income, and would therefore be interested in a scheme whereby they could use those assets twice by becoming an underwriting member of Lloyd's. When the salient features of membership were explained to them landowners agreed and large numbers signed up. Nor were they wrong to do so. Until the disasters of the 1980s Lloyd's produced a run of superb profits, with only one rather severe hiccup in the mid-1960s caused by Hurricane Betsy, which produced losses and led to the average name recording a loss of over £8,000 (approximately £120,000 in 'modern' money) over the two years of 1965/66. Profits are all very well, but are frankly not much use if you are being taxed at 98p in the pound on them. Lloyd's, though, had a 'cunning plan' to get round this one: 'bond washing'. In effect the premiums were used to buy government stock, which was then sold just before the 'dividend' was paid; immediately after the dividend was paid, the same stock was repurchased at, obviously, a reduced price. This manoeuvre had the effect of 'washing' much of the potential 'underwriting profit' (which would have been taxed as income) into capital gains, which were, until 1965, untaxed. The financial effect of all this on a 'name' was interesting. Let us assume he was, in the late 1950s, writing a premium income of £50,000. He had, for the sake of argument, a 'bad' year and notionally declared a loss of £2,000 on his underwriting account, but this was more than made up by a profit of £4,000 on the capital account. The result was that he could set the £2,000 loss against his tax on his other income and therefore recover from the Inland Revenue some £1,800 or so while the £4,000 capital gain was entirely tax-free. In other words, Lloyd's was a most marvellous tax vehicle. Even when a Labour government unsportingly introduced capital gains tax in 1965, the rate of thirty per cent was so low compared to that of income tax that it had little effect on the attractiveness of Lloyd's to names.

Bond washing was eventually outlawed, but its disappearance did little to destroy the attractions of membership. Between 1967 and 1988 Lloyd's produced over twenty years of uninterrupted profits. Little wonder then that by the mid-1980s people were literally queueing to join.

It is an infallible maxim that when everyone is talking about some form of investment or other then the gilt is about to come off the gingerbread and a crash is in the offing. We all know this – or we should – and it is one of the most tried and tested rules of investment: sell and get out when everyone else is piling to get in. Lloyd's reached this point in the mid-1980s. Membership had doubled between 1978 and 1986, reaching a peak of 32,000 as people scrambled to join this club that promised them 'something for nothing'. This sudden avalanche of people interested in becoming members of Lloyd's was caused partly by the surge in property values and partly by Lloyd's decision not to up the wealth requirement of membership in line with inflation. The result was that membership of Lloyd's was now thrown open to a far wider constituency, attracted by the concept of earning a second income by putting up their houses as collateral.

Predictably, it all ended in tears. Lloyd's was hit by a whole barrage of disasters, all coinciding over three years and causing the market to suffer four years of horrendous losses. I do not intend to go into the reasons for the crash, except to say that with the benefit of hindsight it was entirely predictable. That in fact is the primary lesson I would like readers to absorb. If a financial disaster is so obvious after it has happened, why is it so difficult to spot before it happens? We laugh at the stupidity of the Dutch investing in tulip bulbs in the seventeenth century and we used to laugh at the idiocy of the English who piled into the South Sea Bubble in 1720–21. Goodness, how we roared at the gullibility of our ancestors, who got suckered into investing in such ventures as Puckle's machine gun, which 'was to discharge round and square cannon balls and bullets and make a total revolution of the art of war' or – and this took the biscuit – 'a company for the carrying on an undertaking of Great Advantage, but no one to know what it is'. It could not happen today in the modern, sophisticated financial markets; except that it did during the great Internet madness. Companies were floated with little more chance of making money than Puckle's machine gun company of 1721. Hysteria gripped the dinner tables of the country, stories rebounded round the room about how Jack or Jill had put £5,000 into abc.com and their shares were now worth £100,000. People dreamed up ideas, told them to a banker they met at dinner who would, more often than not, get his chequebook out there and then and sign them up. It was madness, and what it proved is that we are no cleverer or more financially sophisticated than our Georgian ancestors were in the early eighteenth century, we just think we are. This is where the danger lies.

It must be remembered that since the beginning of civilization man has been looking for an infallible way to become rich. I call this the philosopher's stone syndrome: the belief (currently held by hedge fund managers in the City) that there is some formula in the economic galaxy which, when discovered, will just spew out never-ending riches to those who possess it. This of course is laughable, or would be if so many people did not believe in it. It was medieval kings who first began the futile hunt for the philosopher's stone, a legendary substance said to enable the possessor to turn base metals into gold. The search for this wonder substance was led by alchemists (the medieval equivalent of hedge fund managers), who persuaded many a monarch to spend vast sums of money on experiments to try to solve the mystery. What none of them seems to have considered was the basic economic fact that rarity has a value – in other words, suppose that the philosopher's stone *had* been discovered, what would the owner of this great secret have done? Would he have kept very quiet about it and only 'minted' enough gold for his basic needs, or would he have gone on a vast spending binge? Human nature being what it is, he would have done the latter and flooded the market with gold, causing the value of it to collapse, as the 'value' of something is always in its rarity and is destroyed by plenty. Oddly, this does not only apply to 'value' but also to 'taste', as in food. So in my youth a salmon was the ultimate treat at a dinner party, but now it has fallen totally out of favour because of the proliferation of cheap farmed fish, while cod, once the fish of the working class, has, as it becomes rarer due to over-fishing, moved inexorably up the social scale and may one day fill the niche, on the super-smart sideboard, vacated by salmon.

At any one time the financial industry in London will have its top dog. Currently the hedge fund manger rules the roost – not in the Square Mile and certainly not in that slum district of the financial industry, Canary Wharf, as hedge fund managers are so much in demand that they can choose where they wish to work and most choose to ply their trade in the environs of St James Street. A mile or so east of St James's lies the City, and still further east is Docklands. These are the two 'financial centres' of London and it is in the gleaming buildings that proliferate there that labour tens of thousands of people whose job it is to try to increase the value of the vast sums entrusted to their care by idiots like you and me. Frankly, they are pretty bad at it and obscenely overpaid. To understand why this is we need to flick back to the early 1960s and the emergence of something called 'the cult of the equity'.

Not that many moons ago, in fact about fifty years ago, the private client reigned supreme in the City. Sober-suited characters trekked into officers clustered around the Royal Exchange on a daily basis, and there they managed portfolios of stocks and shares on behalf of private individuals. That was the old City. It took a long time to die, and even in 1974, when for a brief period I worked for Hoare Govett, a famous broker, there were still many such individuals on the books. Gradually they were killed off by a combination of changes in taxation and the realization, by many stockbrokers, that such clients and their money could be looked after with far greater efficiency – and far more lucratively – if they could be persuaded to put all their money into 'managed funds'. What bliss these 'managed funds' were, and are, for their owners, the banks and the stockbrokers. Under the old system you could make money out of poor Old Lady Snodgrass only if you could persuade her to sell or buy some shares, though when you persuaded her to put all her capital in to a 'managed fund' you could rip her off big time. First, of course, you could charge her an annual management fee of, say, 1.5 per cent then as the 'fund' will be buying and selling shares itself and naturally using you as its broker you can effectively double that basic rate fee by billing the fund transaction charges which, on average, work out at another 1.5 per cent. So, magically, a client who, in all probability, rarely traded her portfolio and thus earned you little commission, has been transformed into a cash cow providing you with a minimum of three per cent a year. Actually I have forgotten the 'upfront' or 'entry' fees normally charged to investors who buy unit trusts, life insurance, endowment policies or any of the other raft of 'financial products' routinely touted by so-called 'financial advisers'. Add in an upfront figure of, say, four per cent of the client's capital and you will begin to understand why people in the City are so much better paid than their counterparts of fifty years ago. To put it simply, they are a lot better at ripping off their clients.

You may be wondering how the City has got away with this great con trick. The answer is in one word: inflation. In the twenty years between 1970 and 1990 inflation in the UK averaged 10.2 per cent. The effects of inflation are many and varied, and as you would expect there are winners and losers. The big losers were the thrifty traditional savers. People who had 'scrimped and saved' and put their money into various government-sponsored fixed-interest saving schemes found that their savings were 'inflated' away. The winners were those who had 'gambled' and put their money into high-risk stocks and shares, as their values tended to increase with inflation. The other class of winner was the house owner. It is forgotten today that owning your own house was not always considered a brilliant investment. It is, in fact, only in the last forty-odd years, since the beginning of the era of inflation, that houses have come to be seen as the best investment anyone can make. Property benefits from inflation. As prices in the shops rise, so does the income of the workers, who are thus able to afford to spend more on their new house; in other words, the attraction of property as an investment is primarily that it is a superb hedge against inflation.

Many companies benefited from this new 'disease' as well as retailers, since in days of inflation there is little point in a consumer saving money. He or she is far better off going out and spending it at once as they know the goods they are buying are likely to be more expensive tomorrow.

So if inflation is 'good for business' and what is 'good for business' is good for share prices, then the long-running bull market in shares, from the depths of the 1974 crash right through to Black Monday in 1987 and then onwards till the end of the century, becomes slightly easier to understand. With the end of inflation and thus the end of 'guaranteed' rising equity prices, the wheels have started coming off the enormous bloated fund management industry. So we have had, in short order, the endowment mortgage scandal, the Equitable Life fiasco and now the 'under-funded' pension fund problem. All of these have, in effect, been caused by the death of inflation. When the various policies and funds were first put together, the managers consulted mysterious beasts called actuaries to advise them on the likely returns they might get over the life of the policies. Now, the actuary is a 'non-brain' species of professional. In other words, he is not meant to think but meant to be a sort of human computer who, taking historical data, can extrapolate them over the future and come up with a forecast. Sadly, the data they took were from the twenty years of high inflation, and the projected gains have thus been non-existent. We forget, though, that these projected gains were a fraud anyway. The fund managers were planning to take your 1985 pound sterling, worth one pound, and pay you back with lots of 2010 pounds which, on paper, looked good but in actual fact were probably going to be only worth, say, 25p of a 1985 pound.

So much of the present prosperity of the City and the inflated salaries that go with it are built on sand or, to be more accurate, inflation. The lesson is that there is no such thing as easy money. There are few people in the City who can take your pound and turn it, apparently by magic, into ten pounds. They may do so one year, they may even do so over three or four years, but they will not be able to keep that performance up for long because certain things will happen. First, their success will mean that they can attract a lot more money, and the more money they manage, the more difficult it will be for them to attain the sort of gains they regularly achieved when they were a small fund. Second, if they have hit on a magic formula that seems to be working, then others in the market will begin to copy them, thus destroying their competitive edge. Finally, study after academic study has been published demonstrating that 'stock picking' fund management is a highly inefficient way of investing money and that, over a period of twenty years, few funds can be seen to have outperformed the market. The result has been the advent of cheap tracker funds, but when I talk to the really big guys in the City and ask them what they do with all that money they make, more often than not they reply, 'I stick it in bonds. Shares are for mugs.'

CHAPTER 13

Taxation

But in this world nothing can be said
to be certain, except death and taxes.

BENJAMIN FRANKLIN (1706–90)
Letter to Jean Baptiste Le Roy, 1789

Taxation has been defined as 'a compulsory contribution of the wealth of a person, or body of persons, for the service of the public powers'. Until the end of the seventeenth century the term 'public powers' was virtually interchangeable with the name of whichever king or queen happened to be on the throne at the time; in other words the level of taxation was set by the monarch and this was primarily what the Civil War was about and why Charles I lost his head. The chief reason why kings had need of taxation was to finance either their lifestyle or their foreign policy which, in the years between 1066 and 1702 (the death of William III), mainly consisted of making war against either one of the Celtic neighbours or France with occasional guest appearances being put in by the Spanish and Dutch. Under the feudal system barons and knights held their land in return for giving the king knight's service, but their obligations were strictly limited. They owed the King only forty days' 'free' service; thereafter, they were on the pay roll, and they did not owe him even that unless their call out was to defend the kingdom. The situation was further complicated by the fact that the Norman kings and their Plantagenet successors also ruled large areas of France and eventually developed a desire to rule all of it. A common mistake that many people make when looking at the performance of some of these early medieval kings of England is to misunderstand what made them tick. It is true that Henry I seems to have genuinely *wanted* to govern his kingdom for the benefit of the whole population (he even spoke Welsh – taught him by a Welsh mistress called Nestor) and the same could certainly be said of his grandson Henry II, but most of these early monarchs seem to have looked on England as a cash cow whose main role was to provide the money to pay for their interminable squabbles with the king of France over the ownership, or otherwise, of some bit of the notional kingdom of France.

In order to hold their possessions in France the kings needed money to pay troops, and it was King John's insatiable appetite for cash, together with the ingenious ways he thought up of extracting it from his subjects, that led to Magna Carta. This is an over-hyped document: everyone has heard of it, but hardly anyone knows what it contains. Most people have a vague idea that it enshrines the concept of the freeborn Englishman and his rights. This is nonsense. What it enshrines are the rights of the *barons* and the Church and various other specified freemen – very much a minority in thirteenth-century England – not to be ripped off by the king with a lot of clever wheezes designed to extract money from them.

There are some sixty-three clauses in Magna Carta and most of them are designed to restrict the king's ability in law to abuse feudal laws and feudal customs. For instance, clause 2 reads:

> If any of our earls or barons or others holding of us in chief by knight service dies, and at his death his heir be of full age and owe relief he shall have his inheritance on payment of the old relief, namely the heir or heirs of an earl £100 for a whole earl's barony, the heir or heirs of a baron £100 for a whole barony, the heir or heirs of a knight 100 shillings, at most, for a whole knight's fee; and he who owes less shall give less according to the ancient usage of the fief.

And you thought death duties were invented by Lord Harcourt in 1894! They were, on the contrary, alive and kicking in 1215, but the barons were not protesting about paying them, merely about the arbitrary increases John had imposed. This was not the only trick John was up to: he had trawled through the minutiae of feudal law and, like a modern-day chancellor, spotted various cunning ploys for raising extra revenue. For instance, as, in theory, all fiefs (estates) were held on condition the holder rendered military service it followed that if the heir was under-age he could not perform his military obligation. The fief then reverted to the overlord, so he could use the revenues to hire mercenary soldiers until such time as the heir came of age. The theory was good, but John had abused the system by 'selling' such wardships to unscrupulous buyers who either pillaged the inheritance and /or 'sold' the heir in marriage. Under-age heirs were not alone in having cause to rue King John's greed; widows too had suffered as clause 8 makes clear: 'No widow shall be forced to marry so long as she wishes to live without a husband, provided she gives security not to marry without our [the king's] consent if she holds of us or without the consent of her Lord of whom she holds, if she holds of another.' It is obvious from reading Magna Carta that what had driven the barons to rebel was the sight of King John plundering the estates of their dead colleagues and the realization that when they died the same treatment was going to be meted out to *their* heirs and widows. As the primary aim of most of the barons in 1215 was exactly the same as that of most landowners today – to pass the estate on to their heir in as good condition as they received it, if not better – it was hardly surprising that they took up arms when they saw how under-age heirs and the like were being treated by King John. In other words, it was the imposition of the medieval equivalent of punitive death duties that led to King John's humiliation at Runnymede.

It is a great irony that England's slow but steady evolution from an absolute monarchy to a constitutional one owes almost everything to bad kings, not to mention the odd thick or mad one, and virtually nothing to good ones. If all the kings had been good and had lived within their income, there is a fair possibility that we could, in theory, still have an absolute monarch. Instead, they wanted to play soldiers and conquer France or Scotland and then hold on to their conquests. All this cost tons of money, and the more money they demanded from their subjects, the more the barons and freemen asked for in return in the way of charters, privileges and freedoms. As kings gave them, so they found, to their dismay, that they had to give yet more next time round, hence the evolution of Parliament. In fact, the kings (with the odd exception such as Henry VII) had no conception of the difference between capital and income. For nearly 700 years kings spent their 'capital' until George III finally, in 1761, gave away the remnants of the crown estates, and most of the remnants of the power of the monarch as well, in return for a Civil List.

The modern history of taxation really begins with the introduction of the land tax in 1692. I say modern because the old feudal dues and duties finally faded into history only during the seventeenth century. The driving force behind the new tax was William III's obsession with fighting Louis XIV, and as war is an expensive business ways had to be found to raise the money required. The land tax was the price the squirearchy suddenly realized they were going to have to pay for having got rid of the Catholic James II in the so-called Glorious Revolution. The new tax was set at a rate of '4 shillings in the pound according to the true yearly value thereof – that is to say that for every £100 of goods and ready money and for every £100 of land and other property the sum of four and twenty shillings'. In other words it was assumed that every £100 of property would produce a yield for the owner of six per cent i.e. £6, and a tax was being levied on that £6 of notional yield at the rate of four shillings in the pound, hence the landowner owed the taxman twenty-four shillings (£1.20) for every £100 of property. In effect it was a type of wealth tax and the squirearchy went into fits over it.

In 1693 Sir James Shaen wrote to Sir William Russell: 'No man knows better than yourself how long and earnestly I have endeavoured to ease all ye real estates in England from ye insupportable burden of 4 shillings [20p] in the pound which must at last infallibly crush and ruin all ye landed men.'

Nothing changes. It is one of the great myths among landowners that taxation of land, and property generally, is a phenomenon of the last hundred-odd years. Nothing could be further from the truth. Until the Industrial Revolution, the vast majority of England's economy was dominated by agriculture and its products while at the same time land, and to a lesser extent buildings, have one supreme advantage as far as a tax gatherer is concerned: they can be measured and recorded and cannot be hidden. As long as four hundred years ago the demise of the English landowner was being predicted because of the heavy burden of taxation. The result of William's tax, however, was that the smaller landowners, the country squires, realizing too late the enormous error they had made in putting their religious principles before their loyalty to the Stuart dynasty, reverted to being Tories, many becoming closet Jacobites.

The land tax was to have a long life, although the rates were to fluctuate over the years. In 1797 landowners were given the option of redeeming it by paying the Treasury a sum equal to thirty times the annual tax. Unsurprisingly, any landowner who was planning to de-velop his land, and therefore increase its value, took advantage of this concession, with the result that by the mid-1930s the yield of this tax had fallen to around £600,000 annually, compared with nearly £2 million when first launched on unsuspecting landowners back in 1692.

One of the reasons for landowners' complaints about land tax was that they were already paying tax on land in the form of the poor rate (introduced in 1601) and the hated tithes (hated, that is, by the occupiers of the land, i.e. the tenants who had to pay it). Poor rates were considerably more burdensome back then than their modern-day equivalent, council tax, is today. If you glance back to Chapter 6 you will see that Squire Steadyman of Wearywork Hall was paying (in 1876) £220 a year in poor rates or nearly £10,000 a year in today's money. Poor rates were also resented because the nature of the beast was that they tended to rise at times of agricultural depression, which of course was exactly the time when landowners and farmers were themselves finding the financial going tough.

No one would deny that today we are taxed more heavily than our nineteenth-century ancestors, if more lightly than our fathers were after the war. The result is that the subject of tax dominates the life of a landowner, and it would be depressing to compute the amount of time and money he spends planning how to die in the most tax-efficient manner possible!

Death duties (or IHT as the charge is now technically called) are often called a 'voluntary' tax, and in some ways this is an accurate description as they can be avoided by the simple expedient of leaving your whole estate to your wife (100 per cent spouse relief) or by simply living seven years after making over your estate to your heir (potentially exempt transfer or PET). Neither option is risk-free. The tragic example of Lord Lovat is a case in point. The Lovats had managed to hang on to most of their vast landholdings and in 1970 still had some 160,000 acres. It was this empire that Lord Lovat tried to ring-fence from the taxman by handing it over to his son Simon and living the requisite number of years. This he achieved, but his son got the taste for horse racing and entrepreneurial investments as well as 'estate diversification' projects which, between them, eventually managed to gobble up nearly all the estate. This is not an isolated incident. Many a father has made over part of his estate, only to see it end up converted by his son into gambling chips or spent on 'investment opportunities'.

If carrying out a PET is not risk-free neither is leaving it to your wife, especially if you have married more than once. By this I mean that if your son and heir is born to your first wife it is the height of foolishness to take advantage of spouse relief and leave everything to your second wife in the fond hope that she will immediately pass it over to your son, thus avoiding death duties. For a start she may not like the boy, second she might rather fancy remaining in the 'big house' and third – and quite likely – she may be a classic gold-digger. While by no means all stepmothers behave like this, there are a fair few who do. Even leaving it to the mother of your eldest son is not completely risk-free, as she may suddenly get a second breath of wind after your death and start enjoying life to the full, in other words start spending money and having fun and, perhaps, even find a replacement for you in her bed, all of which may well spell bad news for your intended heir.

So it is quite possible to be too clever by half with your tax planning. What appears clever today can become a complete bloody mess ten years down the line. It is important when tax planning not just to be aware of the amount of tax you might save, but also of the costs you are going to incur by saving that tax. Oddly, many people never ask this question, although perhaps it is not so strange, as the clever tax advisers might just be embarrassed to reveal the true cost of their highly complex tax-avoidance scheme. I always consider the oddest, and most illogical, tax-avoidance scheme of all is when the very rich insist on going to live in some tax haven ghetto like Monaco where, instead of giving some money to the Chancellor of the Exchequer, they will give great dollops of it to the Monegasques (not really the most deserving people on the planet). If you are rich enough to live in Monaco you are frankly rich enough to live where you like, regardless of the amount of tax you will have to pay.

Back to death duties: modern IHT is a comparatively benign tax compared with some of its predecessors. For instance, the current top rate of forty per cent compares favourably with the top rate of eighty per cent which was extant as recently as 1975. In addition, all in-hand farmland is now exempt, as are 'working' farmhouses, forestry and tenanted farms, provided the tenant did not have possession before 1996. In other words most, if not all, of the land on an estate is free of death duties. The problem comes when you start looking at the cottages and houses. These, fifty years ago, were virtually valueless – as incidentally was your mansion house – but they are now not only valuable but are bringing in good rents. There is a risk that those landowners who amalgamated small tenanted farms as they became vacant and then did up the empty farmhouse to let it as a stand-alone house may well have let their heir in for a substantial death duty bill, which will have made the whole exercise a financial waste of time. They will have converted an 'exempt-from-IHT' asset, a working farmhouse, into a non-exempt one, an assured shorthold tenancy earning, say, £15,000 a year rent and with a probate valuation of £500,000, meaning an IHT bill of £200,000!

Of course if Daddy did make a balls-up of his tax planning and has left you the estate and the big house, together with a substantial potential IHT bill, all is not lost. You must sit down and examine the pros and cons of conditional exemption. This is available if you can persuade the Treasury that your house, contents etc. is a qualifying heritage property. The rough definition of this is any land, buildings and chattels the Treasury considers as being pre-eminent or of outstanding interest historically, architecturally or nationally. If your house is so considered, then land thought essential for protecting the character, amenity etc. of the buildings will also be allowed. In other words, not only will the house become conditionally exempt but also the Capability Brown park, and the follies, temples and lodges scattered over it.

The downside is that the Treasury then demands its pound of flesh. This used to be called 'reasonable public access'. What is reasonable? When conditional exemption was first dreamed up in 1896, only two years after death duties had been introduced, nobody had any doubt in their minds. Reasonable quite simply meant that there should be access allowed to scholars and connoisseurs and anyone else interested enough to go along to the Victoria & Albert Museum and look up the list of such items as were held there. Not surprisingly, many owners of conditionally exempt items who were not open to the public never *ever* got a telephone call asking to see their 'exempt' item. This was too good to last. At the turn of the century (over a hundred years after conditional exemption had first been introduced) the proverbial 'scandal' was 'exposed' and immediately seized upon by every rabble-rousing journalist in the BBC and the tabloid press, as well as by the usual suspects in the political world. The 'scandal', allegedly, was that thousands of 'works of art' worth 'many millions of pounds' had been granted conditional exemption on condition of reasonable public access but that the public were not getting to see them. I am unable to see the scandal in this. The real scandal is that death duties were being charged on chattels in the first place; the second scandal was that the general public was so idle that it could not be bothered to go and look up the register (a copy of which was at every local library). The general public had probably decided that it had quite enough art to go and see anyway without bothering old Lord Thunderbox about looking at his Reynolds or whatever. In this age of 'tabloid government', however, it was hardly surprising that the politicians had to 'act'. What *was* surprising – and disgraceful – was that the government tried to make the changes to conditional exemption retrospective. This aspect of the changes is being challenged and may end up in the courts, because one of the oddities about conditional exemption is that it lasts only for the life of the owner. So on the death of the owner of a conditionally exempt property or item the exemption ceases and the new heir has the option either to reapply or pay the IHT at the current rate.

The nature of IHT is changing. In the old days it was viewed as a tax on a small élite, of little consequence to the mass of taxpayers and voters. House prices have changed all that. The massive inflation in property values over the last twelve years or so has pushed the average value of a house in Britain to £150,000. This being an average, it doesn't take a lot of brainpower to work out that there are an awful lot of houses worth considerably more than the £254,000 threshold above which an estate pays IHT at forty per cent. What was once a tax on the upper classes is now very much a tax on the middle classes and even on the lower middle classes. A tax which has always been virtually impossible to justify on any grounds may well be in retreat. America is planning to abolish it, as is Italy, and other countries may well follow. If there is a fear somewhere that, without capital taxation on death, estates of rich men will grow inexorably richer over the centuries then the legislators can relax. It took some seven hundred years for the late Lord Lovat's ancestors to build up their empire in the Highlands, but it took his son only twenty-odd years to lose the lot. Human nature will always succeed where the taxman fails.

In recent years two other instruments have been created by the government in an effort to enable owners to safeguard their houses from punitive taxation: charitable trusts and maintenance funds. At present there are around twenty large houses owned and supported by charitable trusts endowed by their owners. The big advantage is that, as charities, they are exempt from taxation on rental and investment income and from capital gains tax and IHT, though not – oddly – from profits made from 'commercial' activities. Some of the largest houses in the land are now owned by such trusts, including Chatsworth, Arundel Castle and Burghley House. Charitable trusts, however, are not a panacea for all owners of such properties. For a start the donor loses control and he must remember that gift to the charitable trust is *irrevocable*. To some owners, keen to preserve their house and estate for future generations, but distrusting a rogue genetic trait they know is in the family genes, this might, in itself, seem a major advantage. Most owners, though, will conclude, especially when they fully understand the terms and conditions of charitable status, that the result of going down the charity route will almost certainly be the end of the family's connection with the house. This is due to the fact that charitable status imposes severe conditions on the donor family. A 'market' rent must be paid by them if they wish to continue to live in the house and if they want to use other rooms for entertaining and so forth then they have to pay 'market rates' for those as well, a condition most potential donors would find irksome in the extreme. Finally, the amount of control a donor has over the running of the charitable trust is prescribed, and the law insists that there must be a majority of independent trustees.

In some ways putting your property into a charitable trust is not unlike giving it to the National Trust, except that your own charitable trust has at least been designed by you, the trustees initially selected by you, and the amount of land and property which you have endowed the trust with has also been decided by you. In other words you do not have to beg and crawl to some faceless committee and have the ridiculous Chorley Formula thrust down your throat. You do, though, have to be seriously rich even to consider going down the charity route, since not only do you have to own sufficient property and assets to endow the charity, but you also have to own enough to pay for your rent and for all your family's likely economic needs in the future. In other words, charitable status – like virtually every clever piece of tax planning – is really open only to the seriously rich.

An alternative solution is the setting up of a maintenance fund. In this case the assets vested in the fund are free of the dreaded inheritance tax (IHT), but the income is taxed. The income from the fund can be used only for the maintenance of the house and the fund dissolves on the death of the settlor. When this happens his heir can either opt to set it up again – in which case he will avoid IHT on the assets – or wind it up when he would pay IHT. The attractions of the maintenance fund would appear not to be powerful enough to encourage a large number of owners to opt for it, and only around sixty have so far been set up.

Needless to say, to opt either to be a charitable trust or to set up a maintenance fund would involve large professional fee bills. To me it seems the height of injustice that owners, in order to safeguard something the government insists is part of the national heritage, are forced to jump through a convoluted series of hoops which benefit no one except the lawyers or life insurance companies.

The lack of take-up by most owners of these options speaks for itself. Perhaps, like me, they intensely dislike the surrender of independence attendant upon these schemes and prefer to gamble on getting their tax planning 'right on the night'. If they fail, and the contents of their houses are sold and end up overseas, the houses are broken up into flats, the parks turned into golf courses, the farmhouses sold to weekenders, and the nation laments at yet another 'heritage disaster story', then so be it. After all, if 'the nation' really wanted to help, all it has to do is abolish IHT. In any case, what has 'the nation' ever done for owners of the so-called 'national heritage'? Nothing – unless you consider various vague efforts to staunch the flow of blood caused in the first place by 'the nation's' own taxation policies!

CHAPTER 14

Houses and Villages

Come, friendly bombs, and fall on Slough!
It isn't fit for humans now,
There isn't grass to graze a cow.
Swarm over, Death!

JOHN BETJEMAN (1906–84)
'Slough', from *Continual Dew*, 1937

Most estates have cottages and farmhouses scattered over them and some even still own a whole village. For years, dwellings of any kind were viewed as a disaster by owners. The rents they brought in failed to cover the repairs and could not be increased because they were 'controlled'.

Rent controls were first brought in by our old friend Lloyd George in the First World War, to protect munitions workers who, he feared, were having their housing rents raised by unscrupulous landlords. Gradually the legislation was extended until the dead hand of rent control covered virtually the entire rented-housing sector. Predictably, over time it became accepted practice to sell off any house once it became vacant rather than re-let it and continue to lose money. Such was the rate of loss on rented property that it was generally accepted policy for land-owners to sell whole villages to the sitting tenants at knockdown prices just to rid themselves of the long-term liability.

This is yet another instance of landowners and their advisers failing to look into the future and making wrong decisions based on prevailing conditions. Not that they can be blamed, as the future, back in the

1940s and 1950s, looked bleak. It was not until the mid-1960s that property prices in rural England began to climb steeply.

In 1950 the average rent for one of my father's cottages in Devon was £9.50 per annum, the agricultural wage at that time being about £255 a year. Now the rent for one of those cottages, under a new assured shorthold tenancy, would be in the region of £4,500 to £7,500 per annum, and the agricultural wage around £13,000. To put this in perspective, rents have multiplied 530 times, wages only fifty times. Some may say that the enormous rise in rents versus basic wages is evidence of the importance of rent control, but they forget several things. We are not quite comparing like with like. The modern equivalent of that 1950 cottage now has central heating, mains water, hot-water boilers, fitted kitchens, etc. In other words it has been enormously improved. The current high rents are a direct result of the scarcity of rented accommodation caused by landlords selling off housing over the years because of rent controls. The world has moved on from the 1950s, when regions of the United Kingdom still operated as independent economic areas, relatively unaffected by what was happening in the large cities and towns a hundred or so miles away. The advent of the motorway changed all this. Suddenly it became possible for someone working in London to jump into his car on Friday afternoon and arrive at his weekend home in time for dinner. In other words, house prices in the country were directly affected by the economic performance of London rather than the local market town ten miles away. As I have stressed before, it is a maxim of estate agents that prices of houses are affected by three factors: location, location and location – to which I again add that location is affected by three factors: communication, communication and communication.

Communication, however, is about a lot more than just motorways, rail networks and airports, important though they are in determining the price and attractiveness of properties. For example it is well known that if a railway line is electrified or a motorway built, reducing the journey time to London by some ten minutes, then property prices will increase regardless of what is happening in the property market generally. But communication is also about our ability to communicate *with each other*, in other words, it is about the telephone, the fax machine and nowadays the mysteries of the Internet and the wonders of e-mail. Suddenly the rural cottage is not just for weekends but can become an operating office for a couple of days of the week as well. Gradually people are discovering that in the modern Internet age you do not have to be chained to a desk in London; you can, instead, be chained to one in your back garden anywhere in rural Britain. It is not just individual Londoners who are realizing this, but also people and companies operating in local market towns and county cities. The costs associated with running an office in one of Britain's regional commercial centres are rising all the time as councils operate a love/hate relationship with business. They love the revenue but they hate the cars, so they shove up the rates and try to make life as unpleasant as possible for those who drive into work, assuming businesspeople have no alternative. Many of the smaller businesses are wondering, consequently, whether there might not be attractive alternatives outside the urban fringe, in that old stable block of yours, or in a converted old redundant barn on an estate. So offices and industry are beginning to move out of the towns and back into the country, a hundred and fifty-odd years after they all moved out of the country and into the towns at the time of the Industrial Revolution.

How all landowners today rue their fathers' actions – and their own in many cases – of selling off all those cottages. They are not the only ones who regret this strategy, either. The current chorus of protest at the lack of cheap rural housing is a direct result of this policy. The shortage is real, and few would deny it, but the reasons behind the crisis in rural housing are relatively complex. After all, landowners more often than not sold their houses to sitting tenants and these sitting tenants were local people, so why is there a crisis? The unpalatable fact is that local people then sold them on, at a great profit, to the new breed of incomers who wished to use them as weekend cottages, retirement homes or as bases to commute from. In other words, the crisis in rural housing has been caused largely by local people who, pocketing their gains, moved out of the thatched cottage in rural England and into the modern bungalow of their dreams in the nearby town.

Talking of bungalows, some people may wonder why planners have allowed these excrescences to deface so much of England's green and pleasant land. Many of those found in the open country were built because of a loophole in the planning laws. This enjoined planning authorities to allow planning for agricultural dwellings for farmworkers and farmers. This concession to the farming community was, as ever, abused. Farmers sold their large house and then said that they had no dwelling, so were given permission to build a new one; alternatively, farmers sold fifty or so acres to a third party who bought – for a high price – confident of getting planning permission for the proverbial bungalow, and so on and so forth. Not unnaturally, this privilege has now been withdrawn. Once again we see that government grants privileges on the understanding that people are mature enough not to abuse them. If they are abused, they are rightly removed. History, sadly, proves that no section of the population is ever mature enough to resist the temptation to abuse privileges when there is easy money to be made. As for the proliferation of bungalows on the outskirts of villages, no easy answer is available as to why planning permission was granted for them. Perhaps the easiest explanation is that planners are no different from most of the population and genuinely did not understand that they were playing a vital part in ruining the look of countless 'unspoilt' villages.

It is not only in the villages that the change in rural housing has had an impact. Outside the villages, farms have been amalgamated and farmhouses made redundant. Large pleasant family houses, described by our estate-agent friends as 'character residences', have thus been released for sale to outsiders keen to acquire a 'farmhouse with large garden and five acres, enjoying superb views over unspoilt countryside'. Incidentally, quite a few buyers of such properties will approach local landowners with a view to buying another one or two acres off them for a price above the agricultural land value. Landowners should tell them to get lost: they are no longer in the charity business. For although, on the face of it, an offer to buy an acre of land valued at, say, £2,000 for £5,000 may seem a good deal, remember that acre may add £50,000 or more on to the value of the buyer's property – and why should you make him a present of £45,000? No reason at all. There is in fact a rule of thumb here: the seller of the land is entitled to one-third of the uplifted value the buyer gets from marrying the two properties together.

Fortunately, the Conservative government finally woke up (years too late, as per normal) to the damage the various rent-control measures were doing to the private rented sector and introduced the assured shorthold tenancy. This allows virtual freedom of contract between a landlord and a potential tenant and enables a landlord to repossess if the tenant is in breach of that contract. This measure has breathed new life into the rural rental sector and encouraged many landowners to rent out property that in the past they would have automatically sold on the open market. Also several owners who previously let their cottages as 'holiday lets' now rent them out to local people under assured shorthold tenancies. The result has been a small, but significant, expansion of the private rented sector in rural areas.

The propensity for politicians to bugger up the property market, however, can never be overestimated. Who cares about long-term damage to the nation when important matters like short-term votes in marginal constituencies are at stake? John Major, when prime minister, certainly didn't. In 1992 he brought in the Leasehold Reform Act, which effectively rewrote freely-entered-into agreements between land-lords and lessees in the lessees' favour. This actually was not the first political venture into the minefield of leasehold, as Harold Wilson had already set foot there with the aim of placating Welsh miners. But in those days the reform had been limited to giving lessees the right to buy houses with a low rateable value. John Major acted to extend this right to buy to all lessees.

The immorality of retrospective legislation, changing freely-entered-into contracts between two parties in favour of one side, did not concern Mr Major. Why should it? There are relatively few landlords, while there are many tenants and lessees, all of whom have the vote.

Not that it did him any good – he lost the next election by a record margin. I wonder if a single lessee voted Conservative as a thank you for all John Major had done for him. I doubt it. The common man has no sense of gratitude – and anyway a vast number of the main beneficiaries were foreigners who have made central London their home, but who do not, of course, have the vote!

I make no apologies for forecasting that in twenty years or so the 1992 Leasehold Reform Act will be remembered as a disaster. The good thing about leases was that they allowed a relatively diverse mix of people to live in central London. The leasehold system, by keeping the freehold separate, kept the cost of accommodation in central London down, and if you fancied buying the tail-end of a lease, you could afford to live in the smartest parts of London – provided you did not mind that at the end of your lease you would have nothing.

But, back in the country, is there a solution to the permanent lack of cheap rural housing to rent? Well, there might be. One possible answer might be to encourage landowners to build cottages for rental, just as their ancestors did in the dim and distant past. One of the problems with current initiatives is that they rely on housing associations buying land and then developing the site. The result is that the housing association has to factor in the cost of the land, which might be anything from £10,000 to £20,000 per unit of accommodation. This is cheap compared to what land with full planning permission for residential housing would fetch, but still expensive. If landowners carried out the work themselves, the land could go in at virtually zero and the only cost would be the construction of the house itself at, say, £40,000 to £60,000 per unit. With rents of around £4,500, this could give the landlord a return of between 7.5 and 10 per cent, not that unattractive these days with both interest rates and inflation staying low. If the cost of building the houses could be written off against tax over ten years, and if business relief were available on capital taxation, then perhaps some landowners might be induced to dip their toes back into the water of owning and managing private rented accommodation again, rather than just flogging off that three-acre building site to a developer to build yet more executive homes.

Another sensible solution to the housing problem is our old friend leasing. Say a landowner owned development land but did not have the capital available to build himself. He could lease the property to developers, who would build and sell the leasehold interest on. The result, because the houses were leasehold rather than freehold, would be that they were considerably cheaper, hence affordable. But this ignores the fact that making houses affordable through leasehold is a crime today, and one must never indulge in criminal activity; so much better to make all properties so expensive that only the rich can afford them. What clowns our political masters are!

The selling-off of villages and redundant farmhouses has not only made living in the countryside too expensive for much of the native population, it has also fundamentally altered the character of rural communities. Many of the new arrivals bring with them urban standards and expect country people to abide by them or face the full force of civil action in the courts. But it is not just the urban prejudices which the incomers or foreigners bring with them that are offensive, but their general attitude to the place they choose to make their home. To them they have moved to a rural idyll, but for the long-established residents their village is a living, working environment. Such differing attitudes can and do create conflicts.

A further problem is the actual type of person who buys a rural property. With prices of attractive country and village properties being what they are, it is hardly surprising that most incomers are successful middle-aged professionals. Their children have already grown up, so do not attend the local school; they work in the local town, so call in on the supermarket on their way home in the evening and do not buy from the village shop, and so on. In other words, they do not support the village infrastructure, which is consequently put in danger.

The most abiding threat to villages is clearly development. The vast majority of our villages have already had their beauty ruined by insensitive development since the war. Indeed, it may be said that it is not so much the building of new houses that has caused people to loathe the concept of development but rather the type of houses that are built. It was, and still is, one of the joys of England, that on any journey of a hundred or so miles you can identify three or four or more different types of vernacular building. The reason is that villages were built according to what materials were available locally and it was not until the late nineteenth century that improvements in transport enabled bricks and slates from far away to be imported, to the detriment of the local building industries. These improvements in transport did not just destroy local architectural practices, and the skills that went with them, but they also began the long-drawn-out process of destroying the economy of the village itself. In 1911 my local village boasted a resident doctor, vet, auctioneer, schoolteacher, vicar, wheelwright, baker, black-smith, bootmaker, shopkeeper, edge-tool maker, tailor, carpenter and two pubs. Some of these trades hung on right up to the late 1950s but gradually, as roads improved and car ownership spread, so the village as an economic unit serving its own immediate area saw its trade and its jobs transferred to the local market town.

What the Victorians began, the modern developer has continued, with a vengeance. Planting his ghastly little boxes across the country, regardless of local styles of architecture, intent only on securing a fat profit before moving on, he desecrates the landscape with his puerile designs.

In 1996 the Department of the Environment (DOE) unveiled a new threat to much of the remaining unspoilt countryside in England with its announcement that 4.4 million new houses would need to be built over a twenty-five-year period from 1991. Come 2004, the Treasury, frightened by the spectre of rocketing house inflation, decided that this appraisal needed updating and commissioned one Kate Barker (aptly named), a member, unbelievably, of the Bank of England's Monetary Policy Committee, to write one. Barker, as an economist, had heard of the theory of supply and demand, and had the great brainwave that the answer was to build another 1.4 million houses over the next ten years, many of them in the previously sacrosanct 'green belt'. It must be emphasized that over two million new houses and flats had already been built since 1991; in other words the house-building industry was pretty well on track to meet the targets laid down by the DOE in 1996. What Barker was saying, however, was that these houses were not necessarily in the right place and, in her view, that 'right place' was the south east of England, which was where the demand 'hot spots' were. Why the Treasury needed someone of her eminence to produce such a report is a bit of a mystery, as any schoolchild studying economics at GCSE level could have done as well at a fraction of the cost. Barker made the classic error of looking at the rise in UK house prices in isolation and as a result came to the wrong conclusions. If she had bothered to look around the world she would have found, to her surprise, that the boom in prices of residential property was not restricted to the south east of England, or indeed to the UK as a whole, but was a worldwide phenomenon. All over the globe, in developed countries, house prices were going berserk. So when, at the end of 2002, house prices in the UK had risen by 25.2 per cent, they had also risen by 18.4 per cent in Australia (no shortage of land there, one would have thought), 17.4 per cent in Spain (not notorious for its strict application of planning laws), in the USA by 7.8 per cent, and so on. The boom continued into 2004, as the following table shows, although house price indices have to be taken with a large pinch of salt, as they are notoriously unreliable in showing what is actually happening to a market in the short term, since house markets do not operate in the same way as, say, stock markets. This is obvious if you think about it. House price indices are worked out by looking at the value of property *sold*, so when a market is booming and property is being traded almost as soon as it hits the market the indices are reasonably accurate, but when the market stagnates or begins to fall the indices do not, initially, pick up on it because sellers, instead of cutting their asking price till they attract a buyer, sit on their property in the hope that one will come along at the asking price.

Why this global property boom happened is open to debate and is as little understood as why the lemming population suddenly explodes, but happen it did and all across the globe there was a rush to 'invest' in property. Well, *nearly* all over the globe. Those people who preach the gospel-according-to-estate-agents of continuously rising house prices

Worldwide House Price Inflation 1997–2004		
Country change in months as at	Percentage previous twelve 1997–2004	Increase over prices June 2004
Ireland	181	11.1
S. Africa	168	25.5
Britain	132	13.8
Spain	125	17.2
Australia	110	10.9
Sweden	77	10.0
Netherlands	74	3.9
France	68	14.5
Italy	62	10.8
USA	57	9.4
New Zealand	51	22.1
Belgium	50	8.2
Denmark	44	5.0
Canada	42	7.3
Germany	–3	–1.7
Japan	–24	–6.4
Hong Kong	–55	–28.7

Source: *Economist*

conveniently forget Japan. In the same year (2004) that property everywhere else on the globe was roaring ahead, in Japan house prices fell by 6.4 per cent. Since reaching dizzy heights in the mid-1980s, when it was calculated that the emperor's garden in the middle of Tokyo was technically worth more than the whole of California, the Japanese have got used to seeing their houses and flats fall in value annually, to the point that now, in 2004, some eighteen years off their peak, the average house is worth less than one-third of its value then!

Experts tell us it will not happen here; but then I cannot recall anyone predicting it was going to happen in Japan either, all those years ago, least of all the Japanese banks who lent all that money to property buyers, which enabled them to bid up the market in the first place just as, oddly enough, UK banks did in the 1980s and just as – even odder – UK banks have done again in the 1990s. Some things never change and the collective stupidity of bankers is one of them.

What was the thinking behind the great property boom? People had, it seems – for reasons I have covered in the chapter headed 'The City', ceased to trust traditional methods of saving and instead turned to the one solid object that had never let them down: houses. Houses are for ever, houses only ever go up in value (with the occasional hiccup such as 1988–92, but look what has happened since), so obviously it makes sense to borrow all we can to 'invest' in housing and not in stocks and shares. Actually, as Kate Barker should have known, when everyone believes an asset can only ever keep going up in value then that asset is inevitably going to bomb one day. It is obvious if you think about it. If house prices can only ever go up, then we would all be fools not to buy houses. So we all do, and what happens? House prices rise. So we borrow more money on the back of our now more valuable house and buy another, or bigger, house. It would be madness not to, as house prices are never going to go down. In effect we are now in a classic 'bubble'. Our conviction that prices can only ever rise has pushed the price of property way above the level it should be at: ahead lies catastrophe. Put simply, in words which perhaps even Kate Barker can understand, there cannot, by definition, be any commodity or stock which is guaranteed always to rise in value.

There is some mystery as to why these new homes are needed. England at present boasts a housing stock of around 20 million units of accommodation; with a total adult (over sixteen) population of 42 million, this works out at a ratio of one house or flat for every 2.2 adults. As the population is not set to grow over the next twenty-odd years, the result of the DOE's building boom will be to reduce this ratio to under two adults for every home in England.

The supposed demand for these new houses is from the expected growth in 'single-person' households caused by changing social patterns, the rising divorce rate and, not forgetting probably the largest, but for political reasons least talked-about issue, immigration. If these are the major factors behind the DOE's and the Treasury's obsession with building more houses, then it is obvious that the classic Mr Barratt home in a semi-rural area is totally unsuited to their needs. For a start, single people are not necessarily well off, and living in some new development in a village miles from a town means that a car is a necessity rather than a luxury. The obvious place to build new homes is therefore in the existing towns – and by this I do not mean on the edge of towns, I mean as near the middle of them as possible. Most British towns have been scarred over the last thirty-odd years with jerry-built low-rise office and retail developments; in London developers are buying redundant office buildings and turning them into flats – let us do the same in our county towns. If we do not follow this course of action, then the future for England's towns is dire indeed. The high streets have already been badly hit by the building of out-of-town supermarkets and shopping centres; over the next dozen or so years, a revolution in the banking world is likely to lead to the closure of many branches. It is hard to see a prosperous long-term future for country towns unless people are encouraged to return to them, and this is not as ridiculous an idea as it may seem. Living in towns – as opposed to the suburbs – has much to recommend it, especially for single people. Shops, cinemas, restaurants, pubs and even work may be within walking distance of a person's home. Also if the town centre becomes populated again, then new types of shops and businesses spring up to cater for the needs of the resident population.

But the real key to rejuvenating our cities is architecture. Beautiful cities are successful cities, ugly cities unsuccessful. Places like Bath and Edinburgh are bursting with life and enterprise while those towns and cities that fell victim to the appalling greed of post-war developers and the inane stupidity of 'town planners' are now struggling. It is a fact that scarcely a single building of beauty was built in the United

Kingdom between 1945 and 1980, a grave indictment of Britain's developers. Big financial institutions, such as the Prudential Insurance Company – my pet hate, for putting up an excrescence of an office building in the most beautiful eighteenth-century part of Exeter – and large specialized property-investment companies, like Land Securities, fail to understand a simple fact: if you build beautiful buildings you will be more likely to find tenants for them. That they cannot see this is one of the great mysteries of life. The good news is that most of their buildings are so badly designed and built that few will survive far into this century and future planners and developers will be given a superb opportunity to rectify the mistakes of their predecessors. Will they take it? I am not optimistic, but if they do not the country towns and cities of Britain will end up in deep trouble.

Perhaps the most surprising aspect of the whole debate on where to build these new houses has been the deafening silence from the towns and cities themselves. One would have thought they would be vigorously campaigning against the building of new 'dormitory' estates on their outskirts and demanding that the housing be located in their centres. It is a frightening thing to read of the supposed housing 'need' in a particular area and then to see the price that an inner-city terrace Edwardian town house will fetch in the same town. The key to regenerating the country towns of England is to restrict development outside towns and force (I mean encourage) people to look at what is on offer within the city itself. Then, with luck, a 'halo effect' will be achieved, as has happened in so much of London – i.e. as people do up terrace housing, so others move in to follow suit, then restaurants and shops begin to open to cater for the demand of the comparatively affluent owners of the properties, and so on.

The above is, of course, all common sense; it is just a pity the DOE has so little of it – but then one must remember that the House Builders' Federation (HBF) is a particularly powerful lobby. Politicians should recall, when listening to their blandishments, that no single organization has been responsible for ruining more acres of land, destroying more villages or wrecking more town centres than the membership of this particular – supposedly benevolent – organization.

The reaction of the HBF to the uproar caused by the announcement in 1996 of the proposal to build the 4.4 million new homes was predictable. A Mr Humber, the director of the HBF, made a speech in 1996 to the Town and Country Planning Association (that is not a joke, there actually is one!) from which I cannot resist quoting the odd gem. For instance, on building in towns and cities he said: 'We cannot turn them into dustbins for the shire county NIMBYs.' Now, in my ignorance, I thought he wanted to turn great areas of the countryside into 'dustbins' for those from the towns! But perhaps, in common with many modern men, his grasp of English is not all that it might be. He then went on: 'If the cities become yet more overcrowded, if education gets worse, as does traffic and crime, if the quality of life declines, then more people will try to leave and put pressure on the countryside.' Actually, his argument is rubbish. Sadly, most cities are not crowded; that is what is wrong with them. Walk round the centre of most country towns at ten o'clock at night and they are empty, there is no buzz, no restaurants are open, no late-night shops are to be found; the simple reason is that no one lives in them any more – the members of the Town and Country Planning Association have seen to that, and turned most towns and cities into deserts at night.

If the HBF got its way and was allowed to build willy-nilly over greenfield sites, this would result in the cities declining still further. Crime would rise, education standards fall and the general quality of life deteriorate, because the prosperous and intelligent middle classes would sell up and move to one of Mr Humber's members' ghastly little boxes in the country (although you can hardly call living in a hundred-acre new town 'country'), leaving behind all who could not afford to move. Sadly, it seems that the HBF is closer today (2004) than ever before to getting the government to dismantle many of the planning controls put in place to limit their ambitions to wreck England.

I am afraid I cannot resist one last quote from the absurd Mr Humber, this time complaining about high-density housing being built in London's Docklands: ' . . . they are in some cases building tiny houses, which can only be the slums of the future, on sites which should, at best, be used for road widening or to provide open space'. I wonder if Mr Humber and the members of the Town and Country Planning Association might like to take a trip to Chelsea or Kensington or Mayfair to see how valuable small houses in narrow streets can be and how desirable such areas are to live in. But then, given half a chance, he and his friends would undoubtedly sweep all that away for 'road widening' and to provide 'open spaces'; after all, presumably it was past and, I suspect, a few present members of the Town and Country Planning Association who filled the poisoned chalice with tower blocks and the like!

House builders love 'greenfield sites', not just because they are easy to work but because of an anomaly in the taxation rules. No VAT is levied on new houses, but if a builder converts a disused office building or old warehouse into living accommodation or refurbishes an existing block of flats, he has to pay VAT on all his outgoings. Paradoxically, this discourages builders from doing just what the public wants them to do. The simple solution is to zero-rate refurbishments as well as new houses, but VAT is a complex tax and, because we are forced to give a percentage of the total VAT raised every year to the European Union (so they can give it to the Irish or the Greeks), any change in VAT has to be authorized by that august body.

Britain has so far escaped having to charge VAT on new housing, as it has pretended that new (even 'executive') housing is necessary for reasons of 'social policy'. Unfortunately there is little likelihood of the European Union agreeing to allow us to zero-rate refurbishments and renovations since, once a VAT rate is established, EU law decrees that it can never be reduced. The alternative solution would be to impose VAT at the full rate on new houses built on greenfield sites. Such a policy would elicit howls of rage from house builders, who would make sure the purchaser bore the increased cost.

While on the face of it this seems a logical response, it is Mickey Mouse economics. The imposition of VAT on new homes would not make an iota of difference to the price of the new home. Why? Because builders already sell their houses for the maximum amount they think they can get away with; *ergo* if they had to pay 17.5 per cent on the cost of building the property they could not pass it on as no one would buy the thing at that price. Builders would initially have to absorb the extra cost of the tax, but in the future they would factor it into their calculations when buying building land – in other words, they would pay less for development land to enable them to continue to keep their current profit margins on future developments. The only loser would therefore be the landowner, who instead of getting, say, £400,000 an acre, would get only £300,000.

So now you know why there are 800,000 empty homes in the UK at present, and why no one is that keen on renovating the old warehouses and redundant office buildings that are such a feature of so many of our towns and cities. It is all the fault of our friend the European Union.

CHAPTER 15

The Family

> [Society is] a partnership not only between those who
> are living, but between those who are living, those who
> are dead, and those who are to be born.
>
> EDMUND BURKE (1729–97)
> 'Reflections on the French Revolution', 1790

If the visible features of an estate are a large house and extensive park,
then the invisible element is the people, whose presence make the whole
thing work and without whom it would be just another dead museum.

First and foremost must be the owner and his immediate family.
Whether the estate and house sinks or swims depends totally on them
and their aims and ambitions – or lack of them, as the case may be –
although, as we have seen, a lack of ambition and enterprise can
sometimes have a far more positive effect on the financial health of an
estate than an all-singing, all-dancing entrepreneurial approach. This
has always been true of estates; many in the past were beggared
and eventually broken up by foolish attempts to finance an owner's
ambitions at court, in Parliament, or even in entertaining monarchs
such as Edward VII, while in more recent years others have been used as
collateral to raise money for 'can't fail' business ventures that, sadly,
ended up doing exactly the opposite of that optimistic business plan and
cash flow forecast. (Always remember that there has never been a
business plan or cash flow forecast in history that has predicted disaster
and financial insolvency, yet that is the fate of most 'start-up businesses'.
It is as well to bear this fact in mind next time you are presented with a

'get rich quick' investment opportunity.) Indeed many estates and houses would be in a lot better shape if the owner had spent the day making mud pies with his children rather than playing at business in his office, not just because he was probably losing stacks of cash by trying to be a businessman, but because by doing so he was neglecting his most important asset, one on which the entire long-term future of his house and estate depended: his family.

If this is the case, it follows that the most important decision one makes in one's life is whom to marry because if one gets that wrong the future of the whole estate could be put in jeopardy. Obviously there are qualities you should look for in a wife and traits you should avoid. One of the prime characteristics to be wary of is if the girl comes from bad breeding stock and could bring bad blood into your family, resulting in a string of thick, idle spendthrifts, wastrels or gamblers, or maybe a mixture of the lot, or even – perish the thought – a queer, which will effectively mean the end of your line. So breeding is vital and parents and grandparents of potential spouses should be carefully examined for the sort of faults you do not want in either your wife or your children.

If you should avoid bad blood, then you should equally be attracted to evidence of thrift in your intended. To most house owners the sad truth is that economy is vital for survival. Extravagance in a wife is something few estates can long afford, especially if it is directed at completely useless things such as expensive designer clothes and hair-dressing. Wives who hanker after the bright lights of London should on all accounts be avoided as although the streets of London may be paved in gold, this holds only for those who run shops and restaurants and not for husbands of wives who enjoy walking up and down them with their girl friends on shopping safaris. It is true that in the past impoverished landowners, especially impoverished peers, have managed to attract brides with vast fortunes, which they have used to replenish the family coffers in exchange for bestowing on their beloved their ancient name and title. Never forget, though, that an extravagant heiress may, in the long run, prove a worse bet than a thrifty but dowryless girl.

Ideally, you should marry a girl used to country life and, even better, used to 'big house' life. If you do fall for a town-bred edition, it is wise to road-test her before proposing. So take her down to your mansion in winter, when it is cold and miserable, and see how she reacts to being greeted by a wet muddy dog while still in her smart London clothes. This generally is an infallible pointer to her suitability for the post of *châtelaine*. If she screams with horror, throws up her hands in disgust and later complains volubly about the dog sharing your bed, then you know that you have a problem and you ought to disentangle yourself.

The main thing is that the two of you must be compatible and have shared interests; not that you can ever be completely like-minded, as a woman's brain is radically different from a man's and her ideas of what is important can sometimes drive even the most patient husband to the outer limits of exasperation. I always found the most trying time in my marriage was when my wife was pregnant and spent endless, laborious hours trying to get the house spotless, only for me, with my dogs, to walk into the kitchen in muddy boots in search of a mid-morning cup of coffee. A partner's pregnancy is a very trying time for a man and it is hard always to be totally understanding but if you are more or less compatible, you may avoid a highly expensive and messy divorce some years later.

Once you are married and have moved into your big house, it is probable that your new spouse will put pressure on you to indulge in that most expensive of hobbies, interior decoration. Do not panic. Instead, agree with everything proposed but insist that you have the opportunity to view materials – wallpapers, paint samples, etc. – and play for time. Time is vital. Initially, the paintwork and carpets may have appeared to your wife a touch on the grubby side – hardly surprising, as they date from fifty years ago. But, given time, they will begin to exert their own peculiar charm on her and, if you can persuade your friends and, more importantly, some of hers, to say, 'Oh, you are so clever not to have destroyed the charm of the house by wallpapering everything!' or, 'I just love this faded look, I do think it's so romantic. Promise me you won't ruin my favourite room by painting it!' you are in with more than half a chance of keeping things as they were.

Your main enemies are your wife's friends, especially those who describe themselves as 'interior decorators'. As virtually every other girl one meets nowadays seems to be involved in interior decorating in some form, it is odds-on that your wife will have a number of these as friends. Try and keep them away from the house, if possible, for as long as you can. This will be difficult as they will want to come down and poke their noses around, and give 'free' advice in the hope of picking up some lucrative and prestigious business. The key, of course, is to get your wife pregnant and give her a large family as soon as possible, then she will be too busy looking after the children to think of decorating.

It cannot be overstressed that divorce is the one thing that should be avoided at all costs. It is very expensive, the lawyers charge the earth and are totally unscrupulous in acting 'in the best interests' of their client. Incidentally, whenever a lawyer says this, please remember he is acting in *his* best interests. Divorce is an extremely stressful process for both parties and when your lawyer says smoothly: 'Just leave it to me and let me take care of it . . . ' it is all too easy weakly to agree and let him get on with it – *don't*. Why? Because he will write a stiff letter to his opposite number, who will gleefully show it to his client, who will then go ballistic and authorize his or her lawyer to unleash the full barrage back. In all likelihood the two lawyers will later have a friendly chat on the telephone and agree they have got a really good little money earner here. Divorce lawyers feed on, and create, misery, rather in the manner of J. K. Rowling's famed Dementors in the Harry Potter books; they encourage their clients to exaggerate their needs and find it difficult to see that what they are doing, and how they are going about doing it, is, if not legally wrong then wholly morally wrong.

This brings us to the question of how to avoid divorce. The most obvious answer is to try, if you are a man, to keep your trouser fly buttoned up. A short amorous adventure could lose you several farms or a couple of old masters! If you just cannot help yourself and find the lure of sexual adventure just too tempting, then for goodness' sake select a partner who has as much to lose by divorce as you do and learn to be discreet. Don't, whatever you do, either write her silly soppy letters or keep any she has written to you, as you can guarantee that one day they will come back to haunt you. Personally, I would have thought there was a very good case for the Historic Houses Association (HHA) setting up a private 'escort' service for those of its members who find restraint in this department difficult.

It goes without saying that divorce is not good for your children, and if the most important person on an estate is the present owner then surely the second most important one is his heir. Once again, many people seem to forget this and neglect to bring up their children properly. Time spent rolling around on the floor with your planned successor is not wasted but is, you may be sure, a solid investment in the future. The Jesuits used to boast that a child given to them before the age of seven was theirs for life, and as you have yours from the start, there should not be a problem; sadly, there often is.

It is vital you ensure that your offspring, from the earliest age, take on board your prejudices. I well remember my governess explaining communism to me when I was about five years old. She did it quite brilliantly. 'If the communists ever ruled,' she said, 'then Panda [my number-one teddy bear] would be taken away from you and shared out among the local children.' Such simple explanations are easy for a child to understand and will make an indelible impression on them. For myself, when my children ask for an ice cream, I often say that 'sadly Daddy has got no money'. When they ask why, I answer: 'Because Mummy has gone and spent all the money on plants for the garden.' Mummy then gets a lot of stick but I hope that the message – that if you spend money on one thing you can't have another – lodges somewhere in their brains.

As they grow older, so they should be introduced to the problems of estate management, encouraged to go out with the gamekeeper, taken into the woods, as I was by my father, to prune trees and so forth – in other words, not allowed to fester in some centrally heated room playing infantile games on a computer.

When they leave school the question of careers raises its ugly head. This is a difficult one. What to do with your son and heir while he is waiting for you to die? If he is clever, bright and hard-working then you have, by luck (or good selection?), scooped the pool and he will probably have no problem getting into a good university and ending up with a well-paid job in the City. He may even – as a surprisingly large number of sons of landowners have in recent years – make a fortune. The difficulty is if he is not very bright and totally unfitted for any form of job. Even that old fall-back the armed forces has introduced a nasty two-day series of tests and interviews, which are rather hard – as I found out – to pass.

If he is less well endowed with brains, then probably he will still want to go to university, but it will be not quite such a select one, and the degree with which he eventually emerges will carry little weight in employment circles. In reality, spending three years at a second-rate university is a waste of his time and your money. For some six years, I had students as lodgers, and from closely observing them I was forced to the conclusion that all they learned was how to drink vast quantities of cheap red wine and fuck like rabbits. It is true that in their final year they began to put in a bit of desultory work, which allowed them to walk away with half-respectable degrees, but I was forced to the conclusion that a university degree is overrated. This is not my conclusion alone: many firms are beginning to question the wisdom of a graduate recruitment policy and are beginning to wonder if they might not be better off recruiting direct from schools. School leavers are also starting to think that there might be merit in taking a job with a good firm and working up the ladder rather than wasting three years getting pissed and laid.

As for the City, that too has changed; no longer can a well-placed telephone call assure your offspring of a job in some merchant bank. Strangely, as merchant banks and stockbrokers have become more meritocratic in their employment policy, so they have lost their independence, selling out to fat Americans and even grosser Germans and Swiss, who seem to think that Docklands is a good place to run an investment bank. The attractions of working for such people in such an area are limited until you remember the fat salary cheques on offer.

If all else fails there is still, thankfully, the Royal Agricultural College at Cirencester, where your heir can be punted off to learn the ropes of estate management prior to his taking over control from his agèd father. The concept is praiseworthy – although, as is so often the case with concepts, the results do not always live up to the expectations, for obvious reasons. On the whole, an heir rusticated to Cirencester is not over-blessed with brains, since it is the final solution of exasperated parents who have at last given up on any chance of getting him a 'proper' job. Parents of heirs to estates are no different from any other parents, and intensely dislike having to answer queries from 'concerned' friends which go something like this:

'And what is Johnny up to now?'
'Oh, well, he is at home at present; the job in the City didn't really suit him you know.'
'Oh, poor you, it must be such a worry for you both. Now Charlie's doing very well at Rumbolds and . . . '

After a while even the most long-suffering parent loses patience and gives the heir a one-way ticket to Cirencester. The danger of such a policy is that on his return he may actually want to manage the estate in a 'hands-on' fashion and, as this was supposed to be the reason you sent him on the course in the first place, it is rather hard to deny him the opportunity of showing what he can do.

Some, of course, succeed admirably, but others, convinced that their qualification gives them the equivalent of wings, try to fly and, after spending inordinate amounts of capital, fall to earth like Icarus with a resounding crash. This can be particularly irritating if you have made over a large chunk of the estate to him, in order to avoid inheritance tax, only to see him squander the lot on some stupid project. Because you have to live seven years after making over property to your son for it to be free of tax on your death, the property is sometimes made over too soon; many a parent gnashes his teeth as he helplessly watches his son squander his patrimony.

Since earliest times, landowners have had to find ways of protecting their estates from spendthrift heirs. Over the centuries various legal means have been tried and tested in order to ensure that estates were not dissipated or left away from the family. Most of these forms of 'entailment' fell down because common law does not recognize the creation of a settlement that seeks to secure property in perpetuity, and the law gradually evolved whereby any trust or settlement that tried to tie up an estate for longer than the 'lives of people in being and twenty-one years beyond' was void. Man's ingenuity being inexhaustible, however, a way was found round this problem by means of something called a 'strict settlement'. This, in essence, meant that a landowner agreed to settle his estates on his eldest son and on his, as yet unborn, eldest grandson. It was renewed on the marriage of his son, who, because he was then dependent on his father for allowances in order to live, readily agreed to enter into a renewal of the settlement – thus effectively perpetuating the entail.

These forms of entail were eroded by the passage of Lord Cairn's Settled Land Act of 1882, which allowed holders of entailed estates to sell upon notice to the trustees. While I suspect many landowners welcomed the measure when it was introduced, the long-term consequences were disastrous, as it allowed the Treasury vultures to assess such estates for death-duty purposes as freehold rather than only as a life interest. The many break-ups of estates since then owe much to this act and to the fact that modern landowners can, and do, use their estates as collateral when entering into business ventures. Previously, under the entailment system, an owner had only a life interest and therefore could not borrow money on the freehold value of the property. So if debts became an embarrass-ment, the creditors could not seize the estate and sell it. My own situation is a classic example. In 1863 my ancestor had accumulated debts of over £60,000 and had to flee the country to escape his creditors, but the creditors could not appropriate any assets to sell, apart from renewable ones such as timber. Thus estates could survive even the most profligate owners.

If your eldest son is a problem, what of the rest of your brood? You must pray – as I do constantly – that they are blessed with brains and ability and will be able to make their way in the world, otherwise the future is indeed bleak. It has to be said that the average landowner's breeding line does not afford grounds for optimism. It is unlikely that you yourself have ever held down a highly remunerative job, let alone any of your ancestors. If your other children turn out as hopeless as you and your father probably were then you have a decided problem. For a start your wife is likely to put pressure on you to make some sort of 'provision' for them. This is tempting, but should be resisted, as it is unlikely the estate is large enough to have big slices cut off it to subsidize the laziness and stupidity inherent in your younger offspring, especially if such traits have already manifested themselves in your eldest boy. At such time you should remember the rule: 'Give as you received.' In other words, if you were left the whole estate because you were the eldest and your sisters and brothers were left go hang, then it is not for you to decide that this time you ought to do something different. In short, you should abide by the rule of primogeniture; after all, if previous generations had not rigidly followed it, it is highly unlikely you would have any estate left in the first place. If, on the other hand, you have, by your own efforts, built up a substantial pile of cash, why then it is up to you how you dispose of it.

Finally, of course, and most importantly, the father must know when to go. Too many owners hang on for too long. It is sadly all too common to see an old couple rattling around in a great big house while their son, married now with three children, camps in a farmhouse somewhere on the estate. This is a recipe for strife. Big houses are designed for children and if the grandchildren are not brought up in it they will probably end up loathing the bloody place. For children, big houses are just fun: they can run riot there and amuse themselves for hours. They also have one enormous advantage over adults: they do not feel the cold.

Not only will the children enjoy the big house, your son and daughter-in-law are probably longing to get their hands on it. If you do decide to move out, you must raise no objection when panelling you painted white, at great expense, is stripped and returned to its bare wood; Victorian decorative schemes, considered the height of vulgarity in the 1950s and 1960s and papered over to universal acclaim, are once again exposed to the light of day, and so on. Remember this is but a short episode in the history of the house and daughters-in-law have been behaving thus for centuries. If you deny your son and his wife their opportunity now, they will spend their money and time on doing up the farmhouse, so when the moment does come for them to move into the big house they will quite possibly turn round and say, 'No, thanks, we are quite happy where we are.'

Why do so many owners selfishly refuse to move out of their houses and deny their grandchildren the joys of growing up in one? I myself cannot wait to hand the front-door keys over to my eldest son and retire to a 'sunset home' somewhere on the estate, where I can experience the joys of modern convenience living without worrying about the cost.

CHAPTER 16

The Professionals

'. . . let's kill all the lawyers.'

WILLIAM SHAKESPEARE (1564–1616)

Henry VI, Part 2

Running an estate has always been a intricate business and it is becoming more and more so. It is therefore hardly surprising that professional advisers have come to feature prominently in the lives of most owners. Land management and taxation planning have become a far more complex business of late and thus the professional in his various guises plays a more prominent and more expensive role than his predecessor of, say, a century ago. As every pound spent on a professional is a pound that would be far better off in your own pocket, it is important to ensure that you get both the best and the cheapest professional advice. Oddly, this can often be achieved.

Who are these professionals and how do they fit into the picture? The short answer is that they are symbiotic parasites: we need them and they need us. They are the solicitors, accountants and land agents without whom no estate could function, and who, like anyone else, need feeding and clothing. As in the natural world, however, there are different types of parasite. Some are beneficial to the species; others can destroy it. The fatter the parasite the more it needs to feed, and in country-estate terms there are some pretty fat parasites out there.

Most, perhaps inevitably, are based in London. Estate owners are, after all, no different from ordinary mankind and are as divided into wise and foolish virgins as any other group of people. Some are impressed by deep-pile carpets, swanky West End offices, smooth young men and portly partners. Perhaps it is fear that causes owners to go through the portals of such establishments, fear of losing out because one has not got the *best* advice. This reason is clearly not without merit; more estates have been killed by bad professional advice than by any other single factor. Agricultural depressions, confiscatory taxation, even wayward offspring – all might have been coped with, but bad, even in some cases, dishonest, professional advice has been a killer. It is certainly the case that the vast majority of estates, right up to the late 1960s and early 1970s, were run and managed by local firms of solicitors, and many of these firms proved themselves grossly incompetent, if not actually dishonest – hence, presumably, the rush by so many landowners into the grasping, podgy hands of rapacious London lawyers.

Whatever the reason for changing to top London firms, it is certainly not economy. For as your feet sink into the carpet and the pretty secretary ushers you into a grandiose office for a quiet chat with the senior partner, prior to a light designer lunch, it is worth remembering who is paying for all this: you are!

Like leeches they cling on to your account, sucking the lifeblood from your still living body in the form of indecently fat fees, and incredibly, people happily pay up! This is staggering – especially as the rapacity of lawyers is hardly a new phenomenon. Writing in the late eighteenth century, a landowner in Lancashire, Nicholas Blundell, advised his heir 'to show diligence in taking some care of your own concerns, for when concerns of the moment are left to stewards and attorneys, they grow rich by their master's poverty'.

If the thought of giving so much of your limited funds to these London-based creatures makes you angry, you can always employ local firms of solicitors, accountants and land agents, pay them reasonable fees and enjoy a good working relationship with people who have your best interests at heart. Local firms today are a different breed from those that existed in the pre-war and immediate post-war period; now you are likely to find standards as high among the professionals in your county town as in the grandest London firm. And, after all, if there is a particularly difficult tax or legal problem, you can always wander up to London and pay for top advice, but it is fairly stupid to pay serious money for advice and management from London all the time.

Perhaps the worst form of professional parasites are the 'professional trustee' and the professional executors. Do you hate your heir? Then put his inheritance into a trust managed by London-based trustees. Did your father hate you or was he just plain thick? It has got to be one or other of these reasons, otherwise he would not have saddled the estate with these pariahs. These people have nothing whatever to recommend them; they are not clever, they probably do not even buy you a decent lunch, but they sure know how to type out the fee bills.

Here are some tips for dealing with these dregs of humanity if you are unfortunate enough to be afflicted with them. First, challenge their bills and demand to see all past bills going back, say, six years. I guarantee that if you take this line and make sufficient fuss you will recover around ten per cent, or more, of fees paid over the period. Second, buy a basic law book and examine in minute detail how they have managed your affairs. You never know, you may be able to sue them for negligence. Third, buy yourself one of those chess clocks, the ones that start ticking only when you press the button and then stop when you press it again – never attend a meeting without one. Place it ostentatiously on the desk in front of your trustees and start it only when they stop exchanging pleasantries.

In other words, attack. And don't feel bad about hurting the feelings of that charming old gentleman across the desk – remember he's only in it for the money and has been ripping you and your family off for years. Sadly, it is virtually impossible to sack these bloodsuckers, and why should they resign from a nice little earner? The scenario gets worse if, as well as being your trustees, they are also executors of your father's will, because they will try to charge you fees based, not on the time required to wind the estate up, but on a percentage of its value. If the estate was comparatively small, the same solicitor would charge on an hourly rate. This is a scandalous case of 'having your cake and eating it'. Regardless of the amount of work carried out the executors are guaranteed a fat fee and – in addition – have the gall to charge extra fees for their time!

Your aim should be to keep your professional fees to an absolute minimum, so when you do have to consult expensive accountants or lawyers for goodness' sake have clear questions and clear aims. Avoid wishy-washy questions such as 'How do I save some tax?' Instead, say, 'If I do X will that save tax?' The first question could lead to hours of talk and paperwork, while the latter should be answered in a very short time. It may be argued that as a humble landowner you probably will not know the right question to ask in first place. This is a fair point, but if you are genuinely interested in running your estate and have a modicum of brainpower then you will be a member of such august and important bodies as the Historic Houses Association, the Country Land and Business Association and the Forestry and Timber Association, all of whom actually dish out a lot of good advice free of charge and, more importantly, run seminars and publish leaflets and magazines that contain an enormous amount of relevant material. Take advantage of what is on offer free of charge and you will be surprised how, over the years, your knowledge base expands, until you are pretty hot on most topics. Also there are your fellow landowners, all of whom are in the same boat as yourself and all of whom are only too ready to give you the benefit of their experience and advice. In other words, as an owner you are not alone in a hostile country, with no option but to turn to the fattest and most expensive lawyers in the land; rather, you are surrounded by friends, all of whom will do their utmost to help you avoid falling into said fat lawyers' clutches.

Be all this as it may, trustees are an integral feature of most estates, so if one discards the professionals to whom does one turn to fill this role? The obvious answer is: friends who have had similar problems, who have a knowledge of running estates and are happy to take on the job out of their friendship for you and their love of the estate. If you are appointing trustees for your son, then try and find people who are between your own age and his and, most importantly, have the same aims and ambitions for the estate as you have so that, in the event of your untimely death, they will ensure that these aims continue to be carried out.

If you are saddled with professional trustees and want to get rid of them, it is probably going to cost you money. They are not going to resign meekly from a nice little earner that brings them in regular fat fees, with little work, without a bribe. One estate owner I know was forced to pay his professional trustees £25,000 each to resign.

Moving on from the parasites, we encounter another group of professionals: the vultures. They hang about, eyeing you as you crawl over the desert trying desperately to survive long enough for the agèd relation to drop off his or her perch and leave you the long-hoped-for legacy that will solve your financial problems. These vultures, unlike the real birds, are on the whole charming and friendly people who do you no harm and can normally be relied on to give you lots of good lunches. Prime examples of this species are the large auction houses. It is their job to know as much about you and your current finances as possible, so when Great Aunt Agatha finally does hop the twig, leaving her entire worldly goods to the cats' home, they are there with soothing words and a damp flannel to dab your brow, all geared up to sell your pictures for you. There is the oft-told tale of how some years ago the chairmen of Sotheby's and Christie's were together at the funeral of a noted collector when suddenly the chairman of Christie's noticed that his opposite number, Peter Wilson of Sotheby's, had slipped away; he was already in the house cataloguing the collection for auction!

It is axiomatic in landowning circles that almost the first action of an heir when he takes possession of his inheritance is to sack the entire collection of his father's professional advisers and start again. This happens particularly when Daddy has hung on to the reins of power for rather too long and the heir has had to sit on the sidelines gnashing his teeth in fury as he witnesses the professionals racking up the fee bills. Only the other day a friend of mine innocently asked me if I was familiar with the term 'notional rents'. I cudgelled my brain but could not think what on earth they were and had to ask for an explanation. He was equally puzzled by my ignorance as he was under the impression that they were common to all estates that paid their firm of agents on a percentage of the rental income. It appears, for those of you still wondering, that notional rents are assessed by some agents on houses which are part of the estate but for which, for some reason, no rent is charged, e.g. those housing estate pensioners or employees. The agent will argue that, as he is responsible for managing the property, he ought to receive a fee for the work, which sounds fair on the face of it, although most landowners would regard this as rather hot practice. In this particular case it is jam today but not jam tomorrow for one unscrupulous firm: as when my friend finally takes over they will get their marching orders extremely quickly.

Observing the antics of many firms, one is forced to conclude that 'jam today' is their priority. As an owner gets older he will delegate more and more to these firms and become more and more out of touch with reality. Then it is that the professional comes into his own and makes hay, while the heir can do little but writhe in frustration, vowing vengeance when the time comes for the reins of power to fall into his hands.

Some landowners, especially those who have completed the celebrated course at Cirencester, feel that they are eminently qualified to act as agents on their own estates, thereby saving the fees. Personally, I would advise against this, as it will mean dealing directly with your tenants – people whom you have probably grown up with, perhaps even attended the village school with in early childhood – and arguing with them about rents, repairs and suchlike, i.e. about money, will not be easy. Most gentlemen are not good at negotiations when money is at stake, especially when the result of success will be to remove cash from tenants' pockets and put it into their own. Even people who are as hard as steel and brilliantly successful in negotiations on behalf of third parties quite often find that they are routinely taken to the cleaners when it comes to dealing on their own account.

On balance, few landowners will be worse off for paying an agent to handle the vast majority of estate negotiations, and most will be considerably richer. Among the advantages is the obvious one: an agent acting for you – or, even better, for your trustees – can never be put in a corner by a tenant. He can always use the get-out option of having to 'discuss this with his principal'. It is *de rigueur*, in whatever negotiations you are engaged upon, to have such an option open to you at all times.

Of course professionals come in numerous guises and are not just lawyers, accountants and land agents. Many of us use 'professionals' such as stockbrokers, economists, property experts and bankers in another way altogether: as fortune tellers. We believe that, because they are so closely involved in their business, they must have an inside track into how it is going to develop. Strangely the opposite is normally the case. Virtually no 'insider' foresaw the near collapse of the Lloyd's insurance market, even though, in retrospect, the reasons for its financial problems were so glaringly obvious that a lot of people thought fraud had to be involved. Neither did anyone in the property market foresee the 1988 property crash or, if they did, not before it was far too late to get out. As for the telecommunications/Internet share boom, once again, with the odd honourable exception, few among the highly paid bankers, analysts, fund managers and other assorted experts called the market right. With so many examples of stupidity by highly paid 'experts' to chose from, it is invidious to single out an individual case, but I cannot resist highlighting the stupidity of the board of Barclays Bank in the mid-1980s who had a rights issue and raised £900 million which they promptly lent to the Reichman brothers to fund the development of Canary Wharf. Soon afterwards Canary Wharf went bust and Barclays Bank's money went with it.

In other words, 'experts' or 'professionals' are often fatally flawed when looking at their own markets. Their track record is so universally appalling that it is one of the great mysteries of the world why they continue to be able to command such large sums of money from gullible customers and from employers. Personally, I consider one of the primary reasons for their failures is that they know too much about their specialist subjects and thus cannot see the broad picture, as their vision is so clouded with details and minutiae. Whatever the reason, experience teaches us that we should never trust a professional or an expert, and never ever commit our precious capital to projects whose profitability is dependent on a professional's opinion – *pace* all those poor saps who built golf courses in their parks or on their farms back in the 1980s on the say so of experts. Just remember that it is your money and their advice. When your money goes west, where do you think your adviser will be?

CHAPTER 17

Field Sports

' 'Unting is . . . the sport of kings, the image of war without
its guilt, and only five-and-twenty per cent of its danger.'
ROBERT SMITH SURTEES (1805–64)
Handley Cross, 1843

It is impossible to write a book about the countryside of the United
Kingdom without devoting at least a chapter to field sports. To understand how positive have been the effects of field sports on the country
over recent centuries it is necessary to ask what the countryside would
look like today if landowners had not so often loved to hunt, shoot and
fish. How would the appearance of rural England differ if we had
behaved in the manner of effete continental aristocrats and sponsored
ballets and operas instead of spending our money riding to hounds,
shooting and fishing? There is no doubt the landscape and wildlife of
the countryside would be very different.

For a start it is doubtful if the fox would have survived as part of our
native fauna without the support of the hunt. Back in the nineteenth
century, there was such a dearth of foxes that they were imported from
France and Germany and sold in Leadenhall Market, for around fifteen
shillings a head! The reason for the shortage had little to do with the
numbers being killed by hunts, but far more to do with the fact that
most people in the country kept poultry, and foxes are, to say the least,
partial to chickens, geese and ducks. Such was the virulence of the
campaign waged against foxes – many parishes offering a bounty on the
head of any fox brought in dead – that they would certainly have been

eradicated from great swathes of the United Kingdom but for the sudden popularity of hunting.

At the same time, those who hunted realized the necessity of planting copses and woods in which foxes could make their earths, so hunting not only saved the fox from possible extinction but also helped shape the English landscape. Likewise, red deer on Exmoor were on the verge of extinction and were saved only by the advent of stag hunting.

As with hunting, so with shooting. The red grouse has done more to protect the heather-clad hills of Scotland, and parts of England and Wales, from the ravages of overstocking with sheep or planting inappropriately with trees, than any government-sponsored initiative – and at no cost to the taxpayer. The great enthusiasm for pheasant shooting in the nineteenth century caused many woods to be planted. As early as 1837, Lawrence Rawstrone could write in his book *Gamonia*: 'There has risen of late years a great rage for planting, not only from that spirit of improvement which has displayed itself in adorning the mansions of the rich, but from the introduction of *battues*, which require extensive preserves and numerous coverts.' The author then goes on to deplore the modern (1837) desire for big bags, giving as an example: 'It is a thing scarcely to be credited by our forefathers that two shots should kill in one day three hundred and fifty pheasants, which was done a few years ago at Comme in Worcestershire.'

It is also doubtful in the extreme if our rivers would have survived in anything like their present-day form without the constant vigilance of fishermen, or indeed if the Atlantic salmon would have survived at all. Back in 1896 our rivers were in an appalling state, a mixture of uncontrolled commercial netting and industrial pollution having wrought havoc. The Tyne was virtually empty of fish, having been plundered by netsmen to the tune of over a hundred and twenty thousand fish a year until only twenty years previously. Everywhere in England and Wales the story was same: disaster threatened. That it was averted, the decline in salmon numbers reversed and rivers restored to health, was principally the result of pressure put on the authorities by the riparian community. It is to them we owe the fact that we can still wander down to the banks of so many rivers humming to ourselves the old refrain:

> 'Oh! Grant that I may catch a fish
> So big that even I,
> In speaking of it afterwards
> Shall have no cause to lie.'

Today the salmon is once more threatened, and once again the leading spirits behind the attempts to safeguard it are fishermen; not only fishermen from these shores, either, for the man who has probably done more than any other to safeguard the future of the salmon is Orri Vigfusson, who has led a highly successful campaign to buy off the sea-fishing fleets which were plundering salmon from their feeding grounds. It is true that there is a government body – the National Environment Agency – which has notional responsibility for the health of the nation's rivers, but no fisherman rates them highly or expects much from them. Owners and fishermen everywhere know that their rivers will flourish or fade away solely by their own efforts or lack of them. Evidence of this is a movement by interested parties to form associations dedicated to restoring single-river systems.

And so it goes on. A sportsman by definition does not want to eliminate his quarry but to harvest the surplus. He wants to improve its habitat so it can breed more effectively, and as what is good for game birds is also good for a large number of other species, they too benefit.

Of course, many people abhor all field sports because they think they are cruel. Indeed, the revered National Trust has recently published a lengthy scientific report supporting allegations that stag hunting is traumatic for the quarry. It has therefore banned the practice on its land on Exmoor and in the Quantocks, in defiance of the stated wishes of Sir Richard Acland, the donor of the majority of its Exmoor estate. At the risk of repeating myself, I suggest the National Trust should change its name. If I trust someone, I depend on them to keep their word, without bothering with all the tedious legal niceties that fill our legal friends' pockets at little or no benefit to anyone else. Sadly, that is what Sir

Richard did – he had faith in the organization. Be warned! From now on, remember: you cannot trust the National Trust.

The professor who wrote the above-mentioned report forgot – if he ever knew – that fear in animals translates itself into 'taint' in the meat, which effectively makes it inedible. Stags that are hunted are shot by the huntsman – not torn to pieces by hounds, as mythology has it – and are later sold for venison, which is eminently edible. If, on the other hand, one comes across a deer which has been caught in a barbed-wire fence for many hours and has struggled in vain to free itself, and one shoots it and tries to eat the flesh, it is indeed inedible.

Field sports, especially hunting, are often criticized for the ritualistic approach to the killing of the prey; yet little is said or done about the nauseating ritual killing of sheep and goats by halal and kosher butchers on behalf of Muslim and Jewish communities respectively. I wonder why not. The answer, according to Ben Bradshaw, the current (2004) minister responsible for animal welfare when questioned on this very point, was that to ban religious slaughter would have 'discriminated against religious groups' and that by not banning them he was 'acting out of respect for the religious freedoms and fundamental beliefs of people in this country'.

One man, when he read what Bradshaw had to say, wondered whether hunting with hounds and dogs was not – in parts of the country at least – tantamount to a religion. Rod Brammer, a well-known shooting instructor on Exmoor, conceived the idea of, and has launched, the religion of St Hubert. Broadly, the adherents to the religion believe hunting is fundamental to the exercising of their beliefs and that any attempt to stop them hunting is therefore a breach of their fundamental rights. Over to you, Mr Bradshaw. If a hunting ban is ever brought in, I anticipate much learned debate over what constitutes a religion. Why, though, are so many people in Britain passionately 'anti-hunting'? I have a theory that it all goes back to the Norman Conquest and that somewhere, deep within the psyche of the English, is a memory of mailed and mounted Norman knights arriving in the villages and towns across the length and breath of England dispossessing Saxon landlords, and later ruthlessly putting down any rebellions by the native inhabitants. If I am right, the desire to ban fox hunting is just a manifestation of a subconscious hatred of men and women on horses going back all the way to the beginning of modern English history in 1066.

Finally, it is worth remembering that many of those who are against field sports unwittingly harbour the cruellest killer of all: the domestic cat. It is estimated that the cat population of the UK kills annually some eighty-two million birds! And cats do not just kill, they enjoy playing with their prey and teasing it before they kill it. Anyone who has witnessed a cat doing this will realize that for sheer cruelty the cat has no equal, yet, as far as I know, no one – not the RSPCA, nor the RSPB nor the National Trust, let alone the League Against Cruel Sports – has ever suggested that all domestic cats should be destroyed. Why? A silly question because we all know the answer: a large number of their supporters own cats. It is the hypocrisy of groups such as these that annoys countrymen so much.

This brings us back to shooting and its beneficial effect on wildlife and the environment. I seem to hear mounting cries from the RSPB brigade about keepers persecuting anything with a hooked beak. This was certainly true of old-style keepering. But I wonder if the RSPB's cries are not a little like the pot calling the kettle black, for while old-fashioned keepers may have favoured game birds over hawks, now the RSPB favours hawks over all other species of bird. In short, it carries out what seems to me to be a fascist policy of refusing to admit that hawks need, like any predator, to be controlled. I sometimes wonder how a body can continue to call itself the Royal Society for the Protection of Birds when many of the species it nurtures live by killing – often rather gruesomely – other birds! How would you like to be plucked alive?

Actually, of course, the RSPB does support the culling of predators – but only if they do *not* have hooked beaks. Thus it will, in some of its reserves, sanction the killing of magpies and crows. But if you allow magpies and crows to be controlled, why not sparrowhawks, hen harriers and the like? The RSPB policy is short on logic and long on emotion and public relations.

Even when the RSPB is provided with independent scientific evidence, showing the damage done by an uncontrolled raptor population, it still refuses to admit that there may be a case for allowing the control of hawks. For five years researchers from the Game Conservancy Trust and the Institute of Terrestrial Ecology (part of the National Environment Research Council) carried out a detailed study of the effect of hen harriers on a grouse moor belonging to the Duke of Buccleuch. Their report was published in 1997.

The findings were damning. Over the period of the study, the number of hen harriers on the moor increased from two to fourteen breeding females and the number of breeding female peregrines from three to six. During the last two years of the study, when bird-of-prey numbers were at their peak, hawks killed about thirty per cent of overwintering grouse and a further thirty per cent the potential breeding stock in the spring, and then finished off by killing around thirty-seven per cent of the grouse chicks. The result was that a moor, which in the past could produce – in a good year – annual bags of around two thousand brace, was reduced to recording a bag of only a hundred brace by 1996.

One of the great ironies of the debate over hen harriers – which the RSPB refuses to recognize – is that hen harriers, being ground-nesting birds, benefit from keepered moors. Hen harriers can, in effect, flourish at such densities as they achieved on the Langholm Moor only because the gamekeepers control potential nest predators, such as foxes. In other words, the logical long-term effect of the RSPB's refusal to contemplate any form of control of hen harriers was that the harrier population would itself decline! This has now happened. Hen harrier numbers have collapsed to the same level they were at before the experiment started, i.e. two breeding pairs, but now, in 2004, there are hardly any grouse on the moor, no keepers employed on the hill, no proper burning of heather being carried out, no part-time jobs as beaters, pickers-up and loaders for the locals during the shooting season, and no boost to the finances of the local hotel industry caused by teams of guns, with money to burn, staying for the sport. And there are no more hen harriers either!

Field sports do not just preserve the aesthetic appearance of the landscape, nor do they just encourage landowners to maintain habitats of use to many other species besides game birds and foxes. Field sports are also a major economic powerhouse within the country. Estate owners have discovered in recent years that shooting is now 'chic' with the new rich in the cities and also with rich overseas visitors, who flock to the United Kingdom to enjoy the finest driven-game shooting in the world. This engine of economic demand for field sports has encouraged many landowners to plant new woods, conserve their heather-clad hills and, in parts of eastern England in particular, to farm in a more 'environmentally friendly' way, with the aim of helping game birds to breed successfully in the wild.

It is nevertheless more difficult than people would have you believe to make good money out of shooting. There are perhaps two ways of doing it. The first is obvious. If you have a really premier-division shoot, let it for a large sum of money and perhaps keep a couple of days back for your own enjoyment. The second is, if you have a big house, put up the guns and their spouses or girlfriends at anything between £150 to £250 a night per head (£500 per head per night if you can provide really top-class service and bedrooms) and you should be able to make a significant profit; as you look round the table at dinner, you will find it gives you a warm feeling to count heads and work out the amount of lolly coming your way on the morrow. You may even, with luck, have some extremely amusing and interesting people staying with you.

It is not necessary to tart up the house like some nauseating hotel, but you will get paid a lot more if you do. Remember, your guests are enjoying a unique experience for them – staying in the proverbial stately home – so don't panic if the hot-water system blows up or some other unforeseen disaster occurs, it is all part of the 'unique country-house experience'; relax and let your guests enjoy the 'authentic' atmosphere. I once had a black labrador who liked to climb on the dining-room table and eat off people's plates as he wandered down it. My American guests were ecstatic. It has to be said their English hosts, from the City, did not, initially, see the joke in the same light, but they joined in the laughter when they realized the VIPs appreciated my dog's little ways.

When selling shooting you should not be over-concerned about the numbers your guns shoot; it is far more important that they fire a large number of cartridges. Many people will, when taking a day's shooting, say they want a 'two-hundred-bird' day, but they do not – or if they do, certainly should not – mean it. What they should mean is that they want the opportunity to shoot two hundred birds, which is something different. You are testing your skill against theirs – your ability to show high, testing pheasants, theirs to shoot them. To avoid arguments ensure that you count the cartridges fired and, at the end of the day, if they have fired eight hundred cartridges, but only shot a hundred pheasants, then they are bloody awful shots but still pay for two hundred birds.

Not every shoot is run for commercial parties of guns; some are managed as syndicates and some are still kept for the owner's own private enjoyment – and some are a mixture of syndicate, private and commercial.

The Carnarvon Report of 1992 estimated that shooting and stalking in the UK was now producing a direct expenditure of over £300 million and directly employing around 28,000 people! This is big business. To give you an idea how big, the entire UK offshore fishing fleet turns over only around £500 million a year. But as well as direct expenditure there is the indirect aspect. All those rich Americans who travel over to the UK to shoot tend to fly first-class – often on British Airways – stay a few nights in London at a luxury hotel, kit themselves out from an expensive London gunmaker, and so on. The Carnarvon Report put the total value of this indirect expenditure at a further £258 million, in respect of shooting, making the entire business worth over £550 million to the UK economy. Indeed, in parts of the country it is now a major contributor to the local economy, providing seasonal employment for beaters and pickers-up, as well as enabling hotels and pubs, which in the past might have closed for the winter, to be overwhelmed with moneyed guests. That report is now some fourteen years old and in that time shooting has continued to expand rapidly. I would not be surprised today to find that shooting was worth over £700 million a year.

Incidentally, the report put estimated direct expenditure on hunting at another £150 million, with a further £137 million in indirect expenditure; the figures for fishing were even larger, at £958 million and £788 million respectively, giving a grand total for the amount of direct and indirect expenditure on all field sports of £1.83 billion per annum in 1992.

The thinking behind the production of the report was that most people had not made the connection between field sports and economic activity in depressed rural areas. This aim of the report was achieved and now there is an authoritative source of information to show politicians of all parties just how important, economically, field sports are. It was a pity the work had not been done fifty years earlier. It is almost too depressing to think of the amount of economic damage, especially to the uplands of Scotland, done by ill-thought-out government-sponsored, and grant-aided, so-called 'economic' developments, which have, in the final analysis, produced only a tenth of the once promised employment opportunities and the like, but which have destroyed the one sure-fire economically successful business in the uplands: field sports. So we are confronted by dark alien plantations of Sitka spruce, covering great swathes of Scotland and destroying what could have been first-class and valuable driven grouse shooting moors, but which are now valueless industrial timber plantations. Not only, though, have those plantations destroyed the grouse shooting on the land they occupy, but by providing a haven and breeding ground for every sort of vermin they have effectively and dramatically reduced the grouse-shooting potential of moors for many miles around them. Another classic example of misplaced development was the construction of salmon farms on virtually every suitable site on the west coast of Scotland. The long-term financial viability of these farms is frankly dubious, but the damage they have done to the sea trout runs on the river systems of the west coast is beyond dispute. Rivers, which were once prolific, are now empty, and hotels once filled with anglers are likewise empty. The reason for the collapse of the sea trout runs appears to be that, in nature, the sea trout is a brown trout which, finding not much to eat in its home river, migrates to the estuaries and the sea to feed. Sadly, today when it looks for food in the sea lochs of Scotland, it finds the salmon farms, and round the salmon cages lurk vast quantities of the dreaded sea lice. These lice are kept at bay by the salmon farmers by chemical weaponry, but when an unsuspecting sea trout hoves into view they latch on to it with predictable and gruesome results. There is an argument that salmon farms, by driving down the price of salmon to the consumer, have played a vital role in saving the Atlantic salmon, but for salmon farming there was a real danger that the salmon was entering into a vicious price spiral that might destroy it. The rarer it became, the higher the price it fetched on the fishmonger's slab, the more worthwhile it was to poach or trawl for. Salmon farming thus helped to break this 'vicious circle' and destroyed much of the 'economic' incentive to poach and net the rivers.

Inevitably, the large amounts of money now churning through the field-sports business has led to some practices creeping in that are liable to put all field sports at risk. Put-and-take fishing has been with us for a long time, but in recent years some shoots have begun to practise what is virtually put-and-take shooting. Some – and it must be stressed that it is only *some* and that these are a comparatively small number of the total number of organized shoots in the country – are undoubtedly 'overdoing it'. Putting down too many birds on too small an acreage and shooting the same drives too often – in some cases five times or more a week – are unacceptable practices and are rightly condemned by the vast majority of shooting people. Nevertheless, they threaten the entire sport; the short-term greed of some may yet bring the whole driven-shooting sport into disrepute and lead to calls for legislation to control it. Such practices are not only foolish from the point of view of the long-term public image of shooting, but are bad management, pure and simple. Putting down too many birds of any variety on too small an area brings with it high risks of disease, liable to wipe out large numbers of birds, and leads to the commercial-shoot operator having to cancel days and lose large sums of money.

Driven-game shooting as a commercial exercise is, contrary to uninformed opinion, not a no-risk business but a high-risk one. A big commercial shoot might sell fifty or sixty days' shooting a year and turn over around £750,000 or more per annum, but it will make money only if it sells all its days. Shooting is a fixed-cost business. Nearly all the costs of running a shoot are incurred before the shooting season begins, and it is only after he has sold sufficient days to cover the fixed costs that an operator can start making money. In other words, a shoot selling fifty days' shooting producing, say, an average bag of three hundred birds, would have to sell at least thirty-five days to break even and starts making serious money only once it had sold more than forty days. A sudden downturn in the economy, leading to cancellations from people who thought they were rich in the spring and have found in the autumn, to their distress, that they are poor (as happened in the early 1990s), can lead to major losses. Similarly, outbreaks of disease in stock can have a disastrous impact on the finances of a shoot. The risk of this happening has increased dramatically in recent years with the banning of the drug Emtryl which, when mixed with game feed, had provided reared birds with protection against two parasitic diseases called hexamita and trichomonas which, if they infect birds, can cause death on the scale of a plague.

So how profitable for the operator is the management of a commercial shoot? For amusement's sake I have put together a draft budget for a medium-sized commercial operation in 2004. Each and every shoot is run differently, but the figures in the table will give you an idea of the risks and rewards of running such an operation and, as you can see, the rewards are marginal but the risks, in my view, are considerable. In this case as the operator is a tenant rather than the owner, so his rental charge is a significant part of his budget, and many would advise the 'idle landowner' to run the operation himself and thus take the extra £30,000 profit for himself. Many would so advise, but I would not.

Looking at the 'budget' an observer may wonder what happens to all the birds you put down which are not shot. In our example, of the 30,000 poults released only 12,000 are actually shot – where, then, are the other 18,000? Unsurprisingly, this has always been a hot topic round shoot operators' dining-room tables, but the Game Conservancy has carried out some research and come up with the answers which are, in short, that twenty-six per cent of the birds you release have either died of disease or been eaten by vermin before shooting even begins. These figures should galvanize shoot owners and their keepers into still greater efforts to reduce vermin predation, as just a small reduction in 'early deaths' would have a dramatic effect on shoot economics.

Cause of death	Percentage
Early pen death	3.5
Predator scavenged before shooting begins	23.0
Shot within the boundaries of the estate	30.5
Shot off the estate by neighbours	7.0
Other deaths	7.0
Survived the shooting season	16.0

Running a shoot is one of the most stressful jobs around. There is something peculiarly tiring about being cheerful and welcoming to a party of unknown guns, who have just paid you a very large sum of money for an enjoyable and productive day's shooting. Not only is keeping up the chat and a fixed smile tiring but at the back of your mind is the fear that 'the day will not go right'. All sorts of questions whirl around in the recesses of your mind as you move off for the first drive. Will the weather hold? Will the birds fly? Can the guns shoot? Are they safe? And so on. Then you get to the first stand and wait nervously to see what happens. Fretting as a couple of cracking birds float over the line un-shot at. Wondering where all the bloody birds have got to. Silently cursing the paying guns' inability to load their guns faster when the birds finally do come thick and fast not to mention their inability to hit much. Lead in the air is what you want, especially if you are charging on

Running the Numbers on a Commercial Shoot

OUTGOINGS

Variable costs – day rate	*Total costs*
30,000 poults at £3 per head	£90,000
170 tons of wheat delivered at £100 per ton	£17,000
Breeder pellets at 60p per bird	£18,000
Game crop – say twenty acres at a cost of £250 per acre, includes allowance for 'loss of profit' on normal crop	£5,000
Rent for 4,000 acres of ground at £15 per acre	£60,000
Rent for keeper's cottage	£8,000
Head keeper's wages	£18,000
Wages/cost of two underkeepers/trainees	£20,000
Part-time 'shoot manager'	£10,000
Professional fees and insurance	£5,000
Annual maintenance cost of repairing tracks/pens, etc.	£5,000
Vehicle depreciation – 2 quad bikes, 1 Subaru pick-up and 1 Land Rover	£5,000
Running costs of vehicles	£5,000
Twelve beaters at £20 each for forty days: £240 per day for 40 days	£9,600
Eight pickers-up at £25 per head per day: £200 per day for 40 days	£8,000
Lunch/tea for average party of ten at £25 per head per day: £250 per day for forty days	£10,000
TOTAL ANNUAL COSTS	£293,600

INCOME

Forty days' shooting – average bag 300 birds – giving a net revenue after VAT and agent's commission of £27 per bird: £8,100	£324,000
Game sales at 50p per bird: £150	£6,000
TOTAL ANNUAL INCOME	£330,000
TOTAL ANNUAL COSTS	£293,600
TOTAL PROFIT (LOSS)	£36,400

a 'per-cartridge' basis. Then there is lunch. Now you seriously earn your money, especially if they are all the silent type. It is mind-boggling how utterly lacking in any social graces so many of the mega-rich are. As often as not, these captains of the investment banking world and industry seem almost mentally retarded, socially speaking, which makes for tough work at lunch. Often have I sat down and realized that no one is speaking! If it makes for tough work at lunch, it makes for an even tougher dinner if you are having them to stay as well. The money may be good (£5,000 a night if you can offer five-star accommodation for a party of eight guns and their wives or mistresses), but you do earn it in spades.

Shooting is now on a roll. Once the pastime of country gentlemen, it is now the pursuit of choice of the new rich bankers and businessmen, both English and foreign, and nowhere has the sport of driven shooting been so developed as in the UK. So the future should look good, but there are some small clouds on the horizon. Foreign competition is starting to make inroads into the market and the foreigners are not as hidebound as we are, rightly, in the UK, where most shoots try to do the job correctly according to the code of conduct set out by organizations like the Game Conservancy and BASC. Spain has emerged as a serious competitor, producing superbly managed partridge shooting in beautiful surroundings at competitive prices. Further east, other former Eastern bloc countries are beginning to offer driven-game shooting, so we in the UK must not behave like the British car industry in the 1950s and 1960s and become arrogant and complacent, otherwise shooting here could go into recession with all that would mean for the rural economy.

CHAPTER 18

The Church

Curates, long dust, will come and go
On lissom, clerical, printless toe;
And oft between the boughs is seen
The sly shade of a Rural Dean.

RUPERT BROOKE (1887–1915)
'The Old Vicarage, Grantchester', 1912

It is a lucky rural church today that boasts a curate to look after its
parishioners' spiritual needs. It is only some ninety years since those lines
were written, but in that short timespan the Church of England has
changed as much as any other of the pillars of the countryside.

English rural parish churches are among the greatest glories of the
countryside and can truly be said to be part of our National Heritage.
Every village boasts one; some are relatively humble affairs, but others are
so grand as to be more like cathedrals. The great majority of medieval
churches, however, fall somewhere between these two extremes.

The grandeur or otherwise of a medieval church often bears witness to
the riches, or lack of them, of the surrounding district during the great
periods of church building, while their interiors will demonstrate
whether or not the local 'great family' was sufficiently rich to commission
grandiose monuments to their departed ancestors. It is one of the joys
of the English parish church that sometimes a comparatively humble
edifice can boast a rich interior and vice versa. Sadly, of course, most
of our churches suffered from three traumatic events: the desecration
unleashed by the enforcement of the reformed religion during Edward

VI's reign; the triumph of the puritans under Cromwell, who completed the destruction started a hundred years earlier; and finally the equally fanatical, and often misguided, attempts at restoration undertaken by Victorian incumbents and patrons.

Churches are not the only visible signs of God's influence on rural England. What would our friends the estate agents do without that handsome Georgian property the 'Old Rectory' to offer to successful businessmen and the like? Virtually every village has a fine rectory but virtually every one is now designated 'old' since the Church Commissioners came to the regrettable conclusion, many years ago, that such large and stately buildings were no longer 'appropriate' for their parsons and, incidentally, cost far too much to maintain. The result was that after the war they sold them off in droves for relative peanuts, investing instead in building small excrescences of bungalows in prominent parts of beautiful villages to house their unfortunate clerics.

This was just one more stage in what, over a period of years, has been the Church of England's policy of looting its rural assets for the benefit of the urban church. This process still continues today. So when you wonder why you have to share a vicar with five other parishes, now you know the reason: the assets that once supported those five incumbents have been stolen and given to more deserving causes than you poor rural folk.

What's more, it is not just the assets that have been removed to central control, but the appointment of the incumbent himself; this is now the province of the bishop, whereas previously it used, in many instances, to be in the gift of the local squire. This right of patronage was an extremely important asset. It gave the owner the right to appoint a vicar or rector to his living but – and this is imperative to remember – once the incumbent was installed he then had the freehold of that living for life and there was virtually nothing the bishop or the patron could do to remove him from it till he died or gave it up. This was the reason for many of the great squire-versus-parson feuds of the eighteenth and nineteenth centuries.

This odd system of patronage allowed the Church of England to give a home to many diverse forms of worship and the various High and Low Church sects to live in harmony under the liberal umbrella of the Church, secure in the knowledge that as long as a sufficient number of patrons embraced their beliefs, they would always receive their fair share of parishes to preach to.

But patronage was valuable not just because of the latitude it gave to patrons but because many livings produced exactly that, an extremely good living. In appreciation of this the eccentric Reverend Robert Hawker, vicar of Morwenstow, a relatively poor parish in Cornwall, had the following words carved above his front door:

> A house, a glebe, a pound a day,
> A pleasant place to watch and pray!
> Be true to Church – be kind to poor,
> O Minister, for evermore.

This was in 1837, when Hawker's £364 a year would have been the equivalent of more than twenty times the average income of an agricultural labourer and, in modern money, would equate to at least £30,000 a year, not taking into account what he got from farming the glebe land or letting it out.

Of course, the mixture of private patronage and highly remunerative appointments invited much abuse. Many parsons in the eighteenth and nineteenth centuries collected more than one benefice, put a poorly paid curate in to do all the tedious work, and lived handsomely on the income – a practice called pluralism, the eradication of which had, ironically, been one of Martin Luther's principal aims. Other patrons had their younger sons admitted to livings under their control at a ridiculously early age, while still others traded in them – as they could be bought and sold just like any other piece of property. For example, when my family was badly strapped for cash in 1863, they sold the living of the local parish, for one life only, to a vicar for approximately three times its annual value, which was then £400 a year.

On the credit side, it must be said that the 'good living' the Church offered attracted many first-class brains and fostered diversity among incumbents, which was a great strength. One wonders if there would be any shortage of clergy today if the average stipend for a rural parish was £50,000 per annum, plus the use for life of a lovely Georgian rectory.

Even after the many reforms carried out in the nineteenth century to make pay in the Church more equitable, the Archbishop of Canterbury still received, in 1912, a salary of £15,000 a year – equivalent to over a million pounds in modern money – while many bishops got over £4,000 a year. It is hardly surprising that they were called Princes of the Church.

But the Church's influence on England's country life did not just stop at the church gate. Among the principal sources of an incumbent's income were tithes. These were divided into great tithes and small tithes. Great tithes were levied on all things arising from the ground and subject to annual increase: corn, hay, wood. Small tithes were levied on all things nourished by the ground: the young of cattle, sheep, horses, etc. In effect, a rector owned both the great and small tithes while a vicar was entitled only to the small tithes – which neatly explains why old rectories are far grander than old vicarages.

The Church justified the collection of tithes by quotes from the Old Testament, such as: 'And all the tithe of the land, whether of the seed of the land, or of the fruit of the tree, is the Lord's', and, 'concerning the tithe of the herd, or of the flock, even of whatsoever passeth under the rod, the tenth shall be holy unto the Lord' (Leviticus 27:30, 32).

Nevertheless, it is hardly to be wondered at that by the late eighteenth century the payment of tithes had become a bone of contention between the parson and his rural flock – hence the old harvest song:

> We've cheated the parson, we'll cheat him again,
> For why should the rector have one in ten?

The remaining tithe barns stand witness to the days when the tithe was collected in kind, but in 1836 an Act of Parliament was brought in converting all payments in kind into cash payments. Tithes are now a thing of the past, having finally been abolished in 1936, when tithe owners were awarded government stock yielding three per cent redeemable in 1996!

The year 1836 marked the beginning of a series of Acts of Parliament, the aim of which was the gradual centralization of authority for appointments in the bishops and the centralization of control over assets in the Church Commissioners. So all glebe land, once the rector's or vicar's to farm or rent out as he chose, is now controlled centrally and, when planning is successfully applied for, sold off for building plots with the money going not to the parish but to the diocese. And so the pillaging of rural assets to fund urban churches goes on. Few people realized, as Act of Parliament followed Act of Parliament, that the result of the modernization of the Church of England would be to turn the rural church into a milch cow for the principal benefit of the urban church, but so it has turned out.

I sense a rebellious mood growing among rural parishes, however. People are beginning to ask why they should support churches outside their parish boundaries. It is a good question, too. After all, the investment decisions of the Church Commissioners have not, of late, given much cause for rejoicing. It was these paragons of financial rectitude, you may remember, who entered into a massive gamble on the property market in the 1980s. The Church has always had a large proportion of its assets in property (it owns around 137,000 acres of agricultural land) and so in the 1980's property boom its assets soared in value. So far so good; but then it forgot the lessons of Pharaoh's dream: 'And the seven lean and ill-favoured kine do eat up the first seven fat kine' (which Joseph interpreted to mean that seven bountiful years would be followed by seven years of famine) and instead borrowed substantial funds to invest still more heavily in the property market. The result was a disaster from which the finances of the Church of England have still not recovered.

So where might a rebellion by rural parishes lead? To unilateral declarations of independence? After all, if a parish is routinely raising some £30,000 a year it might just stop and consider that with the average stipend of a priest at £13,500 it could easily support its own dedicated parson and have some change over to put aside. It also strikes me that people might be rather more inclined to give to their local church if they knew that all the money stayed in the parish instead of being siphoned off to fund some new lunacy. Who knows, perhaps the rich banker who now lords it over the village from the Old Rectory might be prevailed upon to make a large endowment to his local church. Then they might be able to raise the stipend level to attract the best clergyman going, instead of taking the bishop's choice.

It is an interesting scenario and one that may well develop over the next decade or so. Put it this way: the Church has taken its rural parishioners for granted for too long – perhaps the time is ripe for the worm to turn?

But when I look at the poor state of the Church of England today I cannot but feel that a major reason for its collapse into mediocrity was amply expressed, in the mid-nineteenth century, by that towering figure from the pages of Trollope, Archdeacon Grantley, who said, on the future of the Church, 'It is not the dissenters or papists we should fear, but the set of canting low-bred hypocrites who are wriggling their way in among us; men who have no fixed principles, no standard idea of religious doctrine, but who take up some popular cry, as this fellow has done . . . '

Can you think of a better description of the vast majority of the so-called 'leaders' of the Church of England over the last fifty years? I can't. No wonder the Church has fallen so far in the esteem of its traditional supporters.

CHAPTER 19

Environment

When green buds hang in the elm like dust
And sprinkle the lime like rain,
Forth I wander, forth I must,
And drink of life again.

A. E. HOUSMAN (1859–1936)
'Spring Equinox'

You think you live in the country, but quite possibly you are wrong because you may well live instead in a 'designation'. Ever since the end of the last war, landowners have suffered a steady erosion of their freehold rights as central government has 'designated' their acres. It is ironic that the landowners who have suffered most by this creeping 'nationalization without compensation' are exactly those landowners who have done most to conserve the environment. Now they must often curse themselves and wish they had drained the marsh, felled the 'ancient woodland', ripped out all the hedges and demolished the servant wing on their house when they had a chance.

Landowners are not alone in this regard. The 'nanny state' has spread its tentacles into virtually every nook and cranny of life in this country, to the joy of the legal profession and those who make their living by telling people what to do. It would be dishonest not to admit that much of the legislation introduced over the last eighty-odd years has been provoked by various people – some landowners included – ruthlessly pursuing profit in total disregard of aesthetic or moral considerations. That these people were a minority, in some cases a tiny one, makes no difference; it is often said that 'good cases make bad laws'. So a farmer ripping out hedges in

East Anglia to make a field of a hundred acres in extent will cause regulations to be brought in that will stop a farmer in Devon removing a hedge to make a five-acre field into a ten-acre one; the wholesale planting up of the Flow Country in Caithness with Sitka spruce as a tax dodge for private investors generates reform of the entire forestry grants and tax regime, to the detriment of thousands of responsible woodland owners. In other words, one rotten apple can, because of the bad publicity it attracts, cause immeasurable harm to all people operating in the same field, whether it be in agriculture or any other profession or business.

The rot started with the setting up of the National Parks after the last war. This attempt to safeguard England's remaining 'wild areas' by designating them 'National Parks', subject to special planning con siderations, was well-meaning in its aim and has – in part – succeeded. The failing of the National Parks has been, ironically, a result of their success – too many people are now flocking to the areas, putting too much pressure on the infrastructure of the parks and on land never designed to cope with the massed tramp of heavily shod feet over its ancient pathways. Watching walkers on the hills, I often wonder why they have to dress as though they were about to scale some mountain peak, and I reflect on the type of mind that can criticize a farmer for 'ruining' the view by storing his silage in black plastic bags without realizing that the bright yellow, red or blue waterproof with which its own body is adorned is a far greater blot on the landscape.

Actually the National Parks were not as new a concept in England as is sometimes made out. The father of conservation in England was none other than William the Conqueror, who had around a quarter of his kingdom designated as 'forest' and the people who lived in them thus became subject to 'forest laws' rather more draconian, it has to be said, than those codes which the National Park authorities currently apply. Gradually, these vast areas were reduced in size as over the years successive kings agreed to 'deforest' large areas in return for money from the inhabitants. Not that these areas were 'forests' in the modern sense of the word, i.e. densely covered in trees. Dartmoor and Exmoor, for instance, are still termed 'forests', although they are now and were then mainly barren upland moor. The term merely defined an area subject to certain laws and where hunting took place.

But the National Parks were only the start of a programme of 'designation' which, like a stone rolling down the hill, has gathered increasing momentum as the years have gone by. The spread of statutory designations over the countryside can be illustrated by the following table.

Designation	Area in hectares	Percentage of rural land
Green belts	1,550,000	12.0
Areas of Outstanding National Beauty (AONB)	2,040,000	13.0
National Parks	1,360,000	9.0*
Sites of Special Scientific Interest (SSSI)	975,000	6.5
Notrate Vulnerable Zones (NVZ)	635,000	4.2
Total	6,560,000	44.7

Source: CLA 1997

Admittedly, these areas are not all exclusive. In other words, land designated an SSSI may well be within a National Park and it is feasible that an SSSI is also a NVZ and is in an AONB. When all is said and done, however, the percentage of land in England and Wales falling under one form or other of the above designations must be around one-third. I do wonder at the amount of land scientists seem to require – am I alone in thinking that at 6.5 per cent of the total rural acreage of the UK they are becoming a little greedy? If the rate of growth continues in this particular form of designation (and at the time of writing it shows no signs of slowing) we shall soon have to rename SSSIs and call them instead Sites of Common Scientific Interest (SCSI).

* Will have increased in size but as most of the 'new National Parks' (the New Forest and, if it is approved, the South Downs) were AONBs the overall 'designation' acreage remains the same. *Source:* CLA 1997.

The list is far from exhaustive; it does not include, for instance, areas of ancient woodland, or heritage coastline, nor does it include other designations such as Environmentally Sensitive Areas (ESA) or Less Favoured Areas (LFA). Admittedly, ESAs and LFAs are less to do with planning and control and more concerned with provision of grants and subsidies to those lucky enough to live within their boundaries.

The good news for those in the designation business, as I write, is that we are about to have two new ones thrust upon us, courtesy of Brussels. These exciting new entrants to the field are called Special Protection Areas (SPA), which have arisen because of the EU Birds Directive, and Special Areas of Conservation (SAC), which are a result of the EU Habitats Directive. At present it is not clear whether SPAs will replace existing SSSIs or whether, as seems more likely, SSSIs will continue and a few will be selected to boast the additional honour of being an SPA or an SAC.

The SAC designation carries a potentially nasty sting in its tail, in that although the designation may actually only apply to, say, a ten-acre site, controls on farming practices, etc. may be enforced on adjacent land as well.

Where will it all end? Probably not until every last acre in the UK has been surveyed and designated, and a whole host of bodies and bureaucrats have grown up to administer the procedures, etc. which designation obviously entails, all at enormous cost to the taxpayer. It is a boom industry and, as in every other industry, Parkinson's law will apply: 'Work expands to fill the time available for its completion.' Except, in this case, land designations will expand to justify the employment of yet more graduates in environmental studies, driving around the countryside in smart new Land Rovers.

I suppose to be truthful it is less the 'designations' that annoy and irritate countrymen as the people who administer them. I suspect the same went for the Saxons living within one of King William's forests. It was not the designation of the land round about his farm as a forest which annoyed the Saxon so much as the mailed Norman men at arms and foresters, who administered it for the king, knowing little of the local language and understanding less of the local customs, yet determined to apply the letter of the law as rigorously as they could, rather like, say, the modern-day representatives of the Environment Agency or the National Parks. They too now speak a language virtually unintelligible to anyone but themselves and the various NGOs (non governmental organizations) such as BEN (the Black Environment Network) – or I kid you not – WIRE (Women in the Rural Environment), all of which makes me sometimes feel up to my neck in the MIRE (Men in the Rural Environment), which sadly does not for some reason exist. Actually the sort of people who work (is that the right word?) for English Nature and the like do not speak to you; they *engage* with you – or try to – if you are a *stakeholder* then they can *connect* with you. They need to *connect* with you, as how else can they formulate their *vision?* This sort of stuff is actually beyond parody, so let me give you a few choice quotes from the English Nature 2004/2005 Business Plan – English Nature does indeed produce a Business Plan, although it is not a business and has never made a profit, so for a start this is a bit of a nonsense. Let us open up a page at random and see what they are planning to do. Apparently a principal target is to 'achieve full statement of Internal Control'. And how are they going to do this? They are going to 'further embed risk management in the way we work and integrate it more fully into the work of Programme Boards'. Excited and inspired? I bet you are. Read on: they are going to 'drive improvements of service delivery throughout English Nature through implementation of the agreed service improvement plans and ensure that appropriate standards are in place, known and applied'. I cannot go on. I dare not go on. You would all fall asleep. If my name was Sir Maurice Doughty, the Chair of English Nature, I would be seriously embarrassed, but I dare say he and Dr Brown, who goes by the title of Chief Executive – Chief Illiterate Cretin, more like – of English Nature are probably both proud of producing twenty-seven pages of meaningless gibberish.

Like the Saxon in the royal forest, though, there is little we can do against the modern-day equivalent of the Norman man at arms. We must learn to live with him and learn ways to manipulate him to our advantage, just as our ancestors did all those years ago and just as owners of listed buildings have learned to live with the planning controls over their properties. Life, however, is not all bad and many may find that grants are available because their land has been designated – indeed, some owners of grouse moors are already finding, to their surprise and joy, that grants can now be obtained for heather improvement and regeneration, owners of parkland are getting grants for restoring it, landowners who have always wanted to try to encourage back wild partridges find that all they have to do is pick up the phone to DEFRA and some helpful official will tell them how to go about applying for money under some new incomprehensible title, which at the time of writing I think is an Entry Level Scheme . . . and so on.

To survive, landowners have always had to adapt so, if today, we have to learn new skills and new tricks and even a new language, then that is no different from what our ancestors have had to do through out the centuries. Even I will 'engage' and 'connect' with the necessary officials to achieve the aim of the survival of my estate, although what I really want to do is to 'engage' my right foot and allow it to 'connect' with a great deal of force with the self-important posteriors of the idiots masquerading as 'expert' environmentalists, who now have so much power over so much of rural Britain.

CHAPTER 20

Scotland

Land of brown heath and shaggy wood.
SIR WALTER SCOTT (1771–1832)
The Lay of the Last Minstrel

When it came to revising this tome, I thought that I should dispense with a chapter on Scotland. My reason: that landownership in Scotland deserves its own book. It is too big and important a story to be set out in a chapter or two. Although I still stand by this, I felt that it would be wrong if I did not skate, however briefly, over Scotland, and relate how the Highlands and Islands have benefited, over the last hundred and fifty years or so, from a massive transfusion of English money, ploughed into them by romantics who fell in love, and do still, with the wild scenery and scattered communities who live there.

Scotland, as the Scots never stop telling us Englishmen, is different from the rest of the British Isles. How right they are! Now it is even more different, with a Scottish Parliament ensconced in a £450 million luxury building in Edinburgh, and many think – and hope – that within the next twenty years Scotland will, to all intents and purposes, revert to its status prior to the Act of Union of 1709. It may surprise most Scotsmen that a large number of Englishmen cannot wait for that happy state of affairs to be accomplished and that many of us would welcome the emergence of a new 'Hotspur', who according to Shakespeare's Henry IV was a man who: ' . . . kills me some six or seven dozen of Scots at a breakfast, washes his hands, and says to his wife, "Fie upon this quiet life! I want work".'

Why this change of attitude among so many of the English? It is difficult to continue to love your wife if she is for ever hurling insults at you, and the same goes for one's neighbours (whatever the 'Good Book' says). A little gentle teasing is one thing and competitive rivalry and banter is to be welcomed, but when venomous hatred becomes the order of the day then it is time for the Englishman to stop 'turning the other cheek' and start seriously considering whether the Scots might indeed be right and the time has come for a divorce.

This feeling among many English is reinforced when they study the statistics. The average Scotsman has £11,000 per annum of taxpayers' money spent on him. Compare this with the figure for the average Englishman of £4,000 and you see at once that Scotland, contrary to the propaganda view, does very well out of the Union. This discrepancy is simply explained. For some time, English politicians have considered that maintaining the Union is vitally important. This is understandable if you are a Labour politician, as time and again the Labour Party has achieved power at Westminster only through its large majority of Scottish seats. It is a puzzle, though, why Conservative politicians have gone along with this 'blackmail' for so long. After all, they, as a party, and the rest of the people of the United Kingdom for that matter, would be very much better off without Scotland. Finally, however, there is a lesson here for politicians and landowners. You never get any thanks. Strange how often we think someone we help will be grateful and thank us – they never do – in fact many of them hate us all the more for the fact that we gave them help, viz. General de Gaulle in the last war, and viz. the Scots of today. So England and Wales are currently lumbered with a nation of people who absorb mountains of taxpayers' money but still hate their benefactors, while they also still enjoy a massive over-representation at Westminster, which insists on voting on purely English matters even when English MPs are excluded from voting on purely Scottish matters. Is this equitable? Of course not, and if this situation is allowed to continue, one day the Union will break apart.

Let us leave modern-day politics for the moment and return to the land. Before we have a brief overview of the modern Highland estates, it would be as well to take a quick overview of Scottish landed history since the Act of Union in 1709, especially as there can be few countries where the role of myth and legend is as important in the thinking of the inhabitants today as it was in the past.

In 1709 rural Scotland was still being run on feudal lines, with the Scottish Parliament dominated by the great nobles. Poor tenants held their land from the lairds on annually terminable leases and hence had little incentive to improve their farms, while the lairds themselves were, by comparison with their English equivalents, poor. A landowner with a rent roll of five hundred pounds a year was considered a very rich man indeed, and had little spare cash to invest in his estates. In short, rural Scotland in 1709 had progressed little since the Middle Ages.

Romantics in Scotland have always regretted the Act of Union, but they forget the harshness of contemporary conditions. Only a short time prior to the Union there had been a period of six consecutive disastrous harvests (1694–1700) when famine had struck rural Scotland and many tens of thousands of people had died of starvation. It is true that since then there had been some good harvests, but the memory of the dark days at the end of seventeenth century, when Scotland had no money to import wheat and its citizens died in droves from hunger, must have been uppermost in the minds of many in 1709.

At the same time Highland Scotland was still a tribal society, depending for its livelihood on selling cattle to the Lowlanders in exchange for corn, and carrying out the odd raid on them when they felt the urge.

One of the many great myths of Scotland is that the large Highland estates were once 'tribal' lands and that it was only after the '45 rebellion that the wicked chiefs appropriated the land for themselves. This is simply not true; even before '45, Highland crofters who wanted land to farm had always had to hire it from the 'tacksman' who in turn had leased the ground from the chief.

Once the Act of Union was passed Scottish agriculture began a century of improvement. At first, go-ahead lairds imported English ploughmen and farmers to teach their tenants the new ways, but such was the Scottish farmer's aptitude for taking on board, and then himself improving on, the new ideas, that by the end of century it was Scottish ploughmen and stewards who were heading south to pass on their knowledge to Englishmen!

The old annual tenancies were terminated and new, larger and more efficient farms were carved out of the land and let on long leases of nineteen years or more; fields were enclosed, drained, limed and manured as, with a longer period of tenure, tenants now had an incentive to improve their land.

As for the Highlands, the end of the '45 rebellion brought new roads, built by General Wade, and this meant that for the first time in history the Highlands of Scotland became part of the mainstream of Scottish life. Because of this, the chiefs lost most of their old feudal power over their tribesmen and began to change into traditional landowners. In short, the 'civilization' of the Highlands had begun. As with the civilization of any warlike people, this was to lead to hardship, since the banding together of families and men under the protection of a strong chief, who could, and did, defend them from attacks by adjacent clans and, on occasion, lead them in raids on their Lowland neighbours, had been one of the *raisons d'être* of the clan system. Once the rule of law was established, the claymore had to be put aside and the warrior ethos of clan life was gone. It is one of the great ironies that those who most deplore the collapse of the 'noble savage', be he Zulu or Highlander, fail to realize that it is the inexorable march of civilization and their own unwillingness to put up with old-fashioned rape and pillage which have brought about the demoralization and collapse of the tribal system they purport to admire. By the start of the nineteenth century the Lowland lairds and their tenants were enjoying a prosperity their ancestors would surely never have dreamed possible, but in the Highlands the 'clearances' (1785–1850) had already begun. This sad but inevitable page in Scottish history was dictated by economic and demographic necessity. The population in the Highlands was increasing and, as a result, farms were getting smaller as they were divided up among a growing population living in poverty. It is true that the economic motive behind many of the clearances was the profitability of sheep, but a large-scale migration from the glens would have occurred sooner or later. It is hardly likely that Highlanders would have been content to remain living in poverty when the Industrial Revolution arrived and jobs in the booming metropolis of Glasgow became available. It could also be argued that the clearances prevented a far greater tragedy occurring. The Highland farmer, like his Irish cousin, had begun to rely on the potato, and so the potato blight that caused the Irish famine of 1847–51 had a similar effect on the remaining crofters. It is less the fact of the clearances than the manner in which they were carried out by some landowners – notably the Duke of Sutherland – which has caused them to rankle ever since in the minds of many Scotsmen.

The beginning of the Englishman's unrequited love affair with Scotland was the triumphant visit of George IV to Edinburgh, so ably orchestrated by Sir Walter Scott; conjuring myth and legend into fact, he squeezed the fat German into flesh-coloured tights and a Highland costume of his own design. With his novels, which became required reading for the rapidly expanding middle classes of Scotland and England, it was Sir Walter Scott who began the romanticization of Scotland and all things Scottish. The public imagination was still further stirred by the paintings of Sir Edwin Landseer, and no Victorian parlour was complete without its print of the 'Monarch of the Glen'. On a series of visits north of the border, Queen Victoria herself fell in love with the Highlands and in 1848 purchased Balmoral, not such an impractical step then as the new railways were thrusting deep into the very heart of the region, making the dream of the Highlands accessible to all.

Even so, by 1880 the concept of rich Englishmen buying a Scottish sporting estate was still a long way off. In 1880 it was calculated that 1,741 Scots landowners held more than 1,000 acres each and owned ninety-two per cent of the country. The descendants of the old Highland chiefs often had massive holdings in acreage terms, although it has to be said that the income generated rarely reflected the land area.

Owner in 1880	Acres	Gross annual value
Duke of Sutherland	1,325,453	£68,939
Earl of Breadalbane	438,358	£58,292
Duke of Buccleuch	432,927	£172,929
Sir Charles Ross Bt	356,500	£17,264
Earl of Seafield	305,930	£78,227
Duke of Richmond and Gordon	269,294	£60,400
Earl of Fife	249,220	£72,563
Duke of Athol	201,640	£42,030
Duke of Argyll	175,114	£50,842
Sir Kenneth Mackenzie	164,680	£9,344

Source: Bateman's *Great Landowners of Great Britain and Ireland*

The top ten landowners in Scotland in 1880 are listed above. The picture today is very different. (I am aware that many of these estates are not 'owned' in the true sense of the word by the people named, but are often held in forms of trust.)

Owner today	Acres
Forestry Commission	1,600,0000
Duke of Buccleuch	270,000
Scottish Office – Agriculture Department	260,000
National Trust for Scotland	190,000
Alcan Highland Estates	135,000
Duke of Athol	130,000
Captain Farquharson	125,000
Duchess of Westminster	120,000
Earl of Seafield	105,000
Crown estates	100,000

Source: *Who Owns Scotland Now?*, Ausian Cramb, 1996

A glance will demonstrate that since 1880 there has been in Scotland, as in England, a vast sell-off by traditional owners. The result is that now over 2,456,000 acres are held by either state bodies, charities (such as the RSPB, which owns 87,400 acres) or public companies, such as Alcan. This is over twelve per cent of the total land area of Scotland.

It must have been a source of great joy to the average Highland landowner, saddled with an enormous estate which yielded only a pittance in income, when he discovered that rich English and Scottish industrialists dreamed of owning a small part of his domain and were willing to pay him good money to translate their dreams into reality. Not only joy to the landowner either, but a cause of rejoicing throughout the Highlands as the new rich were to splurge enormous sums of money on building grandiose lodges and, in some cases, great castles, in the Scottish baronial style; this gave employment first to the builders and then to the vast staff that had to be employed to keep the house and gardens up to the style which the owners not only required but could amply afford, due to the profits being generated by Lowland or English factories. One of the perverse things about the Scots is their inability to recognize the vital role played in the economics of the Highlands by such absentee owners – then and, indeed, now. The absentee landlord is a figure constantly attacked in the press of modern Scotland, and yet, from an economic point of view, it is a jolly good thing he is absentee; it means he must employ a factor to oversee his affairs while he is away; a housekeeper (or couple) to look after the house; a gardener to mow the lawn; in fact, people to do all the sort of jobs which, if he actually lived on the place full-time, he might consider doing himself! It also means, of course, that he is earning – of necessity – lots of boodle, which he will then cheerfully pour down the throat of his voracious Highland sporting estate.

Without doubt, owning a sporting estate, as we have said, is like standing under a cold shower tearing up money. Yet rich men still queue up to buy them when they come on the market. Why they do is a mystery, although a medium-sized sporting estate, which might eat up between fifty and a hundred thousand pounds a year, may seem cheap when compared with the cost of running a string of racehorses or a large yacht in the south of France; anyway, what is the point of making lots of lolly unless you can waste some of it on having fun – and no other type of property in the world, apart from perhaps game farms in South Africa, has the ability to give so much enjoyment to the owner, and his friends, than a Scottish sporting estate. That is why sporting estates are valued less on the area of land they cover than by what they can produce in the way of game, be it grouse, salmon or stags.

A quick glance at the chart below will show that in 1990 the value of Scottish sporting estates soared. The rise, in fishing particularly, had much to do with a wizard new idea called time share, which suddenly became all the rage and made a lot of people (chiefly the sellers of time shares) a lot of money. The best time-share schemes (from the sellers' viewpoint) were those that offered a fixed week's fishing on a stretch of river for a fixed period of time (say, thirty years). This was a brilliant scheme from the owner's viewpoint. Previously he had probably let out rods on the river anyway and had borne the entire cost of managing the river out of the rental income. Now he not only got a large upfront capital sum but the time-share owners would take on the management cost of the river, and in thirty years' time the whole thing would fall neatly back into his son's lap.

	1980	1990	1992	1997
Salmon fishing (per fish)	£1,500	£12,000	£7,000	£6,000
Deerstalking (per stag)	£6,000	£30,000	£15,000	£22,000
Grouse shooting (per brace)	£450	£3,000	£2,000	£3,000

It has to be said that while initially the punters fell for this hook, line and sinker, it did not take long for the realization to dawn on them that such schemes were a bit of a rip-off; as a result, a lot of over-optimistic and rather greedy owners ceased to find many takers. Time shares, with the week being sold in perpetuity, are still being offered, however, and taken up. Personally, I always feel buying one fixed week's fishing is a very dodgy game, because what looks like a prime week's fishing today might in ten years' time yield nothing. In other words, I think that salmon fishing may be cyclical and that the spring run, which used to be the glory of so many rivers but is now a shadow of its former self, may yet return one year and once again be the jewel in the crown of salmon fishing. If this does happen, those who are now buying relatively inexpensive weeks in May or April may have the last laugh over their richer friends who are punting heavily on weeks in September.

It is Scotland's good fortune that so many rich men still have this love affair with the country, but it is good fortune that few if any Scots appreciate. Instead, they indulge in a long tedious whinge about Scotland being 'bought up by foreigners', conveniently forgetting that in the 1930s a large number of Scotsmen emigrated to England and bought up a large amount of East Anglia for a song, which they then farmed rather efficiently. In other words, what is sauce for the goose is sauce for the gander. The latest whinge is that many of the new owners are not even Englishmen, but foreigners from beyond the seas, such as Kjeld Kirk-Christiansen, who runs the Danish Lego company and owns the fifty-thousand-acre Strathconon estate in Ross-shire. Foreigners now own around thirty estates in Scotland. But again my supposition is that these new owners are rich men happily ploughing large amounts of money into their estates, employing many people and being good stewards of their land.

It is salutary to consider the different attitude of the English to the same problem. In London, for instance, some sixty to seventy per cent of houses and flats in the smarter areas of London are now owned or occupied by foreigners, yet I cannot recall ever reading in the English press any demands that foreigners should be deterred from buying property in England, except – come to think of it – by me!

One of the myths ably propagated by elements of the Scottish press is that owners of Highland estates are selfish and have no desire to develop them economically; they are happy to sit on thousands of acres of barren land purely for their own personal enjoyment. It is true that there may be a small minority who take this attitude, but to be able to do so they need to be rich men who employ large numbers of people to satisfy their every whim. The majority of owners undoubtedly rack their brains constantly for ideas that will result in their being able to boast that their estate makes money. Sometimes, as in England, ill-conceived investment decisions are taken, which end up being the cause of the eventual sale and break-up of the estate – the late Simon Fraser's attempt to start a water-bottling plant being a recent classic example.

It is not surprising, given such examples of unfortunate and loss-making investment projects in the Highlands, that many owners have fallen back on what they know and understand and have concentrated their resources on offering sporting holidays to fishermen, stalkers and shooting parties. The attractions of such holidays in Scotland are obvious, and the money they bring in substantial. The Carnarvon Report of 1992 estimated that sporting estates provided about 2,200 full-time job equivalents and that the direct expenditure on countryside sports in Scotland, valued at 1990 prices, was as follows:

Salmon fishing	£39m (*by participants*)
Sporting shooting	£115m (*by providers and participants*)
Grouse shooting	£10m (*by providers*)
Stalking – Highland deer forests	£9m (*by providers*)

The continuing efforts of many owners to make their estates pay, or at least break even, through providing traditional sporting holidays to rich tourists is not only economically beneficial but also environmentally so. The income generated enables owners to manage the heather-clad hills of Scotland in a way that encourages grouse but is also of value to a great many other forms of wildlife, while the rivers of Scotland benefit from having vigilant owners who work hard to ensure that one of their prime assets is kept in good health. It is, as ever, one of the great ironies that owners of such places, instead of being praised for preserving the landscape, are likely to be penalized by having layers of bureaucracy heaped upon them and planning restrictions put on their every improvement.

Those who blame private landowners for the relative economic failure of much of the Highlands and Islands are long on criticism but short on effective solutions. Many of the solutions proposed by planners since the war with such enthusiasm have been disastrous and enormously expensive failures. What, I wonder, would much of the Highlands be like today if all the estates had been nationalized after the war and left to the tender mercies of central planners? For a start, far more of Scotland's wilderness areas would have been planted wholesale by the Forestry Commission, implementing what, back in the 1950s, was 'the preferred solution' to the upland areas of Great Britain. For those of you who are puzzled today as to why this was, the reason was simple: it was assumed that forestry would provide large-scale employment. No one envisaged back in the 1950s the technological advances that would destroy these optimistic projections so that, for instance, in the late 1950s the Forestry Commission's main worry was how they were going to recruit and house the estimated twenty thousand men they were going to need to employ in the Kielder Forest on the Scottish Border, come the year 2000. When 2000 finally arrived the FC found they were employing directly only around sixty men full-time there! Over the last fifty years the taxpayer has poured literally billions of pounds, in modern money values, into the Highlands and Islands in a vain attempt to bring employment and prosperity to the region. The list of failures is depressing: forestry (around twenty-five per cent of which is estimated to be worthless as the cost of felling, extracting and hauling to markets will always exceed what it is worth), pulp and sawmills which time and again have been opened with a great fanfare only to end in bankruptcy and failure some years later; not forgetting aluminium smelting works powered by cheap hydro-electricity; or the great ski resorts of Aviemoor and Glencoe, set up with taxpayers' money and still needing a large annual subsidy just to survive, so large a subsidy, in fact, that it would probably be cheaper to send every Scot who wanted to ski on a taxpayer-funded package holiday to the French Alps rather than keep these ugly and environmentally damaging developments going. The latest 'bright idea' is wind farms. Scotland *is* windy and it has so much beautiful scenery that surely it can spare some to 'save the world' by putting up the odd wind farm? There is, however, a slight problem: most of the windiest sites are many hundreds of miles from the centres of population where, presumably, the electricity generated by the wind will have to go. How is all that power going to get there? By pylons, of course. So a large wind farm is not just going to wreck one small piece of rural Scotland, but the accompanying pylons are going to wreck a far larger area all because of dubious science. So as 'quick-fix', grant-funded industries have failed one after another, many estates have managed to plod on, doing what they know best and do best, and surviving, all to Scotland's considerable economic benefit.

One last thought. There are only two industries in the Highlands and Islands that have a international market and survive with no subsidy: whisky distilling and field sports. Just suppose, back in the late 1940s and early 1950s, some bright politician and his accompanying civil servants in the then Scottish Office had recognized this. Just suppose that, instead of planting up acre after acre with a monoculture of Sitka spruce, they had offered grants to landowners to manage their moors better and poured money into heather and grouse research. Just suppose they had done the same with the salmon rivers and on the deer forests and then fast forward fifty years and imagine the scene at Aberdeen Airport with serried ranks of executive jets parked nose to tail as the rich of the world made their annual beeline to participate in either some of the finest salmon fishing in the world, or to test their shooting prowess against the world's most testing gamebird, the driven grouse. Such a vision is not too far-fetched, as many of the rich men of the world do that today, but if the field-sports industry had received a tithe of the taxpayer's support which has been doled out to all the other deadbeat 'flavour of the month' schemes, there would be a lot more jobs in the Uplands since, although you can mechanize many forestry jobs, there is a limit to how much you can mechanize the job of a river ghillie or that of a grouse moor keeper or a deer forest stalker.

I just hope that those who are now running Scotland do not make the same mistake their predecessors have made over the last half-century ignoring the most successful and profitable industry in the Highlands and failing to recognize its potential to expand and improve and make an even larger contribution to the rural economy of Scotland in the future than it does now. There is an old maxim used by the Russian High Command in the last war: 'Reinforce success, not failure.' Field sports are a Scottish success story, and if I were in charge of giving the economy of the Highlands and Islands a helping hand I would not do anything to jeopardize that industry; instead, I would put in place measures that would encourage it.

CHAPTER 21

The Future

Given for one instant an intelligence which could comprehend all the forces by which nature is animated and the respective positions of the beings which compose it, if moreover this intelligence were vast enough to submit these data to analysis, it would embrace in the same formula both the movement of the largest bodies in the Universe and those of the lightest atom, to it nothing would be uncertain, and the future as the past would be present to its eyes.

PIERRE SIMON DE LAPLACE (1749–1827)

If we look back over the last half-century how we curse our fathers, mothers and grandparents for their stupidity. How on earth could they have sold all those houses for nothing? Surely any bloody fool could have seen that one day that chocolate-box thatched cottage with roses round the door would be worth £500,000 as opposed to the £50 which it fetched in 1956 when Grandpa flogged it to help pay off the deficit on the shooting account? And why did Mamma have to get rid of all the Victorian pictures so lovingly collected by Great-Grandpapa, again for derisory money, and so on *ad infinitum*. Of course each generation throughout history has cursed the stupidity, selfishness, arrogance and short-sightedness of the previous one, and it is a salutary thought that your son will certainly do the same.

So why are we so lousy at getting the future right, especially when, in retrospect, everything looks so blindingly obvious? The main reason is probably a mix of psychology and ignorance, with a dash of arrogance thrown in for good measure. Let us take the 'ignorance' issue first. As I have previously asserted, if you wish to have a stab at looking ahead it is important to study the past, in other words to study history. This is why so much of the preceding book has been about the historic development of the country estate and about how, and why, they survived a political vendetta to destroy them that lasted the best part of a hundred years.

That political vendetta, it seems to me, is over. Partly this is due to rarity value. There are simply too few of us left for there to be any political capital to be made out of driving the remainder of us to extinction. It is a maxim that the British public, and its government, wake up to a disaster only when it has nearly destroyed something of value, and then rush around like a flock of headless chickens trying to save what remains. The heritage industry is awash with examples of this peculiar trait.

It was in just such a way that planners presided over the destruction of town centre after town centre in the post-war period and then suddenly charged around and slapped conservation orders on the few as yet not wrecked. Why it took them so long to realize the enormous damage they were doing is a mystery to anyone but a town planner. So with the number of estates in England and Wales reduced to around twelve hundred, I think that we are relatively safe from direct attack from politicians. Scotland, of course, is another matter.

The primary lesson from the study of history, though, is that most things go round in a circle. This is what I call the 'Beagling Theory'. Beagling is about the hunting of the hare on foot with a pack of hounds called beagles. Those of you who are versed in this activity will know that, more often than not, the hare will run in a huge circle and, eventually, make its way back to where it was originally found. When the hounds first find their quarry, therefore, the wise beagler – though some might call him idle – sits down, lights a fag and gets a book out. An hour or so later the chances are that the hounds will come charging past him, still in the pursuit of the selfsame hare. Meanwhile, some of those who set off in hot pursuit will be tired and bedraggled, while others will have disappeared altogether, having fallen by the wayside.

You, however, will be as fresh as a daisy and now ready to join the fray if you so wish. In short, there is much to be said for the 'do nothing' school of land management of which I am, I suppose, one of the principal advocates. At an educated guess, most estates throughout the UK would be infinitely better off if their owners had followed this strategy over the last fifty years, while those who have sold assets and reinvested the proceeds in various dubious 'flavour of the month' projects rue the day they did so.

Using the 'Beagling Theory', and looking at the dire rural economic scene today, we can come up with some optimistic predictions based on the historical knowledge that, as sure as day follows night, every recession in the history of farming has been followed by a period of prosperity. I know that the mere mention of the word 'optimism', in a 'rural economic' context will cause consternation among many, as one of the oddities of country people is how depressed about life so many of them always are. This may have something to do with genetics; perhaps pessimists are better survivors than optimists, and as landowners and farmers tend to interbreed, the 'pessimist' gene has emerged triumphant. The pessimistic farmer always believes the harvest will be bad and therefore never goes out and spends money in the expectation that it will be good; *ergo* over the centuries optimistic landowners and farmers have done just that and often had a nasty surprise, gone bust and emigrated to the towns, leaving a rural genetic pool of, mainly, miserable bastards. Farmers are particularly prone to this trait and I have never ever heard a cheerful farmer waxing lyrical about his good fortune and the marvellous harvest he has enjoyed. Instead, he will always have something to moan about, even when he is doing the moaning from inside a brand-new Range Rover! Over the last eight years farmers and landowners have had a lot to moan about. Prices for virtually every commodity they produce have crashed, either because of increased world competition or because of the ruthless pressure on prices exerted by the supermarket cartel. All industries, though, need recessions, and agriculture and rural Britain will, in the long run, benefit from what they have gone through. Recessions are dreadful things, painful for those caught up in them, but it is out of recessions that a new vibrant industry is born. So all over Britain farmers and landowners are now using their brains to try to work out how to add value to their produce because, as sure as eggs is eggs, they now know they ain't ever going to get a fair price for what they produce from any supermarket. The result is that for the first time in fifty years farmers are *thinking* about markets and about what the general public *want* to eat and will willingly buy. The consequences can be seen all over Britain: farm shops, farmers' markets and own-label produce – in other words, signs of enterprise and entrepreneurship, which most people thought farmers were incapable of. True, as a percentage of the total food retail market this is still a tiny percentage, but it is an increasing one and the ranks of producer/processor/retailer are growing steadily. If I were running one of the big four supermarkets, I would be worried. Not that they are, because the supermarkets have fallen into the same trap that the farmers fell into in the 1960s and early 1970s: they have become arrogant. The saying 'pride comes before a fall' is wrong; it should be 'arrogance comes before a fall'. It was arrogance that stopped farmers reading the portents and realizing that they were on the slippery slope of turning from heroes into villains back in the 1970s and it is arrogance today that causes the supermarkets to continue to believe that farmers will put up with being treated with contempt and ripped off for ever; likewise, it is arrogance that encourages supermarkets to believe that the public will always want to buy the crap they sell as food rather than pay a bit more for infinitely better quality elsewhere. Not that I am saying that the mighty foursome of Tesco, Asda, Sainsbury's and Morrison's will be faced by a sudden collapse of demand as their customers flock to buy food that tastes of something from people who know and care about what they sell, whether those people be traditional butchers and greengrocers or one of new breed of producer retailers. Sadly, this is just not likely. The vast majority of us will still shop with them for the convenience and for the low prices, even though we know that the food they purvey is pretty tasteless muck. I do, though, think that there will be a steady trickle of customers away from the faceless checkout desks of the supermarkets back towards the friendly and informed independent food retailers and that, over time, this will hurt the supermarkets.

Farming and food, however, is only one industry, albeit the most important and the most visible one, in what passes for the rural economy. There are many others – forestry, tourism and field sports all spring to mind – but out there, under the hedges and in deserted farm buildings, new businesses and new rural industries are beginning to stir, fertilized by the great communications revolution.

Some seven years ago, when the first edition of this book came out, I looked then at the rural economy, both agricultural and general, and this what I predicted:

What of the current state of the rural economy? I have touched on the problems in preceding chapters, but in the last analysis I am a bull of both farming and forestry, in the long term that is. I foresee a boom in commodities brought about by the emergence of China and, perhaps, India as major economic powers. In the short to medium term, however, things look like getting quite rough in the agricultural sector and I expect to see farms continuing to get larger and more efficient in order to survive. Subsidies from the CAP will become less productivity driven and more and more orientated towards acreage payments, with, I suspect, a strong built-in bias against large farmers in the form of a limit on the amount of subsidy capable of being received by any one farmer.

It must be the same with rural property generally. The future must look good. We are conscious of being in the middle of what tomorrow's schoolchildren will possibly call the communications revolution; they will be forced to sit through hours of boring lessons learning about it and how it affected the lives of ordinary people, just like our generation had to learn about the Industrial Revolution.

The Industrial Revolution, of course, sucked labour and capital out of the countryside to feed its insatiable demands, and destroyed small rural cottage industries in the process. It would seem logical that the communications revolution may have the reverse effect: it may suck people and capital out of smelly towns and back into rural Britain and once again make cottage industries possible. Already there are signs that this is happening in a small way, and I expect that over the next twenty years this move will gather pace and those with nice properties to let in beautiful parts of the country will reap the benefit. With any luck the revolution will arrive in time to save many redundant eighteenth- and nineteenth-century farm buildings from falling down. On the debit side the cost of rural housing is likely to continue to rise in real terms, causing shortages of affordable rural housing even to the 'native' population. However as businesses move out of the Home Counties, wage rates and job opportunities will rise in rural areas. The increasing number of 'immigrants' to the country-side will reinforce old hostilities as newly settled townies attempt to force their urban attitudes to life on the resentful native population. There is a need for true countrymen to be protected as a distinct 'ethnic minority', and organizations dedicated to looking after rural interests must give this some thought as a matter of urgency.

On the whole, I am quite proud of the foregoing and it seems to me to have been a pretty accurate forecast of how things *have* developed in rural Britain over the last seven years. Inevitably the meat of my predictions was about the long term, i.e. twenty years and over, but I think that the course I mapped out seven years ago holds good today and some of my predictions have proved spot-on, notably when I said that: 'I forsee a boom in commodities brought about by the emergence of China, and perhaps, India, as major economic powers.' Unfortunately, as yet, that hike in commodity prices has not fed down into farm produce, but it has begun to percolate through to the depressed forestry sector. I am, though, confident that, given time, boom years will return to agriculture. This is partly because history teaches us that over the last thousand years farming has periodically gone through periods of depression but has always come out of it eventually, and I see no reason why this cycle should have been broken for ever. More fundamentally though, I see that over the next twenty-five years the population of the developed world will more than double and perhaps treble as China, and maybe India, join the select club of developed economies, the key word of course being 'developed'. The population of the world as a whole will also grow, albeit more slowly than previously forecast, but it is the population of the *developed* world that we are interested in as, when people become richer, they eat more. So, for instance, in modern China the average Chinese consumes 35 kg of meat per annum but his close relative in Taiwan eats 75 kg of meat a year. If one assumes – and there seems no reason not to – that as the Chinese get richer their meat consumption will rise to Taiwanese levels, then it is likely that Chinese demand for grain will double over the next twenty-five years from its current level of some 450 million tons per annum to nearly 900 million tons. These are the sort of figures that make grain farmers everywhere salivate. We must, though, remember that the enemies of farmers worldwide are the plant breeder, the chemist and fertilizer manufacturer, not to mention the irrigation engineers who have, over the last fifty years, achieved such enormous improvements in crop yields that they have banished any fear of hunger among the inhabitants of the developed world. So average wheat yields in the EU have increased from two tons per hectare to six tons per hectare over half a century – a spectacular achievement, especially when compared to the more modest increase in yields achieved in the USA in the same timeframe, from just under two tons a hectare to just under three today. Undoubtedly there is scope for further improvements in yield, especially in the old Eastern European countries, and perhaps in China itself, which will all help to dampen the large increases in the price of grain which would otherwise inevitably take place. What we can expect, however, is a far more volatile and dramatic market in farm produce in the future, so a drought in the Mid West USA will bring celebrations in East Anglia and the big efficient farmers will find they spend more time on their computers studying world weather maps and talking to their commodity broker than they do on their tractors.

If farming looks as if it is entering into a challenging and fascinating era with periods of boom being followed, inevitably, by periods of bust, then what of the rest of the rural economy? Unsurprisingly, I am equally bullish about the future of forestry; I also stand by what I said seven years ago, that the technological improvements in all forms of 'communications' will make rural locations attractive for both businesses and people. The major challenge over the next fifty years for rural England and Wales will, in fact, be 'how to cope with success'. The primary reason for the preservation of so much unspoilt country-side in the UK has not actually been the planners or the planning laws, though they have helped enormously; it has been the lack of an economic reason to live in the country; in other words, the rural economy for the last hundred and fifty years has been shedding jobs and businesses. What, though, if this changes and suddenly there are jobs galore in rural Britain again? Not just jobs for gardeners or dailies for rich immigrants from London, but real jobs in all sorts of new, small, nimble industries – skilled jobs, managerial jobs, desirable jobs. Such a scenario will put all sorts of new pressures on planners, and I wish I had more faith in their ability to solve them. The problems of success will, they will find, be just as recalcitrant as the problems of failure with which they have been wrestling during the last fifty years.

If we are looking ahead fifty years we cannot avoid the great climate-change debate. One of the oddities of life is that most people are pathological liars. According to opinion polls, the vast majority of people subscribe to the climate-change theory. This states that over the next fifty years temperatures in the UK will increase on average by between two and a half degrees and five degrees Centigrade. On the face of it this might sound inconsequential, but if temperatures were to fall by an average of five degrees Centigrade then we would be in another ice age! So what happens to us in the UK if this happens? Where I live in Devon will effectively move south and, if temperatures rise by only two and a half degrees we will end up in northern Brittany, while if they go up by the full monty of five degrees my son and grandson will scoop the pools and end up in the Loire Valley! It will not therefore surprise you to know that I am a fully paid up supporter of the 'let's have more global warming' party. I admit my friends in East Anglia and on the Somerset Levels are not quite so enthusiastic, fearing that they might well see their extremely valuable fields disappearing under a foot or two of seawater, but actually their fears are disproportionate as it is estimated that sea levels will rise only by between one and one and a half feet. Nevertheless, that rise will be enough to threaten quite a few low-lying areas in the east of England, not to mention our friends in Holland.

So do I believe in global warming, and why do I accuse so many people of being 'pathological liars'? My reasoning is simple: everyone says he believes in global warming but no one is putting his money where his mouth is, no one is *investing* in global warming; even in the City there is no global warming fund busily raising money to invest in properties that are going to benefit from being that few degrees warmer and, incidentally, selling those that are not going to benefit. It seems to me that global warming is rather like Christianity. Most of us believe in it, but few of us go to church on Sunday. As for me, I am agnostic. I believe this country has got warmer in my lifetime and is certainly a lot warmer than it was at the end of the eighteenth century, when a writer on agriculture in Devon referred to the 'snow line' on Exmoor. Statistics seem to support the fact that temperatures in the UK have risen 0.7 degrees over the last hundred years, but I am still sceptical that they are going to rise by as much as five degrees over the next fifty, much as I would like to believe it. Is it really probable that my son will be swilling really great English-made wine and Champagne before he is sixty? And that he will he be looking forward to his retirement not in Spain, now a barren desert reliant on desalination plants for its water, but in Torquay or Bournemouth, where the all smartest people in the world will then migrate in the summer to strut their stuff on the promenades? I do not totally discount the possibility. After all, we know that once hippopotamuses wallowed in the Thames and I have already mentioned that the ubiquitous *rhododendron ponticum* was native to Ireland in pre-Ice Age times (which is why it is such a successful introduction). It just still seems to me a fantasy dreamed up by the scientific community to justify a load of junkets round the globe.

Let us, though, for the sake of argument, assume that the doomsters are right and temperatures do rise by the top-of-the-range five-degree figure over the next fifty years. What will have proved a good buy and what should we be getting out of? I am a bull of any coastal property, for obvious reasons. If the pundits are right, then come 2050 there really will be a Devon Riviera with a consequent massive increase in real property prices, while London property must wilt under the heat, and as for Docklands, that will quite possibly disappear under water. Clearly, as well, the long-term investor should make a geological study of southern England and invest in land which, as near as damn it, matches that of the Champagne district and that of the great white burgundies.

The future of large country houses looks good too. The 'industrial revolution' will continue to invent and perfect devices for making living in such houses easier and less labour-intensive, while the current 'communications revolution' will – in the long term – provide uses for many redundant outbuildings. Great houses with beautiful parks will continue to be a rarity and an increasingly prosperous population, not only home-grown but from all round the world, will be more willing than ever to pay good money to have a taste of a lifestyle invented by the British which is, possibly, the closest any class or people have got to creating a perfect existence in perfect surroundings. In other words, big houses will continue the process of metamorphosing from white elephants to highly successful profit centres for estates, a process begun by such pioneers as the Duke of Bedford when he first opened Woburn to the public some fifty-odd years ago.

I also discern encouraging signs of a resurgence of the rental market in large houses. Back in the eighteenth, nineteenth and early twentieth centuries, it was common if a family had fallen on hard times for them to let their house for a period until their finances recovered. Already owners of reasonably sized properties with in an hour or so of London are cashing in on this idea as an alternative to selling their properties. This is hardly surprising, as renting can be a good deal for both parties: on the one hand, the owner retains the title and the option to move back in at the end of the tenancy, while picking up a large rent, often in the region of fifty to seventy thousand pounds a year; on the other hand, the tenant has the use and enjoyment of a stately home for a fraction of the cost of buying one. If this trend continues, then owners who fall on hard times may find they have a good alternative to consider rather than an outright sale. A tenancy or lease to a rich man might prove an infinitely preferable course of action to the heartache of having to sell up everything.

Ultimately, those of us who own estates and are used to playing the long game will reflect on our good fortune to have had fathers and grandfathers and great-grandfathers who somehow managed to weather the appallingly turbulent years between 1875 and 1979, and give thanks to them for what they achieved in the face of seemingly insurmountable difficulties.

THE COMMANDMENTS OF SURVIVAL

✳

NEVER SELL ANYTHING IF YOU CAN AVOID IT.

✳

NEVER THROW ANYTHING AWAY.

✳

NEVER EVER APPOINT PAID PROFESSIONALS
AS TRUSTEES OR EXECUTORS.

✳

NEVER GAMBLE/INVEST MORE THAN YOU CAN
AFFORD TO LOSE – REMEMBER THERE IS NO
SUCH THING AS A 'RISK-FREE' INVESTMENT.

✳

NEVER APPLY FOR GRANTS.

✳

NEVER BELIEVE THE EXPERTS – THEY ARE
EARLY ALWAYS WRONG.

✳

TRY TO LIVE WITHIN YOUR INCOME.

✳

DON'T PLAN FOR TOMORROW USING THE
CRITERIA OF TODAY.

✳

IF IN DOUBT DO NOTHING – BETTER TO BE IDLE
AND POOR THAN ENERGETIC AND BANKRUPT.

✳

SPEND TIME WITH YOUR CHILDREN – THEY
ARE YOUR MOST IMPORTANT INVESTMENT.

✳